MAN WRITES DOG

DOGS IN OUR WORLD

Dog's Best Friend: Will Judy, Founder of National Dog Week and Dog World *Publisher* (Lisa Begin-Kruysman, 2014)

Saluki: The Desert Hound and the English Travelers Who Brought It to the West (Brian Patrick Duggan, 2009)

Man Writes Dog

*Canine Themes in Literature,
Law and Folklore*

William Farina

Dogs in Our World
Series Editor: Brian Patrick Duggan

McFarland & Company, Inc., Publishers
Jefferson, North Carolina

ALSO BY WILLIAM FARINA
AND FROM MCFARLAND

*The German Cabaret Legacy
in American Popular Music* (2013)

*Eliot Asinof and the Truth of the Game:
A Critical Study of the Baseball Writings* (2012)

*Chrétien de Troyes and the
Dawn of Arthurian Romance* (2010)

*Perpetua of Carthage: Portrait
of a Third-Century Martyr* (2009)

*Ulysses S. Grant, 1861–1864: His Rise
from Obscurity to Military Greatness* (2007)

*De Vere as Shakespeare: An Oxfordian
Reading of the Canon* (2006)

LIBRARY OF CONGRESS CATALOGUING-IN-PUBLICATION DATA

Farina, William, 1955–
    Man writes dog : canine themes in literature, law and folklore / William Farina.
    p. cm.
Includes bibliographical references and index.

ISBN 978-0-7864-7497-4 (softcover : acid free paper) ∞
ISBN 978-1-4766-1455-7 (ebook)

1. Dogs in literature. 2. Dogs—Folklore. I. Title.
PN56.D6F37 2014
809'.9333629772—dc23   2014007619

BRITISH LIBRARY CATALOGUING DATA ARE AVAILABLE

© 2014 William Farina. All rights reserved

No part of this book may be reproduced or transmitted in any form or by any means, electronic or mechanical, including photocopying or recording, or by any information storage and retrieval system, without permission in writing from the publisher.

Front cover images © 2014 Thinkstock

Manufactured in the United States of America

*McFarland & Company, Inc., Publishers
  Box 611, Jefferson, North Carolina 28640
  www.mcfarlandpub.com*

To Humane Societies everywhere
fighting the good fight

Table of Contents

Acknowledgments   ix

Introduction   1

1. Dogs and Law   11
2. Canine Guardians of the Underworld   19
3. Beastly Virtues   28
4. The Wolf as Maternal Figure   36
5. Down, Dog!   45
6. In Defense of Dogs   53
7. The Sensitive Werewolf   61
8. Carnivores Forgiven   69
9. Animal Intelligence and the Wars of Religion   77
10. Natural Rights of Animals   86
11. Devil Dogs   96
12. Everything Is Connected   104
13. Toto Speaks   113
14. Empathy for Wolves   122
15. Canine Heroes   130
16. Justified Predators   138
17. Dogs in Poverty   146
18. Animal Spirituality   154
19. A Man and His Dog   163

20. Last Word in Social Beings	171
21. Summary	180
Chapter Notes	187
Bibliography	207
Index	209

Acknowledgments

Without my wife and partner, Marion Buckley, this book would have never happened for so many self-evident reasons that it seems superfluous to repeat all of them here. Suffice it to say that no aspiring writer ever had a better muse.

Special thanks to the staff of the Marathon County Public Library for guiding and assisting me through the state of Wisconsin's terrific interlibrary loan system. It is like having the world at your fingertips. May they in turn receive the necessary financial support they require, and so justly deserve, for the benefit of all society.

Thanks to Greg and Carol Lamansky for being my occasional captive audience and offering many valuable literary and real-life insights into this topic. Thanks to Pat and Christine Peterson for letting me hang out—I never realized that a Newfy could be so laid back. A word of appreciation goes to Linda Gossett and Mia Fletcher for loaning me books, reading excerpts from my manuscript, and patiently listening to my thinking out loud. All of you are true dog lovers, to be sure.

A Note on Cleo

Behind every canine book is a real-life canine, and this one is no exception. Cleo, aka Cleopatra (b. 1998?), came to us via the Chicago Humane Society (CHS) on September 9, 2000. She is a tricolor (black, tan, and white) mix of mostly German Shepherd and Collie, a sort of cross between Lassie and Rin Tin Tin (see Chapter 15), if you will. The name Cleo was inspired by the dark eye-liner effect characteristic of her Germanic descent, plus she sports a white splotch on her chest known in the Islamic world as "the Kiss of Allah" (see Chapter 1). Soon after her adoption, I viewed an archeological exhibition at the Field Museum in Chicago and noticed a striking similarity between our new pet and an ancient mosaic from Alexandria, Egypt, portraying a first century BCE mixed-breed dog. Anything is possible, I suppose. Cleo's anonymous first owner had done an exemplary job of training her, and she was the only animal at the CHS with a "Do Not Euthanize" order attached to her cage. My wife and I strongly suspect, in hindsight, that we were chosen by Cleo as her new owners, rather than vice versa. Having grown up on a farm  with considerable exposure to the animal kingdom and owning a number of outstanding pets, I have nevertheless over the last 13 years (thanks to Cleo) been forced to rethink much of what I previously thought about canine intelligence and adaptability. Now in the late autumn of her years, Cleo is currently enjoying a plush doggie retirement in Central Wisconsin. She is loved by everyone who knows her, even non-dog lovers. Let it be recorded herein that the close bonds between humans and canines have never been stronger, healthier, or more profound than they are today.

Introduction

The problem is that people have a lot of misconceptions about wolves. —Temple Grandin[1]

Among numerous new scientific discoveries at the turn of the last century, one of the most unpopular, yet one remarked upon to a surprisingly small degree, was a growing consensus among genetic researchers that all domesticated dogs, without exception, are directly descended from wild wolves.[2] This conclusion, though seemingly in tune with common sense, can also be divisive in that many would still deny the reality of evolution, while others acknowledging evolution nonetheless balk at the possibility that one of the most stigmatized creatures in our cultural tradition, namely the Big Bad Wolf, is an immediate forebear of Man's Best Friend. At a glance, the question may seem trivial in today's shrinking, volatile world; yet our slowness in coming to grips with seemingly innocuous revelations such as these may be indicative of larger problems relating to the dissemination of reliable data from mass media, not to mention modern educational systems, both public and private. Why has something that seems so simple and self-evident been so long in coming? If many supposedly well-educated citizens cannot get little things like this right, then it surely bodes ill for our ability as a society at large to get much of anything right within the greater, more pressing spheres of science, politics, and religion. Therefore, let us begin to remedy the situation by modestly addressing smaller but no less interesting matters of ongoing controversy.

Canine literature is, of course, universal in scope, extending back to the very beginnings of written human language. As a body of work it is far too vast to catalogue; moreover, books touching upon mankind's close and frequently emotional relationships with dogs and wolves represent a mere subset of an overwhelmingly larger corpus encompassing the entire animal kingdom. Although this study will occasionally analogize similar historical observations made with respect to cats, horses, birds, etc., the primary focus will remain on *Canis lupus familiaris* and its less reputable near relative, *Canis lupus*. No pretense at comprehensiveness is made herein; moreover, our subject matter has been considerably narrowed by a reluctant exclusion of non–Western literary sources. These distant oriental views of the canine genus have ranged from mere human food source to sacred reincarnations of the human soul, sometimes side by side within the same cultural environment.[3] Our primary focus is on literary snippets produced within a somewhat wider context rather than any specialized canine treatises, of which there are an ever-growing number. Selected Western sources throughout the ages form the basis of each chapter in this volume, representing the author's personal favorites in a highly diverse genre. If anything else links them together it would be a deliberate avoidance of sentimentality, only because there seems to be a burgeoning over-demand for this style in the marketplace, usually in the form of memoirs or novels. We all know the titles, so there is no need to cite them herein. By contrast, I have been often and repeatedly struck by the unsentimental or anti-sentimental manner in which dogs and wolves have made forceful, regular incursions into serious literature. Whether these entail the ferociously realistic portraits by Jack London and Ernest Thompson Seton, the unconventional philosophic musings of Montaigne or Locke, or the detached scientific observations of Darwin and Pliny—certainly none of these authors could be remotely described as maudlin or overwrought in their personal views of the natural world.

The range of topicality can be astonishing. Given that dogs and human beings have always enjoyed a uniquely intertwined social relationship—and that man seems to have always had a uniquely hostile attitude towards wolves—perhaps such variety should not come as too much of a surprise. Within the context of the Judeo-Christian tradition alone canine symbolism has been routinely employed (i.e., Jesus and the Canaanite woman from the Gospel of Matthew), occasionally delving into the realm of theology, as exemplified by the influential legacies of St. Francis of Assisi (see Chapter 8) and C.S. Lewis (see Chapter 18). In a more worldly sense, this work begins and ends with reflections on human law and written legislation, first with concerns of Mesopotamian monarchs over the unchecked spread of rabies within their dominion, and lastly with Temple Grandin's startling but persuasive speculations that modern-day leash laws are affecting the evolution of both dogs and people in ways not to be fully understood for some time to come.

Excluding non–Western literature, we are still left with a staggering range of opinion covering some 4,000 years, originating from geographic locations as varied and dissimilar as the United States, Canada, Brazil, Great Britain,

France, Germany, medieval Italy, ancient Rome, ancient Greece, ancient Egypt, Iran (Persia), and Iraq (Babylon). One comes away with a definite feeling that to date the surface of this somewhat unorthodox subject matter has barely been scratched. The chapters in this book reflect a tentative foray into a topic that most certainly deserves ongoing treatment by other writers with differing or conflicting viewpoints.

While another wolf descendant, the American coyote (*Canis latrans*), will be included as "fair game" for this study, along with its African counterpart, the jackal (see Chapter 2), we will reluctantly exclude from our discussion *Vulpes vulpes* (the red fox), despite its legendary reputation for cunning and stealth. Currently, the majority of scientists have classified the fox as its own canine genus, separate and distinct from dogs, wolves, and coyotes. Perhaps that topic deserves its own book. In any event, Western literary observations on *Canus lupus* and its direct descendents will alone suffice for our purposes. Indeed, it was very difficult to pick and choose among the many works that have filtered into our collective consciousness, not to mention those which deserve more attention than they have received to date. Our primary goal is to demonstrate the highly interactive relationship between mankind, dogs, and wolves over the long course of recorded history. Even a confirmed Creationist must admit that on Noah's Ark the three had to have somehow coexisted at close quarters for a considerable length of time. As for the rest of us (who are supposedly more wise), it may be high time to rethink and reevaluate long-held, entrenched preconceptions regarding our alleged human self-sufficiency and lack of interdependence with the animal and canine worlds.

One cannot meaningfully delve into this topic, of course, without addressing the endlessly contentious issue of recreational hunting and, in particular, the hotly debated respective roles of dogs and wolves in this deadly sport, one so permanently engrained in our collective consciousness. Anyone doubting the timeliness of this debate need only consult the daily headlines. For example, on October 15, 2012, wolf hunting was officially legalized in Wisconsin, which joined several other states in this recently developing trend. Wisconsin, however, is unique in that dogs are allowed to participate in tracking and pursuit of wolves, much to the outrage of animal rights activists and many dog enthusiasts as well. The multiple, thorny ramifications of legislative decisions such as these will be periodically explored within the pages of this study, not the least of which are the strenuous protests of Wisconsin's extensive Native American population, whose objections to wolf-hunting are based on both religious and ecological grounds. Pro–wolf-hunting advocates typically portray their opposition as being overly sensitive and out of touch with the realities of nature; therefore, special care has been taken herein to examine the works of writers no one could ever accuse of being squeamish or faint of heart. Temple Grandin, innovative architect of the modern industrial slaughterhouse, may also be the greatest contemporary advocate for animal rights and humane treatment of animals (see Chapter 20). The ancient historian Plutarch, while writing with penetrating insight and discerning sagacity on the endless overlaps between Greco-Roman societies and the animal kingdom, also admitted how much he enjoyed hunting for sport as a young man, and this was in an age innocent of firearms (see Chapter 4). Even Charles Darwin, it should be remembered, during his English provincial youth was a great enthusiast for the hunt and highly valued field observations of hunters in his groundbreaking scientific works (see Chapter 12). And then there is the unusual case of Ernest Thompson Seton, one of the most successful wildlife bounty hunters of his generation who later became one of its most influential naturalist spokespersons for preservation and conservation.

Each chapter in this study will follow the same general outline. A short biographical and historical sketch for the author and literary work in question is followed by a focus on prominent canine motifs within the work itself. These multifarious themes, as the reader will no doubt quickly discern, all underscore the intense interaction between humans, dogs, and wolves over the ages rather than upon the animals themselves or, for that matter, humankind viewed in isolation. Although many of these writings have a definite scientific or empirical emphasis, over half predate modern science as we normally tend to think of it. Darwin was obviously a pivotal figure in this regard; on the other hand, nowadays most people often forget (or are ignorant of the fact) that contemporary Western science was a much later outgrowth of philosophical thought stretching all the way back to ancient Greece and beyond. Therefore, a Diogenes or Pliny has as much a place in this chronicle as does a Darwin or Grandin. Among fictional writers presented herein, perhaps the most misunderstood is L. Frank Baum, famed author of the *Oz* books (see Chapter 13). Thanks to Hollywood, we too often conjure a rather static notion of Baum's eccentric genius. Those of us who grew up with access to first editions of his books, however, usually view his fanciful world in more complex terms. While movies in relation to the writings will be referenced, effort shall be made to contrast the visual images from the literary sources whenever applicable. In addition, other significant animal and canine-related works by the same author will be explored within the same chapters. Renowned animal fabulists such as Aesop and Rudyard Kipling will be mentioned only in passing, mainly because these writers were concerned with allegory and symbolism rather than reality or perceived reality. In some cases, other famous writers of the same era will be incorporated for purposes of comparison and contrast—for example, Mark Twain and O. Henry in relation to Baum. Nor will musical accompaniment to canine folklore be neglected, as represented by Sergei Prokofiev's masterful 20th century adaptation of *Peter and the Wolf* (see Chapter 16). Lastly, as in all of my previous studies, there will be short detours addressing canine visual symbols in painting, sculpture, architecture, photography, and film, especially as these mediums relate to the specific works under examination.

An Experimental Reaction to New Discoveries

Unless my research has been faulty, few if any books similar to this one, for better or for worse, have ever been produced. This may be understandable given that the concept of point-blank genetic relations between dogs and wolves has been relatively recent in finding widespread acceptance among scientists. In short, canine literature is plentiful, but positive views of wolves (i.e., Seton) are unusual, as are negative views of dogs (i.e., Goethe), however humorous the latter can be. On a basic level, this study essentially represents amateur literary "criticism" of personal favorites in a specific genre; in a more hybrid sense, our survey links ancient ideas with contemporary ones on the same subject matter, thus demonstrating the continuity and universality of these concerns.[4] Because dogs are now thought to be direct descendants of wolves, we anticipate future competition by being the first to comment within this precise context, utilizing multiple viewpoints from other authors in the process. McFarland's *A Dictionary of Proverbs and Quotations About Cats and Dogs* (2001) by Robert and Gwendolyn Nowlan is a useful reference point for anecdotal material; however, ours is a more digressive and diffuse approach, albeit one solely focused on domesticated and wild canines as seen through the ever-shifting prism of Western culture. To further differentiate this work from countless other animal-related books, I have maintained my usual past practice of using short header quotes at the beginning of each chapter, drawn from the individual literary works under consideration, and then tying these quotations into the main discussion.[5]

This is not an anthology (there are already plenty of those) or a memoir; instead we strive to incorporate elements of both anthology and memoir into a single unified commentary. Our intention is that readers will find it both of general interest and difficult to pigeonhole or classify. For example, Darwin dwelled at length upon hunters reporting the mournful songs of birds after a mate had been killed, and this connection in turn will be presented within the context of Ernest Thompson Seton's adventures, in which empathy for his prey helped Seton to become first a superb hunter and then later a powerful voice in favor of wildlife protection, not unlike another well-known hunter and preservationist of the same era, Theodore Roosevelt (see Chapter 14). Another example is Pliny's insistence that many dogs display morally virtuous characteristics (especially compared to some humans), a theme picked up many centuries later by Montaigne in reaction to the appalling savagery of Europe's highly destructive yet indecisive Wars of Religion (see Chapter 9), drawn-out conflicts that in turn played a major role in shaping the philosophical foundation of the United States. In terms of organization, the chronological sequence of this survey should help readers to further appreciate the uninterrupted train of literary thought on myriad canine themes over the last four millennia. Above all, we intend to avoid the all-too-easy trap of bathos, like all of the classic writers on this same topic, as we pay these authors their well-deserved tribute.

Historical (and Prehistoric) Context

Former British Museum curator Catherine Johns has written, quite accurately enough, that "there is no doubt that the attachment between humans and canids was, by a very long way, the first foray into the close inter-species relationship that may be defined as 'domestication.'"[6] The unspoken corollary to this agreed-upon dynamic is that all other pets domesticated by humans came later, in the wake of dogs, and many of these long afterward. This writer grew up on an Indiana farm plentiful with household dogs, cats, birds, and other friendly indoor-outdoor animals and continues to maintain an everlasting affection for all of these creatures. This deep affection, however, does not blind him to the basic fact that dogs set foot in the proverbial human home first, so to speak, and continue to enjoy a unique precedence therein.[7]

A growing school of thought within the scientific community holds that humankind and dogs more or less evolved together, simultaneously and interactively. Our beloved cats, for example, still remain far less social than dogs (as well as more territorial), have far fewer breeds, and were domesticated circa 3,000 BCE whereas it is generally agreed that dogs were fully domesticated by 9,000 BCE at least, causing commentators such as Douglas Brewer to remark that, regarding documented human uses for dogs, "the list is almost endless, as dogs have been intimately associated with humans in every aspect of life, at home, in the field, at work and at play."[8] To repeat, a good part of the reason for this tremendous diversity of practical canine use is that dogs have been in close contact with their human masters for a much, much longer time than any other domesticated species.

Human use of domesticated dogs has not only been vast and varied, it also continues to expand progressively as time goes on. Again, we quote Catherine Johns: "The list of tasks in which dogs assist their human companions is a long one, and it continues to grow."[9] Since canine sensory perception (particularly with respect to smell) and, in some cases, raw physical strength and stamina are effective extensions of more limited human capacities, these advantages have been harnessed since the dawn of civilization for the benefit of people with more than happy cooperation from the dogs being thus engaged. In return for food, shelter, and affection, wild canines gradually, over the long course of time, allowed themselves to be domesticated into the status of human personal property. Traditionally, dogs have been utilized for hunting, herding, guarding, transport, entertainment and companionship, among other basic functions.[10] Later (at some point) these roles expanded into activities connected with warfare, law enforcement, and rescue operations.

Because humans at a very early point in their civilized development noticed that dog owners seem to enjoy healthier lifestyles with more longevity and resistance to illness, dogs became closely affiliated with medicine and religion almost from the moment Western history began (see Chapter 1). Human medical science later repaid this devoted service by cruelly using dogs in lab experiments, then later in the Cold War race for space, much to the justified indignation of humanist philosophers ever since (see Chapter 10). In more modern times, central roles as guide and service dogs for the disabled have been honed, refined and expanded to an impressive degree. Recent years have witnessed the amazing and somewhat controversial deployment of medical diagnosing dogs as predictors or detectors of human seizures and various other hidden illnesses. All in all, humans and canines seem to be inseparably bound together in their ongoing and ever-changing evolutionary journey.

Where did it all start? No one knows exactly, and possibly never will. Currently there appears to be general agreement among archeologists that the presence and influence of domesticated dogs in Asia (including China and India) is a much more recent historical occurrence than in the West.[11] Assuming this is true, our focus then turns to the Middle East, where the earliest evidence exists for canine domestication. This evidence, however, is far from settled and much of it is disputed. For example, precisely where and when it began depends on interpretation of fragmentary discoveries. Most specialists believe that somewhere in modern-day Iraq was the home of the first civilized dog.[12] The exact point in time at which this monumental event occurred is still unresolved. The vast majority of scholars hypothesize that it was at least 9,000–10,000 years before the birth of Christ, which would also make it long before the agricultural revolution centered in ancient Mesopotamia and even longer before metallurgy or the invention of writing.[13] Some scientists now believe dogs could have been domesticated by humans as long as 100,000 years ago during the last glacial period of the Pleistocene epoch. Anyone who has ever seen North American sled dogs in action under blizzard conditions (see Chapter 15) cannot dismiss such far-reaching theories out of hand as being frivolous or extravagant.

Whenever and however these things came exactly to pass, it is clear that, once begun, the process of canine domestication spread rapidly and irrepressibly across the globe. Soon after appearing in Mesopotamia, domesticated dogs became part of the paper and archeological trail in ancient Egypt. As in Mesopotamia, canines—in the form of the ubiquitous black jackal—then became closely tied with Egyptian religious rites (see Chapter 2). Since wolves are not native to the continent of Africa, it is reasonably assumed that these tamed and untamed animals came into Egypt from Mesopotamia to the east.[14] As in most other historical matters, Egypt presents a special case since it subsequently fell under the sway of many other cultures, including Greek, Roman, and Islamic, all the while maintaining its own unique, entrenched set of attitudes and values. With respect to canines, this has translated into a special reverence and respect for domesticated dogs today that is not found as frequently in the Middle East, despite a long tradition of adamant minority support among Islamic philosophers (see Chapter 6). As for the ancient Greeks and Romans, neither are known to have used dogs for food purposes except under emergency conditions, thus recognizing their indispensable value for other tasks.[15] To their philosophers and sages goes the honor of being the first ones known to have formally extolled the moralistic (and even maternal) virtues of canines, both wild and domesticated.

By the Middle Ages, as Western civilization sank into ignorance, war, poverty, and widespread misery, close human-canine relations persevered and at times seemed to thrive more than ever. Welsh, German and French bards even picked up on the old werewolf theme of the Greeks as a thing not entirely to be shunned, and this odd poetic conceit has been going strong ever since (see Chapter 7). With the advent of the Renaissance and modern era, variations on our working and imaginative interactions with canines have assumed multiple dimensions, ranging from the idea of natural animal rights and contemporary anticruelty legislation to the revolutionary proposition that wild wolves are creatures to be treasured and preserved rather than downsized or wiped off the face of the earth. Today, it is a safe assumption that these broad trends, as well as new and previously unimagined ones, will continue to play out in the public arena over both the immediate and the distant future.

From Law to Literature to Folklore

Competing theories of how human language and writing developed are well beyond the scope of this study. The recurring presence of canines within this developmental process, however, is indisputable. From the earliest recorded laws and religious rites of ancient Mesopotamia and Egypt, dogs and their more wild ancestors figure prominently. With the later rise of Greco-Roman civilization over the Mediterranean world, canine themes frequently found new and often surprising variations in the philosophic frameworks and epic storytelling traditions forming the cornerstone of Western culture. Whether discussing the alleged nonfictional and proto-scientific observations of Pliny (see Chapter 3) or the offbeat and pre-aesthetic moralistic teachings of Diogenes (see Chapter 5), one cannot help but encounter profuse praise of canine behavior, usually in tandem with harsh criticism of human behavior.[16] A widely accepted definition of folklore is "the oral, unwritten traditions, legends, and myths of a culture"; yet without writing of any sort, few of us are ever exposed to these treasures.[17] For example, Saint Francis of Assisi is exclusively associated with the poignant wolf legend of Gubbio (see Chapter 8), and yet this beautiful anecdote has come down to us only because an obscure monk from the 14th century decided to record it and did so in defiance of institutional church disapproval. Another example is an outstanding musical drama such as Prokofiev's *Peter and the Wolf* (see Chapter 16), which owes its textual source to the aforementioned tradition of the Big Bad Wolf—itself a complex, tangled web of distant cultural memories—combined with the composer's own considerable powers of creativity and imagination directly in the face of Stalinist rigidity and censorship. The main thing is that Prokofiev saw fit to write it down and hence we are now able to enjoy it. Therefore, we include use of the term "folklore" in our survey, even though purists may object to its strict applicability. Thus the separating lines between literature, law and folklore can become hopelessly blurred. Nowhere is this better illustrated than with respect to canine themes.

Almost everyone has a good animal tale to tell. Typically lost in the excitement, however, are underlying reasons why these stories, both make-believe and nonfiction, will continue to resonate as long as storytellers practice their art. In short, these stories are really about people. Uniquely compelling are narratives featuring dogs and wolves, given the inseparable history of the former as human companions and the seeming irreconcilable hostility of humans towards the latter as presumed natural adversaries. In effect, dogs and wolves consistently teach us lessons about life in ways that few other creatures can—how to live, how to die, how to survive, how to *adapt*. Indeed, some would argue (with good force) that without dogs, humankind would never have gotten as far as it has. These same compelling qualities have caused canine literature throughout the millennia to routinely spill over from the realm of pure entertainment into far more serious endeavors, another striking facet of this fascinating topic rarely mentioned or discussed. Accordingly, this present modest work will hopefully serve as a layman's challenge to more specialized groups of expertise, particularly in the scientific field, to put aside all preconceived notions in their ongoing journey of discovery. We would also sincerely hope that the average recreational reader and all lovers of the natural world will keep thinking about these same questions as well, even if definitive answers often prove stubbornly elusive or, more vexing still, not what we had originally set out to find.

1

Dogs and Law

> *If a dog becomes rabid and the ward authority makes that known to its owner, but he does not watch over his dog so that it bites a man and causes his death, the owner of the dog shall pay forty shekels of silver; if it bites a slave and causes his death, he shall pay fifteen shekels of silver.*—Laws of Eshnunna, Mesopotamian Anonymous, 20th century BCE[1]

In late 2011, the United States officially ended its war in Iraq by withdrawing military personnel from that country, thus concluding extensive operations first commenced over eight years previously, during the spring of 2003. Ostensibly triggered by the 9/11 terrorist attacks, the Iraq War was in truth an outgrowth of the Gulf War of the early 1990s, in which Operation Desert Storm successfully contained the illicit territorial ambitions of Iraqi dictator Saddam Hussein. Although Hussein's wicked and oppressive regime was quickly overthrown by a second American invasion, the U.S. then found itself embroiled in a relentless cycle of sectarian violence that took another seven years of police action and over a trillion dollars to subdue (relatively speaking), not to mention thousands of lives being sacrificed by all sides represented in the conflict. In a region overrun with remorseless warfare since time immemorial, none of these more recent events seemed especially unusual when viewed within the broader context of Middle Eastern history; yet there seemed to be a somewhat greater degree of tragic irony, even in comparison to the pitiless standards of the past. As noticed by countless coalition veterans who participated in these campaigns, modern Iraq is also the site of ancient Mesopotamia, the cradle of Western civilization. It was on this same ground, some 4,000 years ago, that the very first human laws were transcribed, so that any literate citizen would know the difference between acceptable and unacceptable behavior. Remarkably, some of these official pronouncements took the trouble to include specific provisions relating to the misbehavior of domesticated dogs.

As American-led coalition forces in Iraq strove to enforce international law—oftentimes with the deployment of military working dogs (MWDs) for bomb detection—it probably occurred to few (if any) that some of the earliest Mesopotamian legal texts also happened to address issues involving third-party disputes with canine handlers. Nevertheless, it was in northeast suburban Baghdad, at a site today known as Tell Abū Harmal, where, at the dawn of the second millennium BCE, the Sumerian city-state of Eshnunna once prospered and flourished. Though not nearly as well-known or infamous as the nearby Old Testament landmarks of Babylon and Nineveh, Eshnunna enjoyed its own brief heyday of political supremacy in the region, serving as a trading center conveniently located between the rapidly developing urban centers of the Tigris-Euphrates river valleys and the Elamite frontier of Persia (modern-day Iran).

Sometime around the beginning of the 18th century BCE, perhaps shortly after the biblical patriarch Abraham migrated from Mesopotamian Ur of the Chaldaeans to the land of Canaan, Eshnunna reached the zenith of its power and influence under its most renowned king, Dadusha, son of Ipiq-Adad.[2] Even before this early period, however, royal proclamations and decrees had been committed to writing, a relatively new form of communication invented and more or less monopolized by Mesopotamian culture.[3] Among the oldest of these surviving texts, written in Semitic Akkadian cuneiform, are the Laws of Eshnunna, covering a wide range of civil and criminal matters. Though fragmentary and far from comprehensive in scope, this codex includes not one but two provisions specifying punishment for cases of lethal dog bites.[4] These particular statutes appear to be a natural outgrowth of the very prominent and visible role of *Canis lupus familiaris* within Mesopotamian society. In short, as mankind first emerged as a civilized creature from the Fertile Crescent, domesticated dogs were there right alongside him.

This unusual discovery of ancient tort legislation concerned with the payment of monetary damages by negligent dog owners occurred only 67 years ago. As World War II came to a close in 1945, an archeological team led by Sayid Taha Baquir, curator for the National Museum of Iraq, began excavations which almost immediately unearthed the tablet containing the Eshnunna inscriptions in question.[5] By way of backdrop, the artificially mapped Kingdom of Iraq had been primarily promoted and sponsored by the postwar British government, maintaining its traditional colonial posture towards the Middle East, even though the stability of this colonialism was quickly fading long before the Second World War began.[6] In reality, the Tigris-Euphrates Valley has always been (and remains) a teeming, clashing interaction between multiple cultures and peoples, extending north all the way from the Persian Gulf to the southwestern borders of Turkey. The Laws of Eshnunna, despite their great antiquity, would have been written during a time of political and religious instability, not unlike that of modern-day Iraq. Upon their discovery in 1945, the tablets rightfully became objects of considerable scholarly interest, with inquiries into their meaning—and parallels with the contemporary world—today still being discussed and debated among specialists. Currently housed with other priceless treasures within the National Museum of Iraq, the Laws of Eshnunna tablets have thus far fortunately been spared the ravages of more recent damages sustained by the museum during Baghdad's ongoing civil and religious strife.

Earlier English translations of the Eshnunna laws by Mesopotamian scholars such as Albrecht Goetze and Yaron Reuven were deliberately less specific in meaning, substituting the word "vicious" for "rabid" in the text.[7] No doubt 4,000 years ago, society did not understand or label rabies in the modern scientific sense; they simply understood that any dog bite could be potentially lethal in the long term, and that if death in fact occurred, then the dog owner should be punished. More recent scholars, however, such as renowned Chinese Assyriologist Wu Yuhong, have concluded that the ever-present threat of rabies was truly the main concern behind this particular legislation. Yuhong has identified numerous other Mesopotamian references to rabies in letters, omens, spells, incantations, and prophecies, drawing a fairly conclusive preponderance of evidence in this regard.[8] In their engrossing new book *Rabid: A Cultural History of the World's Most Diabolical Virus*, authors Bill Wasik and Monica Murphy point to a recorded ancient Akkadian joke about a dog bite victim who takes the trouble to travel all the way from Nippur to Isin (20 miles) just to receive a special incantation from the high priest of Gula, goddess of healing, whose main shrine and temple was affiliated with the latter city.[9] Given the overall weight of these findings, it appears likely that early civilized man, with domesticated dogs accompanying him, was concerned enough with the effects of rabies (or what was then understood as the disease) to have royal decrees addressing the issue transcribed. In their definitive work on Mesopotamian religious symbolism, Jeremy Black and Anthony Green tacitly acknowledged that "it has been suggested that the disease of rabies was present in Mesopotamia by the beginning of the second millennium BC and more widespread during the first millennium BC."[10]

Such legal specificity comes as less of a surprise after considering the importance of dogs within the framework of Mesopotamian culture, as reflected by the religion, politics, and art of that time and place. The aforementioned Gula, Babylonian and Assyrian goddess of medicine, a deity with very distant roots in history, had a dog as her own sacred and symbolic animal, with the dog itself sometimes presented as an independent magical figure.[11] Elaborate dog figurines, some made of precious metals and dedicated to Gula by her worshippers, have come down to us. The practice was noted in a surviving inscription by Babylonian king Nebuchadnezzar II (reigned 604–562 BCE of Old Testament notoriety.[12] This close association with the healing process (as well as rabies) can in turn be linked to the traditional canine role of therapy dog, which included not only restorative licking but also giving patients sympathy and encouragement to fight their illnesses, especially where these same aids might be lacking from fellow human beings.[13]

Just as trained dogs were considered important within the sphere of religion, so were they visible components of Mesopotamian secular life. Distant ancestors of the famed but now extinct Molossus, a fearsome but controllable mastiff-like breed, were certainly used for security and peacetime hunting, as evidenced by period artwork.[14] They were likely utilized for military purposes as well and had definitely become a fixture in ancient warfare by the 6th century BCE. While Shakespeare is usually given credit for coining the English "dogs of war" expression, war dogs have, in fact, frequently been used for that literal purpose from the earliest dawn of Western history.[15] Probably because of their courage and ferocity, all canine breeds were mistakenly (but not surprisingly) considered by the ancient Mesopotamians to be animal kingdom relatives of the lion family.[16]

The central role of tamed dogs in the process of human evolution during the Fertile Crescent milieu is best illustrated, however, by the surprising abundance of canine art that has survived from that period. Outstanding examples of Mesopotamian dog sculpture can today be found within most of the world's great museums, particularly the Louvre, where incredibly sensitive, realistic depictions of mastiff and saluki-like breeds dating from the second millennium BCE can be studied and admired. Another good place to see some of the oldest visual images in canine art (as well as many newer ones from both Western and Eastern cultures) is the British Museum. Former curator Catherine Johns has conveniently collected many of these striking works in her superb study disguised as a coffee table book, *Dogs: History, Art, Myth* (2008). Included in this dazzling anthology are numerous Babylonian and Assyrian mastiff look-alikes being exuberantly led by their warlike wranglers and handlers, which, as Johns takes the trouble to underscore, are hardly to be found in ancient Egyptian art (see Chapter 2).[17]

Whether or not these animals were actually used for military purposes is almost beside the point; one still gets a definite sense, for example, why the Old Testament Hebrews, like most other Semitic tribes in the region, were typically no match for Babylonian or Assyrian armies in the field, given the mood of disciplined ferocity conveyed through these pieces. Also emphasized in this same volume are the important, multiple functions of canine imagery in Mesopotamian religion and medicine.[18] In short, to contemplate these artifacts and then try to deny how much these animals profoundly meant to our ancient human forebears is, at best, an exercise in futility. As for those who might question the true extent of human affection for such intimidating beasts, recall that Molossus descendents include much-beloved modern-day breeds such as the St. Bernard, Great Dane, Newfoundland, and Swiss Mountain dog. It is entirely possible, if not likely, that the now-extinct hunting and fighting mastiffs of Mesopotamia could also display the similar gentle, laid-back qualities of their contemporary counterparts.

Extinct though the Molossus now is, it long outlived the kingdom of Eshnunna, whose harsh, sudden, and unexpected downfall was typical of so many ancient city-states in the Fertile Crescent. Probably as Eshnunna reached the pinnacle of its luster under King Dadusha, in the Euphrates River valley to the southwest a young Babylonian prince named Hammurabi was coming of age.[19] Hammurabi's long reign (over four decades) as king of Babylon during the first half of the 18th century BCE began quietly enough as the city grew in strength and prestige, enjoying mostly peace and security. Then towards the middle of the century a series of crises hit Mesopotamia that rapidly catapulted Babylon to the top of the heap.

First came a devastating Elamite invasion from the east which subjugated most of the old Sumerian kingdoms along the Tigris River, including Eshnunna, whose weak monarchy after Dadusha failed to anticipate or counter the threat. Then as the Elamites continued to push into the heart of the Fertile Crescent, and no doubt to the surprise of many (including the Elamites), Hammurabi proved himself a vigilant and inspirational leader in battle, possibly with war dogs in his train. After the Elamites had been successfully beaten back into Persia, the now-feared Babylonian king went so far as to militarily chastise erstwhile allies who had underperformed during the conflict. This should have sent a regional message. Instead, in a final act of civic folly, Eshnunna declared rebellion against its new Babylonian overlord and attempted to resume status as an independent city-state, notwithstanding its having been lately saved from serfdom by Hammurabi's energetic counter-attacks against the Elamites. The Babylonian response was swift and ruthless. In the 38th year of Hammurabi's reign, Eshnunna was attacked, overrun, and this time utterly destroyed, never to rise again, all of its inhabitants presumably killed or enslaved. It is altogether possible that the buried rubble in which the surviving Eshnunna tablets were discovered in 1945 was the direct result of the city's total obliteration in the approximate year of 1754 BCE.

Today, of course, none of these distant events are remembered. Eshnunna has been almost completely forgotten, and the Babylonians, for the most part, are cited only within a biblical context. The name of Hammurabi, once the political stabilizer, savior, and terror of the Fertile Crescent, is now associated (at least among the educated) not with agriculture, trade, or war chariots, but with written legislation. In a final act of ego, or as a gift to civilization, or as both, Hammurabi bestowed his ubiquitous written "Code of Law" to a now extensive Babylonian dominion, which itself would temporarily recede in the face of Assyrian ascendancy not long after his death in 1750 BCE.

Claiming (and illustrating) in a lengthy preface to have received these laws directly from Shamash, the Mesopotamian Sun God of Justice (not unlike the manner in which Moses received the Ten Commandments directly from Yahweh), Hammurabi had his legal code engraved in Akkadian cuneiform—the same language as the Laws of Eshnunna—on a diorite stele, discovered in late 1901 by archeologists working in Iran, and now on display in the Louvre.[20] The code contains 282 provisions covering a broad spectrum of concerns. As the early 20th century scholar and translator Robert Francis Harper summarized, "He [Hammurabi] codified the existing laws that the strong might not oppress the weak, that they should give justice to the orphan and widow, and for the righting of wrong."[21] Though Mesopotamian laws, including those of Eshnunna, had been written down as early as the third millennium BCE, the Code of Hammurabi has become by far the most famous and comprehensive of these, as well as its namesake's greatest and most permanent historical legacy.

Unfortunately, the Code of Hammurabi, unlike the Laws of Eshnunna, do not delve into canine jurisprudence. While dealing extensively with livestock regulations and veterinarian fees (including standards of malpractice), the code fails to address dog ownership and control, for which there are at least two possible good explanations. One is that such comparatively minor and domestic civil issues were beneath the royal dignity of a king who boasted divine inspiration as the source of his statutes. Another possible reason, and one not totally beyond the realm of likelihood, is that canine matters were widely considered to be more of a religious matter, especially given the previously outlined centrality of dogs within the sacred Babylonian pantheon. Perhaps these things were viewed as more appropriate for the priesthood to decide, particularly since the Code of Hammurabi does not generally address religious concerns, except to adopt religious and royal authority as its wellspring, and almost in passing to regulate the moral standards of priestesses (not priests). It is also worth noting that in the code's famous preface, Hammurabi is self-described as a "mighty" or "charging" bull in warfare, although "raging" or, better yet, "rabid" bull could easily be substituted, according to no less an authority than pioneering Assyriologist and translator C.H.W. Johns of Cambridge.[22] The military self-descriptor of "rabid" is noteworthy. In their recent study on rabies, Wasik and Murphy observe that the ancient Greeks often conflated the two meanings as well.[23] Last but not least, the very name "Hammurabi" in the Akkadian language literally means "relative of a healer." Given the deep and widespread veneration given by Babylonians to their healing goddess Gula (along with her symbolic dog), it would not be out of the question if the king opted to promote personal associations with canine religious symbolism, one which most likely came automatically through his own family name. This, however, is speculation.

Far more concrete is the exact legal content of the Eshnunna laws, which, to repeat, certainly predated the Code of Hammurabi and possibly influenced its later creation as well. Of immediate note is that these laws do not expressly require destruction of the animal, even though it may have caused a person's death in a horrific manner. Eshnunna assigned responsibility for such tragedies to the owners and classified the acts as civil offenses, leveling hefty monetary fines at individuals deemed liable, but no eye-for-an-eye capital punishment, torture, or incarceration. As for the dogs in question, assuming they were rabid and not yet dead from the disease, their fate goes unremarked by the laws. Perhaps it was considered a discretionary matter for the authorities and aggrieved parties. One might suggest that implied destruction of the dog in such instances was a fait accompli, but later ancient laws, including Hebrew law, did in fact (in some cases) expressly mandate the death of an animal that had killed a human being. Another possibility is that in Mesopotamia all domesticated animals, including dogs, were considered too valuable or sacred to automatically condemn simply because they had caused something bad to happen. Recall this was a society that heartily endorsed human slavery and one in which the monetary worth of a slave was quantified as being less than half that of a free citizen. Furthering this more cautious reading is a qualifying clause within the legislation itself mandating official warning by government authorities to the owner (before the crime is committed) in order for subsequent legal proceedings to have legitimacy. All of this suggests that the domesticated canines of Eshnunna were widely considered to be far more than mere companions or pets for their owners. Indeed, if we could, one would be tempted to ask the Mesopotamian owners how much more, if any, a human slave was valued than a domesticated dog.

Four thousand years later in the Middle East, during the 21st century CE, dogs continue to be crucially important to mankind in diverse ways too numerous to catalogue herein. One outstanding example, however, is the distinguished saluki breed, whose ancestors were known to have become Man's Best Friend in the Sumerian city-states of Mesopotamia long before writing itself was invented.[24] A remarkable hunting sighthound famed for its blinding speed, endurance, and tenacity in the chase, the saluki then does a reversal, becoming extremely tender and affectionate towards its human owners.

From the Fertile Crescent, nomadic owners of the saluki fanned out to

Egypt, North Africa, and Asia, introducing the breed as far afield as India and China. Later, European crusaders brought the saluki back home with them. Later still, Renaissance artists were struck by the breed's beauty and grace, incorporating them into nativity and adoration scenes.[25] In America, the saluki has become a college mascot.[26] Everywhere it has been highly prized by royalty, commoners, and everyone in between. Despite a comparative aversion to canines by Islamic law (see Chapter 6), the saluki stands out as a great exception. Being bestowed many special privileges by the Bedouins and viewed as a holy gift from heaven, the breed rarely changes hands. Distinctive white neck markings are often reverently dubbed "the Kiss of Allah" by Muslims and non–Muslims alike. There has been speculation that occasional mentions of dogs in the Old Testament, particularly those made in a positive light, in fact refer to salukis.

Regrettably, war has always been too frequently the ultimate law enforcement vehicle. Whether dogs definitely participated in the early military struggles of the Middle East remains an open question, although it seems more than likely that they did. Beyond doubt is the fact that they participate in today's conflicts. The best, most recent example of this are confirmed reports that a military working dog was part of the American Navy SEAL team overtaking Osama bin Laden near the Pakistani-Afghan border in 2011.[27] While details and the identities of both men and beast have remained understandably under wraps for security purposes, this lack of specificity seemed to give even more free reign to public imagination certainly captured by the idea of a canine hero in the war against terror.

The incident confirmed that dogs continue to be used unapologetically as enforcers in the modern world, as well as being the objects of legislation, just as they were thousands of years ago in the very same geographic region. Moreover, after some four millennia, we do not foresee this dynamic changing anytime soon. The only things likely to change are the justifications that humans use to put their adaptable and more-than-able canine assistants to work. Some will continue to use religious motives; nevertheless, even within spiritual realms, whether these be real or imagined, there is no escaping the actual or symbolic presence of the Canidae clan. As we have shown, this lofty status certainly held true for Mesopotamia and its venerated goddess of healing and medicine. It was also a commonality with Mesopotamia's great rival of the distant past, ancient Egypt. Here, even in the afterlife, one was confronted with an abundance of canine imagery.

2

Canine Guardians of the Underworld

Words spoken by He who is in the embalming chamber: "Pay attention, to the decision of truthfulness and of the plummet of the balance according to its stance."—The Egyptian Book of the Dead, Anonymous, 13th century BCE[1]

While reporting on recent (2011) developments in the wake of the "Arab Spring" revolution in Egypt, leading American journalist William J. Dobson repeated a Tunisian dog joke shared with him by an Egyptian colleague. The joke went something like this: A Tunisian dog met an Algerian dog in the Sahara Desert. The Algerian dog was mangy, scruffy and underfed. The Tunisian dog was healthy and well-groomed, with an expensive collar. The Algerian dog asked the Tunisian dog why it had left beautiful Tunisia for the wilderness. The Tunisian dog replied it was there simply so it could bark.[2] That was the punch line. North Africans laugh; Americans are typically bewildered. Beneath the sly humor, however, lay some very serious and ancient Egyptian wisdom: namely that canine species often get a grip on reality long before humans do. When a lone Tunisian suicide protest—the kind of incident for which that country has been somewhat notorious for thousands of years—set off a wave of revolutions and government overthrows all across North Africa (including Egypt) and the Middle East, it starkly exposed how many Arab leaders, or rather dictators, had become indifferently out of touch with the day-to-day problems of their respective countries.[3] One of these vexations was repressed freedom of expression, which had become so extreme that, proverbially speaking, not even a dog was allowed to bark.

And yet, there were far more serious problems that Egyptian and other North African leaders failed to notice, fully appreciate, or come to grips with, thus leading to their inevitable and swift demise. Perhaps the most pressing of these domestic issues was that of rapidly rising food prices in the face of stagnant wages. This factor alone and overnight radicalized more otherwise peaceful citizens into revolutionaries than did Internet social media or, for that matter, any widespread violation of civil rights. The food problem in particular was exasperating for Egypt, a country whose Nile River Valley was once upon a time the breadbasket for the entire Roman Empire and Mediterranean world. While the ravages of time, climate change, and human mismanagement have diminished (but not extinguished) the Nile as a major agricultural producer, the humiliating quandary of the average Egyptian having trouble affording groceries proved a little too much for the body politic to tolerate. Nonetheless, it seemed as though the only ones who noticed the dire situation were those directly affected by the inconvenience. In effect, to not experience the shortage personally and firsthand equated with firm denial that any crisis was pressing upon them. A dog, wolf, coyote, or jackal would never have made such a mistake. Simply because a canine animal may not be hungry at any given moment does not mean that it is not keenly and simultaneously aware of growing or ongoing hunger all around it—quite the contrary, in fact. Canines tend to notice everything; moreover, their judgments are generally less clouded than humans by any vanities or pretensions.

Long before Islam, Christianity and Judaism left their heavy respective marks on North Africa; however, ancient Egyptian religion had given a prominent, respectful nod of sorts to canine objectivity in the form of its afterlife god Anubis and a number of other jackal or wolf-headed deities. Arguably the most famous visual images of these exotic figures are to be seen in *The Egyptian Book of the Dead* or *The Book of Going Forth by Day*, a complex and sometimes impenetrable collection of spells and rituals designed to guide devoted pagan Egyptians safely through the mysterious uncertainties of the hereafter. Numerous versions of similar texts had been rediscovered by Europeans during Napoleon's campaign into Egypt circa 1798–1801. Then later, in 1887, during the Victorian era, the British Museum purchased (under somewhat dubious circumstances) the most famous and spectacular example of this literary type, known today as *The Papyrus of Ani*, named after its original designated owner, a royal scribe from the mid–13th century BCE.

This was the New Kingdom period in Egyptian history, when Pharaoh Rameses II, also of Exodus and Hollywood fame, ruled absolutely an extensive Egyptian empire at the height of its power and prestige for over two-thirds of a century, between 1279 and 1213 BCE.[4] For those of us acknowledging the historical existence of a Moses or Moses-like figure, this would have been the same approximate era in which that venerated prophet led a less than fully cooperative Israelite people out of Egypt across the Sinai Peninsula into the Promised Land. Given its context and circumstance, *The Papyrus of Ani* represents the apotheosis of ancient Egyptian religious art combined with hieroglyphic text, commentary, and captioned illustrations.[5] One of the most dominant visual symbols found within this imposing document happens to be canine, specifically that of a black jackal (or head thereof). These repetitive jackal-like images appear no fewer than 20 times out of 37 illustrative plates in the lavish 1994 Chronicle Books edition, variously representing the Egyptian gods Anubis, Wepwawet, and Duamutef, or human priests in the guise of divinities.

This limited study is not the proper place to delve into the seemingly endless subtleties and nuances of ancient Egyptian religion. Suffice it here to emphasize that Anubis, son or nephew of Osiris, and his divine, jackal-headed cohorts were very important and popular deities within the realm of Egyptian religion. In essence, they were guardians of the underworld. Anubis, in particular, was crucial, having a three-fold task: to oversee the embalming process, to act as a guide for human souls in their journey through the afterlife, and most crucially, to weigh the heart of the deceased in the balance scale of justice to determine whether paradise or damnation would follow.[6]

Anubis delegated various embalming tasks to other deities, including Duamutef, son of Horus, overseeing preservation of the stomach during mummification. Wepwawet, son of Anubis, was a wolf-headed god of war and hunting, and opener of all roads, including that which led to death. Anubis, Duamutef, and Wepwawet all were closely associated with Osiris, supreme Egyptian god of the afterlife, and acted under his authority.[7] Any dog owner will immediately recognize how well these multiple roles of canine-headed Egyptian deities relate to canine-associated behavior—emphases on searching, hunting, eating, etc. Interestingly, *The Papyrus of Ani* offers numerous examples in which divine acts of licking and spitting are considered to have curative and restorative powers.[8] In this particular respect, Egyptian religion had similarities to that of its counterparts in ancient Mesopotamia (see Chapter 1).

It is also interesting that the ancient Egyptians adopted the aspect of the wild African jackal or wolf for so many of their religious symbols, notwithstanding their morbid emphasis on physical preservation (through mummification) and insistence on retaining material possessions in the afterlife. Transcontinental desert cousins to the American coyote, modern-day descendants of the African jackal so enthralling to the original inhabitants of the Nile River Valley include the black-backed jackal (*Canis mesomelas*), the side-striped jackal (*Canis adustus*), and the golden jackal (*Canis aureus*).[9] The English word "jackal" is itself, appropriately enough, of Arabic derivation. Portrayed in Egyptian art almost exclusively as black in color, jackals represented death, as well as transition from life to death. Given the seemingly limitless adaptability and stealthy demeanor of these animals as desert scavengers, it is not too surprising that they long ago should have become the very emblem of physical survival for emerging civilization in northeastern Africa. During that time and place, one surely wanted to be on the good side of a jackal and stay that way lest one's less-than-securely buried corpse be devoured.

The flip side of this remorseless, unrelenting quest for food was the jackal's well-known penchant for monogamy, devotion to small family units, and independent initiative quite apart from pack behavior, which tends to be combative. Jackals may not have been cuddly house pets for their human neighbors, but they clearly possessed abilities far beyond those of mortal men. No small wonder these adaptable, resilient creatures eventually came to represent manifold extensions and manifestations for the divine power of Osiris. Similar to the monstrous Cerebus from Greek mythology (see Chapter 5), this peculiar Egyptian manifestation of canine divinity served as a perfect guard dog of sorts for the human afterlife, an ideal combination of unsleeping vigilance and impartial judgment.

Various hypotheses have been presented by experts to explain why canine imagery dominated the religious symbolism of ancient Egypt.[10] This study will offer its own theory. Contemporary animal science guru Temple Grandin (see Chapter 20) has recently observed that nonhuman intelligent life forms appear to be totally lacking in the psychological illusions so characteristic of humans. All animals, and canines in particular, more so than their human counterparts, seem to be (in the popular parlance) the ultimate masters of reality. As Grandin has written, "another huge difference between animals and people: I don't think animals have the defense mechanisms Sigmund Freud described in humans. Projection, displacement, repression, denial—I don't think we see these things in animals."[11] Grandin then goes on to use two contrasting situations in which humans and dogs find themselves in dangerous situations.

Humans are notorious for denying the existence of imminent danger if doing so serves a perceived immediate purpose. A canine, on the other hand, would never do this. It might pretend not to be afraid of danger if it believes showing fearlessness might help diffuse a situation, but this is quite different from convincing itself (as a human might) that a clear and present danger does not really exist.[12] For dogs there is no such thing as denial; something simply is or is not. Add to this basic trait the extended and heightened senses of desert jackals (smell, hearing, sight) which allowed them to dominate the ancient Egyptian landscape, and we are left with a creature whose perceptive abilities are probably unsurpassed among the living.[13] Since canines, in the words of Grandin, have no Freudian illusions, they would therefore make perfect keepers of the balance for the scales of justice used in the Egyptian

Last Judgment. Human beings may kid themselves one way or another but never the impartial, jackal-headed deity Anubis. Indeed, one could well say that the primary role of Anubis was to guide the departed human soul back to true reality, for better or for worse.

In regard to the opening quote for this Chapter, never was a more terror-inspiring directive uttered in religious literature. The "He" who orders us all to "pay attention" is none other than Anubis himself, after having guided the departed soul (in this case, that of Ani the royal scribe) to the scales of justice in which the "plummet of the balance" will determine its fate. The physical heart of the deceased is measured against that of the feather of Ma'at, goddess of truth and justice. If the heart is lighter than her feather, then the soul obtains eternal bliss, if heavier, then it is devoured by the demon goddess Ammit. Anubis oversees the scales. The scene is brilliantly illustrated by *The Papyrus of Ani* in one of the most famous masterpieces of Egyptian papyrus artwork. With respect to Anubis, as Egyptologist Ogden Goelet has remarked, "There is something almost frightening about his red eye, as he steadies the right-hand pan with one hand and the plumb bob with the other."[14] The emotionless objectivity of Anubis, as portrayed in this work and consistently throughout earlier depictions, vividly captures the essence of this important Egyptian deity as a literal gatekeeper to the afterlife.[15] Loyalty to his master, Osiris, is absolute, and his mastery of the judicial scales infallible, if not outright terrifying to any mortal subjected to its pitiless scrutiny.

While *The Papyrus of Ani* includes perhaps some of the best-known representations of Anubis and other canine-headed deities in ancient Egyptian art, there are countless similar examples to be found, from the beginnings of the Old Kingdom period (third century BCE) straight through to the latter stages of the Roman Empire in the fifth century CE and well into the Christian era. As with Mesopotamian canine art, the British Museum alone houses numerous treasures (besides *The Papyrus of Ani* itself), and many of these can be conveniently admired in former curator Catherine Johns' superb anthology. Here Anubis and his cohorts can be seen in almost every then-known artistic medium, sometimes as half-man, half-beast, sometimes in full canine glory as a black jackal.[16] Apart from religion, Johns also shares examples of mortal, domesticated dogs represented in Egyptian funerary art (along with their names inscribed) as early as 1800–1850 BCE.[17] Mummified pet dogs were not uncommon. For reasons of its consistently dry regional climate, combined with the comparative imperviousness of its culture, more artwork quantitatively speaking, and therefore more canine-related art, appears to have survived from ancient Egypt than from ancient Mesopotamia.

Another prominent dog lover of distant Nile Valley yore appears to have been the teenage King Tut (Pharaoh Tutankhamun), whose short reign during the 14th century BCE predated that of Rameses II. Discovery of his nearly pristine tomb in 1922 revealed a treasure trove of precious objects, including an admirable bronze puppy figurine. Recently, in 2011, in a well-publicized gesture of goodwill, this artifact was returned by the Metropolitan Museum of Art to the Supreme Council of Antiquities of Egypt, which oversees most of King Tut's relics, as well as ancient Egyptian archeological treasures in general.[18] On a less benign level, and one far more in earnest, Tutankhamen (no doubt like other pharaohs and probably like Mesopotamian kings) appears to have employed dogs in a military capacity, as images of his formidable Salukis can be seen alongside his war chariot in a bas relief depiction.[19] Salukis to this day are surnamed the Royal Dog of Egypt, even though Egyptian royalty, strictly speaking, ceased to exist after a 1952 revolution and establishment of a republic in 1953.[20]

In a narrow sense, we possibly have Tutankhamen to thank for much of the magnificent Egyptian canine art following in the wake of his reign from the New Kingdom period, not the least of which is *The Papyrus of Ani*. It was Tutankhamen, or more likely his surrounding adult advisors, who severely rolled back the monotheistic religious innovations of his father and predecessor, Pharaoh Akhenaten, thus paving the way for a powerful resurgence of traditional pagan worship in the centuries that followed. It also may have helped push the exodus of the monotheistic Israelites from Egypt into the western Levant, to whatever extent that historical event actually occurred. Regardless of how these things precisely transpired, it is well established that polytheistic worship in Egypt was stronger than ever by the end of the second millennium BCE, by which time some of its most accomplished painting, sculpture, and architecture had been produced. This was the prevalent image of Egypt encountered by subsequent Mesopotamian, Persian, Greek, and Roman invaders during the first millennium BCE, and one that continues to filter down most forcefully to the modern imagination.

Yet another manifestation of this Egyptian worship in relation to canine imagery was the prominent "dog-star" Sopdet (Sothis or Sirius to the Greeks) within the constellation of Canis Major ("Big Dog"), the heliacal rising or maximum brightness of which marked the high tide and inundation of the Nile River, hence agricultural abundance for the valley's inhabitants.[21] When prominent, the dog-star Sirius is in fact the brightest star in the sky. It almost goes without saying that its waxing was considered a crucially important natural phenomenon in the Nile Valley. The Egyptian calendar understandably evolved around this annual event on which lives and livelihoods of its residents depended. As Sopdet gradually came to be widely viewed as a divine manifestation of Isis, Egypt's universal mother goddess, Isis-Sopdet was in turn portrayed by artists as being accompanied by, or sometimes even riding, a symbolic canine known as the Sothic dog.[22] Thus both supreme Egyptian deities, Osiris and Isis, had personal canine associations in pagan artwork, Osiris through his jackal-headed surrogate Anubis, and Isis-Sopdet through her cosmic Sothic dog companion. In short, to make any serious study of ancient Egyptian religion is to be repeatedly confronted with these symbols that seemed to link canine attributes with both the Day of Judgment and the annual renewal of earthly agricultural life.

Perhaps the first foreign invasion into Egypt to make any lasting cultural impression on its inhabitants was that of Alexander the Great and his Macedonians in 332 BCE greeted by the natives (for the most part) as liberators from longstanding Persian tyranny. Possibly accompanying Alexander into Egypt was his favorite dog, Peritas, one that had been personally raised and trained by the conqueror, then later, according to Plutarch (see Chapter 4), becoming the namesake of a town in India established by the Greeks.[23] In addition to the founding of the illustrious Egyptian city of Alexandria, the invasion of Alexander the Great also inaugurated a period of relative political stability not known since the decline of the New Kingdom pharaohs during the previous millennium. Upon his death at Babylon in 323 BCE Alexander's extensive Egyptian acquisitions were bestowed upon his trusted general and close companion, Ptolemy Soter, who proceeded to establish a Greco-Egyptian dynasty lasting nearly three centuries and ending only with the death of his more famous descendant, Queen Cleopatra VII, in 30 BCE.

It was this Cleopatra who first seduced Julius Caesar and then later his lieutenant, the triumvir Marcus Antonius, before both Anthony and Cleopatra were defeated by Octavian Caesar during the final phase of the Roman civil wars.[24] Whether one is speaking of Ptolemy Soter or Mark Anthony, it is notable how both Greek and Roman rulers opting for residence in Egypt tended eventually to be absorbed by and assimilated into Egyptian culture. For example, Cleopatra is typically thought of as Egyptian in spite of her Greek pedigree. Greco-Roman conquerors may have initially scoffed (as many Greeks and Romans in fact did) at the Egyptian custom of worshipping animal-like deities, but then they usually found themselves, at the very least, having to accommodate these deeply engrained local habits and prejudices. Furthermore, it may be asserted that one of the keys to Greco-Roman staying power on foreign soil, at least whenever successful, was a consistent ability to honor local customs, rather than employing attempted, outright opposition or reform.[25] By allowing themselves to be influenced, they in turn proved to be the most influential of occupiers. Their extensive relations with Egypt, spanning several centuries, resulted in countless amalgamations of social mores, including some relating to dogs.

A perfect example of theological canine amalgamation can be found in the Greco-Egyptian god Hermanubis, a creation of comparative late antiquity whose very name represents a combination of the Greek god Hermes and the Egyptian god Anubis. Greek invaders began by scorning and laughing at the Egyptian jackal-headed deity, confidently informing the natives that Hermes (Mercury to the Romans) was the true messenger of the gods and guide of human souls in the afterlife. The eventual result, however, was a compromise. Hermanubis had the body and accoutrement of Hermes but retained the jackal head of Anubis.[26] Apparently, the extraordinary canine sensory capacities of the jackal—and probably his impartiality as well—were considered essential to the god's very essence. By the time the Romans had begun to assert their will over the Levant during the final centuries of the first millennium BCE, Hermanubis had become the popular successor to Anubis in Egyptian religion. Another good example of this linking process occurred during the Hellenistic era as the important Egyptian agricultural goddess Sopdet became closely associated with Anubis as well.[27] Since Sopdet, whether viewed as herself or as a manifestation of Isis, was always symbolic of the Greek dog-star Sirius and dog-constellation Canis Major, Greco-Egyptians gradually came to associate this heavenly divinity with the inherent canine nature of Anubis. This link was not too far-fetched, given that Isis-Sopdet was mainly responsible for providing earthly food to mortals, an activity in which jackals of the Nile Delta appeared to have absolute supremacy. At this point, it should also be clear why limited space cannot possibly do any kind of full justice to such a multifaceted topic.

The stubborn refusal of native Egyptians, along with that of their occupying Greek and Roman overlords over centuries past, to abandon the canine character of their more important deities is, to say the least, noteworthy. Afterwards, during the first millennium CE, both Islam and Coptic Christianity would come to dominate religious worship in North Africa. These faiths continue to define modern Egypt. With this dramatic monotheistic shift in belief systems, there would be no more room for jackal-headed gods or dog-accompanied goddesses. As a corollary to this trend, *The Egyptian Book of the Dead* would sink into gradual oblivion and disrepute until its hieroglyphic symbolism evolved into new languages, was eventually superceded, and finally relegated to the status of superstition by Muslims, Christians, and Jews alike.[28] Centuries later as these long misunderstood ancient works were reencountered by Europeans during the Napoleonic wars, so too was an important artifact today known as the Rosetta Stone, conveniently transcribed in both the old hieroglyphic script and classical Greek.[29] It seems somewhat fitting that our modern understanding of distant Egyptian culture was facilitated by a proclamation from a successor to one of Alexander's Macedonian generals. Thus enabled, scholars and specialists have been gradually deciphering the world of the pharaohs ever since. By the time the Caesars had consolidated their control of North Africa and the Levant, however, the Ptolemaic line of Egyptian kings and queens had been extinguished, thus opening up a whole new chapter in Western civilization's understanding and perception of canine intelligence.

3

Beastly Virtues

> *"[D]omestic animals are worth studying,
> and before all the one most faithful to man, the dog."*
> —Pliny the Elder, *Natural History*, first century CE[1]

Surely the most famous volcanic eruption in recorded history occurred on August 24, 79 CE as Mount Vesuvius, with little warning, exploded off the Bay of Naples, burying or obliterating within a matter of hours at least nine densely populated cities and towns along its southern leeward face. The substantial violence of this eruption has become less remembered than that which it destroyed, a large swath of affluent seacoast resorts and villas representing the absolute pinnacle of Roman luxury during the mid–Flavian Imperial era; moreover, significant aspects of this distant world (including the victims themselves), especially at the celebrated city of Pompeii, were frozen in time by the suddenness of the catastrophe, preserved for future study by the lethal falling ash and flowing mud.

Among the countless thousands of aristocrats, plebeians, and slaves who perished in this disaster, by far the most famous and distinguished was Gaius Plinius Secundus (24–79 CE). Better known to history as Pliny the Elder, he was arguably the leading scientific author of his day (although that exact descriptor was not then in use, the natural sciences being bound together indistinguishably with philosophy and religion). When not studying the natural world, the elder Pliny served as military commander, friend of emperors, and prolific writer in an age where such a wide range of activities in one individual was not unusual among the more talented of the patrician class.[2] Pliny, like so many other great minds of the ancient world, found time and inclination to write about canines, among many, many other topics.

Much of what we know regarding the Vesuvius eruption of 79 CE comes from the only eyewitness to have later recorded the event, Pliny the Younger (61–113 CE), nephew and adopted son of the elder Pliny. In two letters written by request of the eminent Roman historian Cornelius Tacitus, the younger Pliny first relates how his uncle was commander of the Roman fleet stationed at Misenum, roughly 20 miles northwest of and opposite the volcano on the bay, when disaster struck.[3] After a leisurely, ordinary morning in which the elder Pliny devoted his usual amount of time to relaxation, study and writing, his otherwise-engaged attention was drawn to an imposing column of smoke rising from the summit of Vesuvius. In short order, he received an SOS from a friend living in the danger zone and without hesitation ordered the Roman fleet launched to the rescue. By the time his flagship approached shore near the soon-to-be annihilated town of Stabiae, Pliny's terrified subordinates were advising him to turn back. Replying with his conviction that "fortune stood by the courageous," Pliny instead led his rescue team in, where they met plenty of refugees, but were unable to sail back out because of prevailing winds and violence of the surrounding atmosphere.[4]

After spending a terrifying night protecting themselves from falling ash while Pliny rallied the spirits of all those around him, the group made a break for it, running south along the shoreline. Some in the party apparently found safety and lived to tell the tale, but Pliny did not, collapsing either due to toxic gases, cardiac stress, or both. His unmolested body was recovered two days later, according to those who found it, "looking more like sleep than death."[5] Back in Misenum, the younger Pliny, his mother (sister to the elder), and other locals got the scare of their lives, first with violent earthquakes followed by pitch-black darkness in broad daylight—probably due to blowback from pyroclastic flows which covered the town in ash—and finally (perhaps worst of all), widespread outcries of apocalyptic doom. Near the end of his second epistle to Tacitus, the younger Pliny, all of 17 years old at the time of the cataclysm, writes of personal calm throughout the ordeal only because of his temporary belief that the entire world must have been coming to an end.

Before his death, Pliny the Elder wrote at a time in which canines were first being seriously evaluated, however imperfectly, in the modern scientific sense. He was born during the reign of the second Julio-Claudian emperor Tiberius, when Jesus of Nazareth was alive as an adult but had not yet begun to preach. Pliny never married and never had children, even though Roman society strongly encouraged both. He may have been gay, but this was also a time and place in which sexual orientation was no barrier to civic advancement for citizens possessing extraordinary abilities. By the time Vesuvius took Pliny's life at age 55, the second Flavian emperor Titus ruled the empire after having earlier sacked and leveled Jerusalem, subduing the Jewish rebellion of 66–70 CE.

This had been preceded by persecutions of Christians in Rome by Nero in 64–67 CE that had killed the future saints. Peter and Paul, among many others. Then Nero's own downfall was followed by civil war from which Vespasian, father of Titus and friend to Pliny, emerged victorious. Almost needless to say, Pliny had lived through and survived much, only to fall victim to a natural disaster in which he opted to help others rather than flee to safety. Interestingly, there is little indication that most Romans in 79 CE even realized that Vesuvius was a volcano, it having given little previous signs of activity other than earthquakes, which had always been a routine occurrence in the Italian Campanian region. Early accounts, including surviving murals from Pompeii, portray Vesuvius as just another mountain, although some period writers had taken note of the ancient volcanic quality of surrounding soil.[6]

Pliny's voluminous *Natural History*, dedicated to Titus, was completed not long before the writer's death and represents a lifetime's worth of observation and study. It is one of the finest works of its kind in Latin, in spite of including an understandable amount of superstition, misinformation and prejudice. Book 8 (of 11 total) delves into canines, beginning with wolves, or, to be more specific, werewolves. Pliny, to his credit, mocks the notion and, not unusual for a Roman leader of the time, blames the Greeks for origins of the myth. "It is astounding to what lengths Greek credulity will go; there is no lie so shameless as to lack a supporter," he complains.[7] Underscoring the important entertainment aspect of his study, Pliny has little to say about actual wolves, dwelling instead on the more extravagant aspects of werewolf legends, including the possibility of future redemption for those thus allegedly transformed. Despite his scorn, whether actual or feigned, Pliny by his topical emphases alone acknowledges the enduring popularity of man-wolf themes for future audience generations (see Chapter 7).[8] He also comments briefly upon exotic (and likely fictional) hybrids such as the stag-wolf.[9] Pliny's fascination for these sorts of oddities may have been partly due to more recent and substantial arguments by historians that the unification of the ancient Western world under the Roman banner probably helped to facilitate more breeding varieties among all canines, both wild and domesticated.[10]

As a writer whose thinking was obviously grounded in Stoic moralistic philosophy, Pliny saves his most serious commentary for the virtuous qualities of domesticated animals, particularly dogs. Foremost among these admirable qualities is fidelity to man, upon which he expounds at length, giving numerous and extraordinary examples.[11] Many of these anecdotes include specially trained war dogs (see Chapter 1) fighting to death against all odds, not so much out of pure aggression as unswerving devotion to their masters, many of whom included notable kings. Other believable cases are cited in which dogs seem to consciously choose death after the passing of their owners or in the case of murder determinedly identified the perpetrator. A dog is even reported to have bitten its master's unfaithful wife.[12] Pliny's implication in this famous passage is clear: human beings would typically not show nearly as much virtue as these beasts in similar situations. For Pliny, a dog's worth therefore extended far beyond its capacity for mere physical work or temporary companionship. Last but certainly not least, it would be remiss not to observe in passing that the elder Pliny showed similar virtues of loyalty and courage to endangered friends appealing to him for help, and paid for it with his life. In a similar manner, the younger Pliny (along with his mother) refused to flee the deadly environs of Mount Vesuvius until they had learned the fate of his uncle; he then later wrote a tribute to the elder Pliny that now ranks among the most famous and oft-quoted letters from ancient history.[13]

In his study, the elder Pliny the scientist goes beyond praising the moral virtues of dogs; he forcefully asserts that dogs are also highly intelligent creatures with formidable powers of memory and audio response to human vocabulary.[14] "No creature save man has a longer memory," he insists.[15] Their powerful physical senses, he notes, seem to be a natural extension of man's own and particularly well-suited for the hunt.[16] Once again, there is a provocative subtext in Pliny's writings that canine animal intelligence in some instances might be superior to that of humans. Fifteen hundred years later, the great Renaissance humanist Montaigne, who knew Pliny's Latin book inside and out, would pick up on this same theme as he tried to make sense of Europe's then-raging and seemingly insane Wars of Religion (see Chapter 9). Curiously, as Pliny expounds at length on canine intelligence, he pauses to note that aggressive behavior in dogs can often be diffused by passivity in the object of its rage. A dog, it is suggested will usually not be aggressive unless it has very good reason to be so. In all of these casual observations, Pliny proved to be a great forerunner of modern animal science and animal behaviorism—perhaps the first ancient writer to seriously evaluate the canine species in this specific and quite original manner.

Pliny winds down this section of his treatise with miscellaneous, fascinating observations on both dogs and wolves that seem to reinforce their reputations for intelligence, adaptability, and social order. Having earlier noted that in northern climates wolves tended to be "cruel and fierce," he remarks that these same wolves were then being cross-bred with hounds in Gaul, presumably to develop toughness and ferociousness in the latter.[17] As an extreme, perhaps legendary, example of how formidable these creatures could become, Pliny cites an enormous dog, presumably a Molossus breed (see Chapter 1), given as a princely gift to Alexander the Great and reportedly capable of holding its own with an elephant in single combat.[18] Almost as an aside, Pliny inserts a very believable anecdote to the effect that Egyptian dogs or jackals are well known to lap up water from the Nile River while running so as to dodge hungry crocodiles.[19] After making some good empirical observations on canine breeding and pack behavior, Pliny concludes on a surprisingly misinformed note regarding rabies, perhaps indicative of widespread ignorance and uncertainty on this topic at the time. Repeating a number of old wives' tales regarding cures for rabies, he even throws in the colossal misassumption that rabies was only a threat whenever "the dog-star," Sirius, was prominent in the sky (see Chapter 2).[20] These errors demonstrate yet again that even the greatest minds are capable of occasional missteps, or perhaps Pliny was once again consciously fulfilling a role as imperial entertainer rather than one of strictly observational scientist.

Notwithstanding Pliny's frequent overreliance upon anecdote, there can be no denying that his enthusiasm for canines was shared by many of his aristocratic fellow Romans in and around Pompeii. Abundant evidence for this enthusiasm can be found today in the surviving Roman artwork long buried by the Vesuvius eruption of 79 CE today on display both in the extraordinary Museo Archeologico Nazionale di Napoli (Naples National Archeological Museum) and the even more extraordinary living museum of excavated Pompeii. Undoubtedly one of the more famous of these ancient relics is the mosaic floor piece situated in the vestibule of the so-called House of the Tragic Poet, prominently located on Pompeii's Via di Nola, realistically portraying a fierce black shepherd breed and boldly labeled "CAVE CANEM," or (roughly translated) "Beware of Dog."[21]

The House of the Tragic Poet itself is one of the most amazing artifacts found within the city, so named because of its elaborate interior frescoes depicting scenes from Homer's epic poems. The house has in turn fired the imaginations of writers and artists ever since its discovery during the early 19th century—the most well-known example being *The Last Days of Pompeii* (1834), a British novel by Edward Bulwer-Lytton—spawning a seemingly nonstop proliferation of plays, films, and musicals. The specific vestibule mosaic in question is hardly an isolated example of its kind from the Roman era (as similar ones have come down to us), although to this writer's untrained eye it is by far the most visually striking and sensitively executed. The unknown artist for the unknown house owners—all likely victims of Vesuvius like Pliny—obviously saw domesticated dogs as far more than mere living home security systems.[22] Today, the Pompeii "Cave Canem" mosaic continues to inspire creative writers everywhere, including one of its direct namesakes, the venerable society of African American poets based in Brooklyn, New York City.

Modern visitors to the ruins of Pompeii and the Naples museum are repeatedly struck by the detailed realism and immediacy of surviving artwork, particularly the still-vividly colored frescoes showing mythological and legendary scenes, as well as those from real life. Canine artwork is no exception in this regard. A sampling of these works include Actaeon being torn apart by the hounds of Diana (in punishment for being a Peeping Tom) from the exquisite House of Menander; Meleager and Atalanta reposing with their almost cutely portrayed hunting dogs after slaying the formidable Calydonion boar; and a mysterious image sometimes interpreted as Oedipus meeting the Sphynx with a passive, sitting dog situated between them as a kind of bystander or witness to the momentous event.[23]

Dogs were also used for allegorical caricature, such as in a private villa mural in which Aeneas, his father, Anchises, and his son Ascanius together flee Troy—a very popular subject matter among ancient Romans—but in this particular case given the grotesque, farcical bodies of monkeys with heads of dogs, perhaps representing another Roman commentary on the alleged Greek credulity of which the elder Pliny was so openly contemptuous. Then there are the incredibly elegant and anatomically accurate sculptures of dogs from the Imperial Roman era which surpassed anything the world had seen up until that time, sometimes subject matter unto themselves as opposed to simply window dressing for human events. Taken as a whole, these treasures speak volumes on Latin attitudes towards canines, often giving eloquent testimony to the same virtues of fidelity, intelligence, and skillful instincts to which Pliny paid homage in his great encyclopedic catalogue of the natural world.

Not all of these relics, however, are beautiful, or even artistic, for that matter. As a densely populated urban area that was suddenly snuffed out by a huge natural disaster, Pompeii contains more than its fair share of pathos and tragedy. The most poignant of these remains are surely the countless plaster reconstructions of the victims themselves, many of whom died by asphyxiation, suffocation, or concussion before being buried, along with their entire city, in falling volcanic ash, lava, and pumice.

During the late 19th century, Italian archeologist Giuseppe Fiorelli developed a method of creating plaster reproductions of those victims whose decomposed bodies had left vacuums in the volcanic residue.[24] The disturbing level of intricate detail achieved by the process is astonishing, as any casual observer will attest, sometimes capturing grimaces on the faces of the victims themselves. Of all these unfortunates, some would say the most moving is that of a guard dog tethered to a chain at the House of Vesonius Primus and left to its fate in the general panic ensuing on that fateful afternoon of August 24, 79 CE. Tellingly, the dog had instinctively climbed as high as its chain would allow to escape the accumulating ash before perishing.[25] One cannot help but wonder if whether, without the chain, the dog would have been able to survive. Given the well-documented rational behavior of dogs and other animals in natural disaster situations such as these (especially compared to frequently less-than-rational humans), the possibility at least cannot be completely ruled out.[26]

Now almost two thousand years later, the dogs of Pompeii continue to display a resilient knack for survival. While Pompeii maintains its status as one of the world's leading archeological tourist attractions, multiple challenges have been presented to Italian authorities, and not all of these issues are directly related to historic preservation. During the summer of 2010, in a noted piece published by the *New York Times*, foreign correspondent Elisabetta Povoledo reported on the growing problem of stray dog packs roaming Pompeii, alarming tourist groups the dogs followed. Although there had been isolated cases of individual dogs attacking people (some of whom possibly provoked the attacks), by far the more serious nuisance involved these packs tracking guided tour groups "in hope of scoring tasty treats" from "potential food dispensers" (i.e., tourists).[27]

In response to the unique type of crisis that only southern Italians seem capable of generating, the government, having first declared a state of emergency at Pompeii, then introduced a state-sponsored program for the adoption of theses strays, appropriately christened (C)Ave Canem, a wordplay on the famous mosaic vestibule warning found at the House of the Tragic Poet.[28] In typical Neapolitan fashion, as soon as word spread of the program's modest success, Pompeii subsequently became a popular anonymous dropping point for abandoned dogs, further aggravating the original problem. Leaving this conundrum aside, most everyone can at least agree that the stray dogs of Pompeii are not dummies—far from it, in fact. They do what they have to do in order to survive, and biting, or threatening to bite, the hands that feed them ordinarily is not part of this agenda. When Mount Vesuvius erupts the next time (as it surely will one day), we are confident that these same stray dogs will be among the first creatures to evacuate the area, and all the humans will do well to follow their lead.[29]

Returning to the ongoing (C)Ave Canem project, journalist Povoledo's profile cleverly focuses upon the fate of one dog in particular, a one-year-old mixed-breed named Sallustius, whose irresistibly "sweet" photograph amidst the Pompeian ruins is featured on the lead page of the article. Sallustius, like most of the adopted dogs in this program, was given a Roman name, after the House of Sallust in Pompeii. This classic urban dwelling, like the aforementioned House of Menander, happens to include yet another well-known fresco depicting the same myth of the miscreant Actaeon being torn apart by the hunting hounds of Diana. According to the profile by Povoledo, however, the real-life mongrel Sallustius has little in common with these vicious hunters of yore. On the contrary, during an interview with the rescue program's director, Giacomo Bottinelli, the young male adolescent dog clung anxiously to the side of the interviewee, knowing all too well who his ultimate benefactor was and even demonstrating an instinctive show of cuteness for the benefit of the press. As of the interview date, Sallustius had yet to be officially adopted by anyone, the program director was careful to point out. Thus the urgency of the stray dog problem in Pompeii was boldly delineated for an international reading public to fully appreciate. Pliny the Elder would have likely approved.

Among many other useful qualities, canines can teach us much about mortality and vulnerability—that is, if we pause long enough to pay attention. We may delude ourselves as to the extent of our alleged individual strength, resourcefulness, or determination; nevertheless, we are all at the mercy of the world surrounding us. Consider Pliny the Elder. Here was an accomplished, successful human being by anyone's standards, one who had somehow survived several reigns of terror imposed on the Roman world by emperors such as Caligula and Nero. Then, as if this were not enough, he survived "the year of five emperors" in which Rome was engulfed in yet another bloody, chaotic civil war.[30] From all this and more Pliny had emerged unscathed, only to heroically meet his end, along with thousands of others, during a great natural calamity that hardly anyone could have foreseen or anticipated. It is likely that he would have even escaped this final catastrophe had it not been for his sense of duty and loyalty. These qualities had apparently won him the trust of the Flavian emperors Vespasian and Titus, and the admiration of subsequent historians, not unlike the manner in which Pliny himself expressly admired certain animal species, including dogs.

About the same time Pliny met his fate at the base of an exploding Mount Vesuvius, however, a younger Greek contemporary from the other side of the Mediterranean world was beginning to make his own mark as a historian, one who would go on to influence nearly everyone and everything coming after him, from Shakespeare and Montaigne to the 1954 musical film *Seven Brides for Seven Brothers*. Like Pliny, this writer was particularly interested in canines, especially the manner in which human frailty and vulnerability could be overcome with unlikely help from Man's Best Friend, or in one famous case, from Man's (supposed) Worst Enemy.

4

The Wolf as Maternal Figure

And they were called Romulus and Remus (from ruma, *the dug) ... because they were found sucking the wolf.*—Plutarch, *Life of Romulus*, second century CE[1]

Not long after Mount Vesuvius exploded in 79 CE a well-traveled Greek nobleman and scholar took detailed note of the recent natural disaster in a curiously titled philosophic treatise, "Why the Pythia Does Not Now Give Oracles in Verse."[2] In providing an explanation for the skeptically perceived fashion of prose prophecies delivered by the Sibyl-Oracle at Delphi, the author first steps back, beginning with a strong assertion that unforeseen catastrophic events such as volcanic eruptions can only occur, and be predicted, through supernatural guidance. He concludes, "It is hard to believe that such things have happened at all, let alone that they were predicted long ago—unless with divine assistance."[3] In other words, seemingly fantastical occurrences, as well as human visions foreseeing these, are directed by higher causes—by God, if you will—such things being well beyond any rational human understanding. As most students of history will recall, by the time the quoted words were written, Greece, along with the entire Mediterranean world, had fallen under the complete political and military dominance of the Roman Empire. Recalled by fewer students of history, however, is the well-documented fact that many (if not most) of these non–Italian Roman subjects were more than happy to be under the imperial jurisdiction and protection of the *Pax* Romana ("Roman Peace"). Many, in fact, including Greeks, were even proud of it.

One may well ask what any of this has to do with canines. The short answer is that the Greek-born author of the Pythian treatise would later go on to record some of the most best-known and oft-quoted anecdotes on canine behavior in the ancient world. Lucius Mestrius Plutarchus, better known to future readers as Plutarch, was probably born sometime between

45 and 50 CE to a notable family in Chæronea, Bœotia, not far from Delphi and Thebes, also site of one of the most famous battles in history, one in which Macedonian forces under King Philip and his teenaged son Alexander defeated all other combined Greek confederates opposing them in 338 BCE long before Rome became a world power.[4]

By 66–67 CE the teenage or "college" age Plutarch was in Athens studying Platonist and Aristotelian philosophy when the Roman emperor Nero, fresh from ordering massive Christian persecutions that killed future saints Peter and Paul, toured Greece in search of fulfilling his own artistic pretensions.[5] Somewhat later (no one is sure exactly when), Plutarch also visited Egypt and then Rome itself, where he befriended powerful patrons, including the future consul Quintus Sosius Senecio (a friend of Pliny the Younger) and another future consul, Lucius Mestrius Florus, later acting as Plutarch's sponsor to obtain the then-coveted status of Roman citizenship.[6] By the time Plutarch was age 30, he was already making an international name for himself as an author and lecturer, and may well have been somewhere in Italy when Mount Vesuvius erupted and killed Plutarch's older literary contemporary, Pliny the Elder (see Chapter 3). In any event, Plutarch's obvious brilliance, versatile talent, privileged background, humanist education, extensive travels, and well-placed connections—as well as the fact he was born in the right place at the right time—all made him, by anyone's estimate, one of the most formidable and long-term influential intellects of the Greco-Roman epoch. It is no wonder that most of his surviving work continues to be read, studied, and enjoyed well into the present day.

Plutarch's greatest literary legacy would of course be his comparative *Lives of the Noble Grecians and Romans*, mostly written and published later in life sometime after the beginning of the second century CE. Although he had been born and came of age during the unstable, violent eras of the Julio-Claudian and Flavian dynasties, Plutarch found himself in 96 CE by then in his late forties and likely at the top of his game, witnessing the accession of the Roman emperor Nerva, who ushered in the golden age of Roman imperialism throughout the Mediterranean region. The next 85 years, through the successive reigns of Nerva, Trajan, Hadrian, Antonius, and Marcus Aurelius, would represent the high tide of the Roman Empire and *Pax* Romana, in which, according to the judgment of historians such as Edward Gibbon, civilized mankind possibly enjoyed its greatest age of overall happiness and prosperity.

Some historians believe that Plutarch may have lived as late as 120 CE (implying an advanced age well into his 70s or 80s), as the Christian historian Eusebius later wrote that he was in fact still alive during the reign of Hadrian, who came to the throne in 117 CE.[7] It was sometime during these later years that Plutarch produced his voluminous biographical studies (in Greek), including that of Romulus, historical or legendary founder and namesake of Rome during the mid–eighth century BCE.[8] The most interesting aspect of this legend, as one may expect, were the origins of Romulus and his twin brother, Remus, both of whom depended for their survival during infancy upon the unlikely, if not miraculous, behavior of a she-wolf.

Plutarch was far from the first author to give an account of Romulus (and in fact may have been the last word of sorts), but his was certainly the most extensive and appears to have been the most oft-quoted. The first Roman to systematically write down the tale had been Quintus Fabius Pictor during the mid–third century BCE at the unresolved height of the Punic Wars between Rome and Carthage. This titanic 118-year struggle between two geographically proximate world powers, astonishing in the sheer magnitude of its remorseless carnage, in hindsight makes most if not all wars fought ever since appear like brushfires in comparison. Fabius at the time was obviously using an extant traditional story to boost the morale of the Roman people, but he acknowledged that the first writer on the same subject (approximately half a century earlier) had been a Greek, Diocles of Peparethus, also later given a nod as the original source by his fellow Greek Plutarch.

In brief, after giving a lengthy discourse on etymology, Plutarch tells of how several generations after Trojan refugees led by Aeneas settled along the west central Italian coast, twins were born to a royally descended virgin who claimed that the father was none other than Mars, Latin god of war. Family rivalries and shame caused the twins to be exposed on the banks of the Tiber River, where instead of perishing they were protected and nursed by a she-wolf before being rescued out of pity by a local swineherd.[9] Growing into formidable manhood, the adult twins then turned on each other, Romulus in a fit of passion causing the death of Remus, symbolically representing the first of countless, debilitating civil conflicts that would plague Rome throughout its long history.[10] Romulus went on to establish his birthright by military force, founding the city of Rome as its first king and uniting the new kingdom (through an act of gang rape, however ambiguous) with that of the neighboring Sabine tribe before himself falling victim to either internal unrest or divine intervention, depending on how one chooses to interpret the conflicting accounts presented by Plutarch.[11] Less ambiguous is Plutarch's underlying message that divine intervention in earthly affairs trumps all human planning, scheming, and conventional wisdom, no matter how prudently and deliberately made.

The crucial role of the she-wolf in this legend is noteworthy and has been the subject of considerable unresolved debate among commentators. It is understandable to create a myth in which the founder of Rome was a mortal offspring of the Latin war god Mars; but why literally add a feral, beastlike element to the character of this individual? We are not aware of any documented real-life cases in which a she-wolf gives voluntary sustenance to abandoned human newborns; to the contrary, common sense and experience insist that in reality the infants would have become food for the she-wolf.

Then again, taken in context, that seems to be Plutarch's main point: the twins were saved and nourished only by decree of divine providence. Not only were they the children of divinity, they survived and benefited through supernatural protection alone, despite human efforts to destroy them. Moreover, the unique, often animalistic personality of Romulus was both his primary advantage as a cunning and fierce military captain and the eventual source of his downfall in peacetime, as he later became intolerable as a king to his fellow countrymen. His wolf-like character first made him and then later broke him, in a very real sense. The very fact that he instigated or caused the death of his twin brother, Remus, at a very early stage in his career alone suggests that—not unlike the behavior of wolf pack leader or alpha canine male—Romulus was quite capable of behaving in a decidedly unnatural manner, at least by normal human standards. To underscore this fault (or tragic flaw, one might say), Plutarch remarks upon the propensity of Romulus for sudden, unexpected violence as being one of his chief faults both as a man and as a leader.[12]

As for the she-wolf itself, the choice of a wild canine as nourishing infant savior by those who created the legend also has some logic to it. One might ask, why a wolf and, say, not a bear, a large feline, or an eagle? For one, the wolf (and no other mammal) was long considered sacred to the war god Mars.[13] In this respect, one sees a close parallel with the ancient Egyptian god of war, Wepwawet, typically portrayed in art as wolf-headed (see Chapter 2). For reasons that will be explored in greater depth throughout this study, it was the wild canine that, for many of the ancients, best embodied the full package of military virtues—toughness, fierceness, stratagem, cooperation, and above all, intelligence. The very fact that trainable, domesticated canines were often used in various military and hunting roles from a very early period in civilization onwards (see Chapter 1) further reinforces this connection. Lions, tigers, and bears, despite their formidable natures, could never be used in such capacities. In addition to their specialized rational, cooperative capabilities, canines also offered yet another rather frightening "military" virtue of sorts, namely their close association with occasional rabid, lethal behavior.

As discussed in the first chapter of this book, many of the ancient Western powers, including those in Mesopotamia and Greece, considered it a compliment of sorts to equate warrior demeanor in combat with that of an attacking rabid animal, although rabies as a disease was not as clearly understood then as now. In this regard the Romans were no different than their predecessors, although the decisive organizational virtues of their legions over opponents was something not previously seen in the Mediterranean military world. This same organizational virtue happened (by necessity) to have been perfected at the bloody height of the Punic Wars when Quintus Fabius Pictor first pushed widespread popularity of the she-wolf legend among his countrymen. Then, appropriately enough, at the absolute pinnacle of the Roman Imperial era, it again found full, complete expression with Plutarch's retelling of the same tale.

Plutarch's fascination with the she-wolf as savior of Rome was not an isolated instance of his keen interest in canines or the animal kingdom in general. Perhaps the best-known of these other examples is to be found in one of Plutarch's earliest surviving works, comprising part of his collected *Moralia*, or miscellaneous philosophic writings apart and separate from his parallel lives of Greeks and Romans. Probably written before the earlier quoted Pythian treatise (as well as before the eruption of Mount Vesuvius), his short essay "Whether Land or Sea Animals Are Cleverer" (better known in amateur literary circles under the somewhat misleading title "On the Intelligence of Animals") may well have been written around the same time Pliny the Elder was composing his *Natural History* in Latin and making similar observations with respect to animal behavior.

The form of the piece itself is constructed as a semi-fictional discussion between Athenian students, none of whom include Plutarch by name but surely contain many of his views and ideas. The students have their discussion, mostly a dialogue between the two main characters, while waiting for designated debaters to arrive who will argue the various mental capacities of sea creatures versus land game, essentially fishermen arguing with hunters over which of them has the more challenging quarry to stalk. The pre-debate discussion, however, focuses upon the merits of hunting itself, as well as the human-like qualities or lack thereof in the animal kingdom, a much more controversial proposition both 2,000 years ago and today. This informal discussion (and the essay itself) ends abruptly with the arrival of the official debaters.

The main instigator of this spirited, pre-debate discussion is one Autobulus, named after Plutarch's own highly esteemed father, and his comments likely align most closely with the son's own personal opinions on the same subject matter. The work concludes with an extraordinary proposition, especially by Greco-Roman standards of the time, that all hunting activities engaged in for the sake of pure sport, including the tremendously popular games publicly displayed in the arena involving animals (never mind humans), are morally indefensible. While defending man's right to use animals for his own benefit, including killing for basic food or in self-defense, Autobulus takes a dim view of those who would spill animal blood for the sake of mere recreation or luxurious living. He finishes his powerful, climatic speech with this: "The fact is that it is not those who make use of animals who do them wrong, but those who use them harmfully and heedlessly in cruel ways."[14]

At this point in the narrative, his alarmed companion Soclarus (named after one of Plutarch's fellow students) warns Autobulus to be quiet since hunters and fishermen, all personal acquaintances of the latter, are then approaching to begin the main debate. The passage is doubly remarkable given that Plutarch strongly suggests at the beginning of the dialogue that he himself had been an enthusiastic hunter in his youth and even written another treatise titled "Praise of Hunting."[15] Clearly the author of this rather surprising work was an individual who had personally experienced all of the excitement and thrills of the hunt much earlier in life but now had some second thoughts on the subject to share with his audience.

While Romulus and Remus were both noted by Plutarch as reportedly being excellent hunters in their youth—a quality no doubt passed along to them by their she-wolf surrogate mother—this was not the primary theme of his comparative biography. The biographer is far more concerned with the character of Romulus, his incredibly quick rise to power and his even more sudden, unexpected downfall. While the founder of Rome obviously benefited from divine protection and, to some degree, supersensory, canine-like ferocity, these very same extraneous forces seemed to play an active role in his forced exit from the stage of Roman history. Again harking back to the climactic speech of Autobulus in the "Pythia" dialogue, Plutarch writes about rabies with apparently more firsthand knowledge and authority (as a Greek provincial) than the Roman aristocrat Pliny had during the same era.

Before praising dogs in their oft-designated roles as guards and herders, as well as criticizing unnecessary animal cruelty, Autobulus compares rabies in canines to human madness, a malaise which (as in humans) nullifies a dog's otherwise "by no means despicable intellectual faculty."[16] Given the frequent ancient comparison of warrior dominance with rabid animal behavior, Plutarch's moral—when one considers his writings as a whole—seems to be that virtue in war can also be a liability in peacetime. Specifically, violent instincts may have their designated place if properly channeled into military aggression; however, successful statecraft must, above all, be tempered with reason. Romulus proved ultimately to be a failure at the latter activity, despite a natural penchant for reflection and cooperation. In the end, he was probably murdered by Roman senators (like Caesar was after him), a coup passed off by the perpetrators as an alleged act of divine intervention. Romulus, the wolf-like first king of the Romans, rising to the top with a combination of cunning and violence, then became the victim of wolf pack-like behavior. Above and beyond his own personal strengths and weaknesses, however, Romulus became founder of the Eternal City only through divine intervention in the affairs of mankind in the iconic form of a maternal she-wolf.

As one would imagine, such a vivid, legendary image has provided a field day for artists of all mediums throughout the last three millennia. From the British Museum alone a large sampling is displayed over the course of six pages in Catherine Johns' magnificently illustrated compendium.[17] Other outstanding examples are to be found, not surprisingly, all across the Western world and beyond. Most, if not all, of these works, whether sculpture, painting, or coinage, feature the nurturing mother wolf naturally dominating the scene over the infant twins. The presence of both Romulus and Remus in these depictions without exception is a subtle reminder to all beholders that one later instigated the death of the other, as well as an overarching theme of the children's total dependence on divine favor through a creature otherwise often perceived as their natural enemy. Thus multiple dualities of meaning are conveyed through a relatively simple artistic composition, which perhaps explains its enduring fascinating and popularity.

Poets would also pick up on the same theme, the most famous possibly being Shakespeare some 23 centuries later, but in a more purely negative fashion. In the rousing English history play *Henry VI, Part III*, Queen Margaret is vilified (with a qualifier) by her antagonist, the Duke of York, as "She-wolf of France, but worse than wolves of France" (I.iv.111). Shakespeare the writer, no stranger to either Plutarch or Roman history, hits upon the same duality of canine nature when deriding one of his greatest villainesses. Margaret possesses the deadly viciousness of a wolf, and yet (the Bard adds), this may be an insult to wolves, since even they, including the legendary she-wolf that nourished and saved Rome's legendary founder, have certain virtues. As an interesting footnote to Shakespeare's drama, we can see that the playwright takes repeated trouble in his work to remind audiences that Margaret was of Italian rather than English birth, further underscoring an implied lineal descent of sorts from canine surrogate parentage.[18] Like Romulus, Margaret (both in Shakespeare's play and in actual history) appears to have been politically undone largely by her own incapacity for controlling rash, ill-advised outbursts of violence, as well as an increasingly haughty demeanor towards her English subjects over the passage of time.

Although literary and archeological evidence on this topic is scanty from the specific period in question, probably the second most famous canine image from the Roman world, at least in the popular imagination, is the sacred wolf-skin military headdress worn over the helmets of specially designated legionaries. The closest thing to factual confirmation of this custom can still be viewed in modern-day Rome on Trajan's Column, an imposing monument erected in 113 CE to celebrate the emperor's Dacian victories along the Danube River valley and still having the power to overawe casual bystanders with its triumphal magnificence. This was the same period in which Plutarch was alive, active, and possibly writing his parallel biographies, including that of Romulus.

On the column itself can be seen a Roman *cornicen*, or military horn signaler, whose helmet is adorned with what appears to be a wolf skin. Although there is somewhat more evidence that these military animal-skin headdresses were in fact more frequently than those of a bear or lion—and the idea of a wolf skin in particular may have been considered sacrilegious in some quarters of the ancient Roman mindset—there is also no good reason to dismiss it out of hand. For example, the authoritative military historian Polybius mentions in passing the wolf-skin helmet markers worn by Republican-era Roman light infantry, or *velites*, to distinguish themselves in combat.[19] This popular tradition was endorsed (using Trajan's Column as visual confirmation) by no less an authority than the prolific British scholar and artist Peter Connolly (1935–2012), whose detailed, influential renderings can be perused within impressive, comprehensive volumes such as *Greece and Rome at War* (1998).[20] Discerning authorities such as Connelly have provided a bonanza for ancient military reenactors, however overdone and exaggerated some amateur enthusiasts can become in their fanciful depictions of supposedly authentic Roman legionary fashions.[21]

Plutarch wrote numerous other Greek and Roman biographies besides the *Life of Romulus*, many of which are considered definitive despite occasional flaws or inaccuracies. Of these, none is more famous than his life of Alexander the Great, who had subdued the Western world long before Rome represented anything more than a regional Italian republic. Although Alexander made his considerable mark on history several centuries before either Plutarch or Pliny the Elder was born, one of the Macedonian conqueror's most distinguished philosophic contemporaries had his own definitive biography written by yet another Greco-Roman chronicler during the third century CE. The connection is noteworthy because not only did Alexander's professed admiration for this philosopher provide one of the most colorful anecdotes in Greek history, the very school of thought founded by him also had a moniker with canine associations.

While the Romans came to have religious worship respectful of wolves as animals sacred to their war god and surrogate mother of their city's founder, the ancient Greeks had no such professed veneration of the canine species, at least not among the more respectable elements of their society. This was also long before it became desirable for a Greek native such as Plutarch to become a Roman citizen. Nevertheless, some six centuries after the fact, the distant memory of this unconventional sage, along with Alexander's respect for him, would be preserved for the edification and, dare we say, amusement of all future readers.

5

Down, Dog!

> *Being asked what he* [Diogenes] *had done to be called a hound, he said "I fawn on those who give me anything, I yelp at those who refuse, and I set my teeth in rascals."*—Diogenes Laërtius, *Lives of Eminent Philosophers*, third century CE[1]

Plutarch's biggest advantage in writing his classic biographies of Romulus, Alexander, and other prominent figures of the Greco-Roman world was that he wrote during the pinnacle of that distant society's achievement and prosperity. At the time, it must have seemed like Western civilization had gradually built itself into something uniquely durable and desirable over the previous millennium, that is, if one had full access to the benefits of its privileged membership. It would be only natural in such a setting to praise the virtues and analyze the faults of past heroes and villains for the benefit of future reading generations.

Plutarch, the Neo-Platonist and Greek provincial, was also writing, quite understandably, to underscore the considerable extent to which the Roman Empire owed its cultural and political heritage to colonial Greek predecessors. There is no indication, however, that the Neo-Platonists (or Plato himself, for that matter) were any great lovers of dogs, despite Plutarch's politic care in giving full credit to the she-wolf who saved the founder of Rome (see Chapter 4). To the contrary, Greeks were known for their open animosity towards wolves, as noted by Plutarch himself in his *Life of Solon*.[2] A little over a century after Plutarch's death, as the Western empire faced the first in a series of major crises leading to its ultimate decline and fall, the general public mood would have been quite different. By then, some may have even felt that a dog's life was one to be envied rather than despised.

It was during this later, more troubled, unhappy era that *The Eminent Lives of Philosophers* was written in Greek by one Diogenes Laërtius, an author of whom virtually nothing is known and whose moniker may or may not represent a pseudonym. Because of the language and first name, it is surmised that he came from the east, perhaps from the Roman province of Bythnia in modern-day Turkey, also birthplace to Diogenes' presumed namesake, the Greek philosopher Diogenes of Sinope (Sinop), who lived during the time of Alexander the Great, at least five centuries earlier. Laërtius may represent a place name in Bythnia or the family name of a Roman patron. He divides his philosophic biographies into those thinkers active in Greece itself versus Italy to the west, a psychological precursor of the empire being divided into two sectors by the emperor Diocletian in 285 CE. The date of composition is one of the most uncertain in all of ancient literature. Laërtius makes reference to the early third century CE but to no prominent philosophic figures of the mid-third century (such as Plotinus), leading to a reasonable surmise among scholars that he wrote sometime during or before mid-century. There are no direct references to the writings of Laërtius himself, however, until after the Western empire had fallen towards the end of the fifth century. The oldest surviving manuscript dates from the Middle Ages. During the Renaissance, Laërtius became widely admired, especially among distinguished humanists such as Montaigne (see Chapter 9), for the wealth of colorful and detailed (though not always reliable) information presented.

Assuming that Laërtius wrote during the early or mid-third century, this period would have represented the destabilized tail end of the Severan dynasty, terminating with a military assassination of the eastern-born emperor Alexander Severus in 235 CE.[3] This melancholy event was immediately followed by a prolonged era of economic chaos, internal power struggles, and external foreign threats which seemed at the time to presage the imminent demise of the empire itself, often referred to by historians as the "Crisis of the Third Century." Ultimately, during the latter half of the third century, the Roman Empire was saved by a series of brilliant military emperors, culminating in Constantine, all of whom managed (when not fighting among themselves) to beat back barbarian invasions while restoring civil order and prosperity. This same epoch, however, in large part because of the stressful nature of the times, saw the origins of Christian monasticism, as many people from all walks of life abandoned worldly affairs and the seemingly no longer extant benefits of Roman citizenship in favor of a more secluded, peaceful existence.[4] In this sense, the writings of Laërtius were a literary secular harbinger of the monastic movement.

It was also an era in which the Greek-speaking east appeared to be a more stable society than the Latin-speaking west. The word "ascetic" was itself Greek in derivation, the original ascetic in terms of lifestyle having been, in a very real sense, Diogenes of Sinope. Diogenes was the same philosopher who popularized the so-called school of Cynics, less a formal school of thought than a general attitude of contempt towards anything resembling conventional respectability. "Cynic" was also a Greek word, meaning "dog."[5] Cynics such as Diogenes embraced the intended insulting descriptor as a compliment. Laërtius, in all likelihood, was writing during very cynical times, and the centerpiece from Book IV of his *Eminent Philosophers* is, predictably enough, his own namesake, Diogenes of Sinope.

Diogenes of Sinope belonged to a wider milieu described by some historians as the Axial Age, a roughly 500-year period (800 BCE to 200 BCE), during which most of the influential philosophers and religious teachers of the ancient world were active. Besides Diogenes (412?–323 BCE), other prominent figures in the Greek sphere alone included Socrates (469–399 BCE), Plato (424?–347? BCE), Aristotle (384–322 BCE), and the lesser-known teacher of Diogenes, Antisthenes (445–365 BCE). Diogenes, Plato, and Aristotle all were contemporary with Alexander the Great (356–323 BCE); in fact, Aristotle was hired as the young Alexander's personal tutor by his father, King Philip of Macedon. It was Diogenes, however, who seemed to fascinate Alexander most, for reasons to be examined presently.

Except for his own guru, Antisthenes, and the universally venerated Socrates, Diogenes held his contemporary philosopher colleagues in low regard, especially Plato. As Laërtius wrote with considerable understatement, "He [Diogenes] was great at pouring scorn on his contemporaries."[6] Curiously, Diogenes was the son of a banker and, along with his father, early in life, had been caught up in a scandal involving the debasing of local coinage, and he seems at this point to have renounced the material world. Moving to Athens, he persuaded a reluctant Antisthenes to take him on as a student, then upon the latter's death became Cynic-in-residence on the streets of Athens, as well as a tourist attraction of sorts. Just as he had debased currency in his youth, so Diogenes continued to debase and discredit the dominant philosophical fashions and trends of his day, much to the delight or outrage of many.

Later in life, Diogenes was captured at sea by Greek pirates and sold into slavery. His subsequent unconventional, reckless demeanor on the auction block led to his being purchased by a wealthy Corinthian as a tutor for the man's unruly sons, an unlikely role for which the aging Cynic nonetheless proved to be a rousing success in the eyes of both parent and pupils.[7] Spending the remainder of his years in prosperous Corinth, Diogenes died in 323 BCE at age 90, according to tradition, on the same day that a much younger Alexander the Great died in Babylon.[8] Like Socrates, Diogenes wrote nothing, or at least nothing has been preserved, only anecdotes written down by others such as Laërtius. Indeed, Diogenes is portrayed by Laërtius as possibly the all-time master of the one-line zinger, surpassing even Plutarch's similar portrait of the Roman orator Cicero as a formidable trial lawyer. Like Laërtius during the third century CE, Diogenes had been active during a period of extreme civil unrest, namely the demoralizing aftermath of the Peloponnesian War in which Greek city-states had torn each other to pieces (not unlike wild dogs), thus leading to the swift demise of Athenian prestige and ascendancy of the Macedonian kingdom. In less than three decades, Athens had gone from being the Mediterranean's leading political and military power to total subjugation at the hands of its Greek neighbors (including Sparta), setting the stage for many a philosophic reflection on how such a sweeping thing came to pass so swiftly.

Describing himself as a "Socrates gone mad," Diogenes derided Greek astronomers for paying too much attention to the heavens and too little to more pressing, earthly matters.[9] His publicity stunts were notorious; for example, he wandered around Athens in broad daylight with a lantern in search of an honest man, as he explained to anyone who asked. The Athenians responded by calling him a dog and throwing bones at him; he retaliated by relieving himself in places they least expected.[10]

Diogenes, however, saved his most cutting barbs for Plato, the preeminent philosopher of the day, with whom he had a running war of words for several decades. Declaring Plato's lectures a "waste of time," Diogenes "scoffed at him [Plato] as one who talked without end."[11] Their exchanges were famous, with Plato usually receiving the worst end. According to Laërtius, the following took place: "When Plato styled him a dog, 'Quite true,' he [Diogenes] said, 'for I come back again and again to those who have sold me'"—a cutting reference to Diogenes' victimization by the Greek slave trade, one presumably endorsed, or at least not condemned, by Plato.[12] After Plato had returned from Greek Sicily somewhat more prosperous and under suspicion for his dealings with Dionysius the Younger, Tyrant of Syracuse, he tried offering the impoverished Diogenes helpful advice: "Had you paid court to Dionysius, you wouldn't be washing lettuces." The retort from Diogenes was harsh: "If you had washed lettuces, you wouldn't have paid court to Dionysius."[13] Later, when Dionysius was exiled to Corinth, Diogenes followed him around in the streets hurling verbal abuse at the former Sicilian tyrant for his evil past behavior.[14]

By far, Diogenes' most renowned interaction with a powerful personage, however, involved his encounters with Alexander the Great, who seems to have put up with his barbed commentary out of admiration for the great Cynic's transparent honesty and lack of hypocrisy. Alexander's father, Philip, had also liked Diogenes, one of the few things that father and son had in common. After being detained for loitering like a snoop dog in the wrong place at the wrong time in the wake of Macedonian victory at Chæronea (see

Chapter 4), the fearless philosopher was dragged before Philip for judgment, only to inform a bemused conqueror to his face that he [Diogenes] was "a spy upon your insatiable greed."[15] Instead of having Diogenes executed, Philip freed him with honors, possibly by then having heard of the famous Cynic's contempt for money and well-known animosity towards the Athenian establishment. Later, Alexander too was amazed at Diogenes' fearlessness towards him, a quality he was certainly not used to encountering.[16] At their first meeting, Alexander introduced himself with, "I am Alexander the great king," to which the philosopher responded, "I am Diogenes the Cynic."[17] Their most famous exchange, and possibly the most famous exchange to come down to us from ancient times, involved Alexander's visit to Corinth circa 336 BCE Finding the Cynic living in the street (as usual) and sunbathing in the open air, Alexander, in the presence of his entourage, asked Diogenes if there was anything that he could do for him. "Stand out of my light" was the curt, canine-like response. The master of the Western world then turned to his attending military staff and announced, "Had I not been Alexander, I should have liked to be Diogenes."[18] Given such accounts, it may well be that Alexander, like many others of his younger generation, preferred the rebellious insolence of Diogenes to the more flattering, diplomatic bearing of Plato, or for that matter, his officially assigned schoolmaster, Aristotle.

Alexander, unlike many of his supposed more civilized Greek contemporaries, seems to have been a dog enthusiast as well (see Chapter 1). The point could be easily overstated, but this may have partially accounted for his fascination with Diogenes. It is certainly true that Diogenes seems to have been more popular with the younger generation of the times than with his elders or contemporaries. As boys typically like dogs, so, too, those of the past tended to like Diogenes. As for Diogenes, he appears to have reveled in the comparison. Laërtius writes that "he [Diogenes] described himself as a hound of the sort which all men praise, but no one, he added, of his admirers dared go out hunting along with him."[19] For young men frightened of being bitten by his acerbic wit, he assured them, "Never fear, boys, a dog does not eat beetroot."[20] A contemporary Greek poet praised him as a "hound of heaven," and Diogenes himself went so far as to say that he would not mind being deified as Serapis, the Greco-Egyptian god sometimes portrayed with a canine-headed companion by his side.[21] Another tradition had the death of Diogenes being caused by a dog bite, just as he had bitten so many others with his sharp tongue while alive.[22] Most agree that his grave monument in Corinth, long since disappeared, consisted of a marble dog, in a sense fulfilling his own earlier wish.[23]

His greatest legacy, however, was the flourishing of Cynical philosophic thought in the Mediterranean world over the next 500 years. Long before

Laërtius promoted Cynicism by writing in the third century, we find Cynics being banished from Rome during the reign of Vespasian (69–79 CE), a contemporary of Pliny and Plutarch. Vespasian, well-known for his irrepressible sense of humor, one day chanced upon a displaced Cynic on the road who, according to Suetonius, while confronting the emperor "made no move to rise or salute him, and barked out some rude remark or other," causing the famously fast-witted Vespasian to respond matter-of-factly with "Good dog!"[24] A less good-humored response might well have been "Down, dog!"

The canine connection to Greek mythology forming part of the Diogenes tradition is noteworthy in that, despite a marked pre–Macedonian cultural hostility, Hellenic thought still always allowed a prominent place for dogs in its religion and epic poetry. Perhaps the most renowned pet in all of Greek literature is Argos, faithful dog of Odysseus, who, according to Homer, though aged and on the threshold of death, was the only living creature (wife Penelope included) to recognize his old master upon return to his native town of Ithaca after a 20-year absence. On a more ferocious level, certainly one of the most popular subjects in ancient Mediterranean folklore is the hunter Actaeon being torn to pieces by the hounds of Artemis in retribution for his spying on her nudity. The most intimidating supernatural canine, however, was Cerebus, three-headed guardian of the Hellenic underworld and mascot of Hades-Pluto. Other divine or legendary doglike creatures abound in Greek mythology, including Orthos, multiple-headed canine sibling to Cerebus (eventually slain by Hercules); Laelaps, the invincible hunting dog given as a present to the doomed Procris by Artemis; Scylla, another dog-headed monster guarding the hazardous Straits of Messina (along with Charybdis); and, on a more benign level, the goddess Hecate and god Aesculapius, divinities of magic and medicine, respectively, typically represented in art with friendly canine companions, possibly throwbacks or analogies to Gula, Mesopotamian goddess of healing (see Chapter 1).[25]

Canine references in Greco-Roman artwork are in fact too numerous to catalogue or categorize. Several interpretations of the same theme in relation to the traditions and legends of Diogenes, however, are worthy of mention. In a more modern vein, the 1860 painting *Diogenes* by French artist Jean-Léon Gérôme (1824–1904), today exhibited in the Walters Art Museum of Baltimore, portrays the great Cynic seated in his emblematic street barrel, holding his infamous lantern, and surrounded by affectionate street dogs seeming to possess more common sense than the average human. The sitting or reclining animals appear to be begging for food from a beggar who has nothing to offer except his extensive wisdom and insight into the world. Even more provocative is the 1848 painting by British artist Edwin Landseer (1802–1873), *Alexander and Diogenes*, included in the collection at the Tate Gallery in London. The meeting between the two personages in which Alexander is requested (if not ordered) by Diogenes to stop blocking his sunlight has been favorite artistic subject matter throughout the ages. Landseer, however, a sensitive and skilled painter of animals, dogs in particular, gives the encounter a new allegorical twist by portraying both Alexander and Diogenes as canines. Alexander the Great becomes a proud, strutting bulldog surrounded by a menagerie of sniveling hounds and groveling smaller breeds, while Diogenes, situated in his street barrel as usual, becomes a placid, downtrodden mutt, nevertheless completely unimpressed with Alexander's pomposity and affected grandeur. Charles Darwin (see Chapter 12) was known to have later criticized this wonderful painting for its alleged lack of realism, but realism is not the point. The hyperbolic symbolism speaks for itself, particularly for Diogenes, who manages to draw in the viewer's attention despite the outward dominance of the bulldog Alexander and his obsequious train of followers. Landseer's striking composition is also said to have influenced Walt Disney in the creation of his 1955 animated dog film classic, *Lady and the Tramp.*

In terms of pure, overpowering drama, the meeting between Alexander and Diogenes has never been more vividly portrayed than in a bas relief circa 1685 by the great Pierre Paul Puget (1620–1694), now on display in the Louvre. Puget distorts the legend by presenting Diogenes as a pathetic beggar and Alexander as a haughty passer-by; but Alexander's chained war dog Peritas is also shown in a pose either threatening to, or empathizing with, the Cynic, depending on one's interpretation. Puget, however, was far from the first artist to portray the two men together with a canine companion. An early imperial-era bas relief at the Villa Albani in Rome shows Alexander, Diogenes, and a street dog in respective poses far more faithful to ancient literary sources, with the dog obviously in allegiance to the Cynic, perched on top of the philosopher's barrel like a kind of sympathetic observer. As for Alexander, it is a shame that the famed Pompeii mosaic for which his semi-authentic image is perhaps best remembered was partially defaced by the Vesuvius eruption, since the complete work may have revealed a Roman-period artistic interpretation of his dog Peritas as well. On the other hand, there can be no mistaking in this work the deliberate, canine-like, rabid intensity of Alexander and his Macedonian "companions" as they rout the Persian forces of Darius at the historic battle of Issus in 333 BCE.[26]

The Villa Albani also houses an ancient Greek statue of Diogenes, sympathetically portrayed as a street beggar with cup and staff, accompanied by a dog. Unfortunately, the dog is considered by most experts to be an 18th century restoration, but a skillful one that accurately represents the authentic tradition of the philosopher. More disappointing is the recent unveiling of a civic sculpture in Corinth, Greece, boldly depicting (yet again) the meeting in that city between Alexander and Diogenes, but with no canine imagery included. Over two thousand years after the fact, the Corinthians are still apparently ambivalent regarding dogs in public places. One could even postulate that the disappearance of the original marble dog monument for Diogenes in Corinth may have been the result of disgruntled local vandalism. No such ambivalence is to be found, however, in the hometown of Diogenes. Today Sinop, Turkey, boasts an elaborately melodramatic but affectionately detailed public park statue of perhaps its most distinguished native son, still holding his symbolic lantern while in search of an honest man, side-by-side with a proudly seated pooch assisting him in his difficult quest. Both man and dog are placed astride the ubiquitous street barrel, complete with explanatory inscriptions in Turkish and English.[27] The site is not only a poignant reminder of the city's ancient heritage, but also of the educated Islamic world's deep respect for the philosophical heritage of the Greco-Roman world, one which they inherited (and helped enormously to preserve) along with the Judeo-Christian West.

The same reverence that Islamic society held for ancient Hellenic thought did not extend to their Byzantine contemporaries after the fall of the Western Roman Empire in 476 CE. For that matter, one could easily argue that the rapaciousness and arrogance of the subsequent Eastern Roman Empire towards its non–Greek subjects was a major factor in the sudden rise and spectacular growth of Islam during the seventh century. If a Greco-Roman biographer such as Diogenes Laërtius was a product of an era witness to a declining West and ascendant East, then the versified teachings of the Prophet Muhammad less than five centuries later would foreshadow the eventual fall of Constantinople, though its eventual demise would prove to be even more excruciatingly gradual and drawn out than that of Rome's. By the time the dust had settled, a good part of the Western world previously subdued by Alexander the Great had embraced a new religion emphatically separate from the older, supposedly more established Judeo-Christian traditions. One unfortunate by-product of this new cultural trend would be, with a few grand exceptions, a general aversion to canines. Interestingly, one of the most delightful of these exceptions—at least in written form—originated from the old Persian Empire overrun by Alexander (and his dog Peritas) during the previous millennium.

6

In Defense of Dogs

You should know—may God exalt you!—that a dog is more affectionate towards his master than a father towards his son or one blood brother towards another. He guards his master and protects his household, whether the master is present or absent, whether he is sleeping or awake. The dog does not shrink from this task, even if he is treated harshly. He does not let people down, even if they let him down.—Ibn al-Marzubān, *The Superiority of Dogs Over Many of Those Who Wear Clothes*, 10th century[1]

With the fall of the Western Roman Empire in 476 CE came long-term instability for the Mediterranean world, which subsided only somewhat in the Greek-speaking East with continuance of a thriving Byzantine Empire centered in Constantinople. After the death of Eastern emperor Justinian I in 565 CE however, began a prolonged period of war, plague, corruption, territorial shrinkage, and general decline. This set the stage for the most significant event of that epoch—the forcible expulsion of the Byzantines from a good part of the Middle East during the mid-seventh century by the explosive, militant spread of a new religion emanating out of the Arabian Peninsula. Farther to the east, the old Sassanid dynasty of the Persian Empire (modern-day Iran) was toppled in less than a decade (633–642 CE by the same new conquering force. Although the Prophet Muhammad (570–632 CE was by that time no longer alive, armies fervently marching in his name seemingly swept everything before them, being stopped only temporarily at Constantinople itself in 678 CE and more permanently by an emerging Frankish kingdom under Charles Martel at the epic Battle of Tours in 732 CE.

As former Greek colonies in Anatolia and the Levant began to pay tribute (sometimes preferably) to their new Arabian overlords, it might be easily said that one of the few things shared by traditional Greek and Arab cultures was a certain ambivalent attitude towards canines. Persia, however, was a different case. While slowly adopting the religion of its conquerors over the course of several centuries, Persia simultaneously and stubbornly retained many of its non-Arabian customs. Included among these was a longstanding veneration for domesticated dogs, a social convention extending all the way back to pre-Islamic religious worship in the Zoroastrian tradition.² Therefore it seems only natural that one of the most passionately written praises of canines from the Islamic sphere of influence should also come from the pen of one who in all likelihood had strong and longstanding personal roots in ancient Persian culture.

Although there appears a growing consensus that wild wolves were first tamed by mankind somewhere in western Asia long before the written word came into being, whether the honor of this important breakthrough belongs to Mesopotamian Iraq (see Chapter 1) or Persian Iran remains an open question. While the proliferation of highly developed city-states along the Fertile Crescent certainly marked the beginning of Western civilization in the historical sense, the concurrent rise of urbanized Susa and attending Elamite culture in southwest Persia provided the former with dynamic neighboring antagonists from the get-go. Elam's then somewhat less civilized populace may well have had better, and more, opportunity to interact with canines. In any event, definitive answers to such questions are lost in the remote annals of history. Fast forwarding several millennia, by the 10th century Persia, a word meaning literally "land of the Aryans," was flourishing under its first home-grown Islamic dynasty, the Samanids. Though themselves Sunni Muslims, the Samanids officially tolerated Twelver Shi'ism, thus setting the stage for that distinctive branch of Islam that permanently became the majority faith of Persia during the 11th century under the subsequent Buyid dynasty. Hence Persian Iran became perpetually and decisively separated in religious doctrine (as well as secular culture) from the dominant Sunni-majority of the Muslim world. The Samanids, however, also proved to be great patrons of native Persian literature. It was probably while under the distant spell of this intellectually friendly, enlightened environment that Ibn al-Marzubān of Baghdad produced in Arabic his offbeat, going-against-the-grain treatise in favor of domesticated canines.

Very little is known of the life and career of Abū Bakr Muhammad ibn Khalaf ibn al-Marzubān (?–921 CE), other than that he appears to have been active in and around the precincts of Baghdad during the early 10th century, the height of the "Islamic Golden Age" in which classical learning flourished while a destabilized Europe simultaneously sank into the depths of the Dark Ages.³ Although writing in Arabic at the then–Arabic center of political and military power, al-Marzubān seems to have had strong Persian connections. The very name of al-Marzubān is of Persian derivation, suggesting that the author's family came from the east or that he himself was born there.⁴ Near contemporaries credit him with translating over 50 works from the Persian language into Arabic; moreover, al-Marzubān sometimes employs Persian words, as well as drawing upon material from Persian and Indian sources, particularly the timeless *Arabian Nights* tradition.[5] All evidence suggests that as a writer he participated in the torrential influx of classical Persian literature and learning into the Arabic language during that period. The collection, tersely known in Arabic as *Fadl al-Kilab*, wonderfully translated by Egyptian-born Professor M.A.S. Abdel Haleem (University of London) as *The Superiority of Dogs Over Many of Those Who Wear Clothes*, today survives in various printed and manuscript texts found in Cairo, Beirut, Berlin, and Paris.[6]

Of the many wonders in an endlessly surprising treatise, perhaps the biggest surprise is al-Marzubān's obviously deliberate failure to credit his primary source, his great contemporary al-Jāhiz of Basra (781–869), the foremost Arabic prose writer of his day from whose voluminous *Hayawān* no fewer than 15 stories in *The Superiority of Dogs* appear to be taken. Otherwise scrupulous in giving credit to source materials, it has been reasonably surmised that the younger al-Marzubān was writing in rivalry or opposition to the non–Persian al-Jāhiz, the latter also feeling obliged to present extensive anti- as well as pro-canine views in his work.[7] As a native of Mesopotamian Basra, al-Jāhiz most likely was attempting to achieve a delicate balance between the dog-friendly attitudes and customs of Bedouin tribesmen and the less-than-friendly canine traditions of more cultivated Islamic urban dwellers from the Arabian Peninsula. The pro–Persian al-Marzubān, on the other hand, apparently saw no such need to be ambivalent, diplomatic, or tactful on this particular subject matter, one that no doubt was so near and dear to the traditional Persian literary sensibility.

In English translation, the text for *The Superiority of Dogs Over Many of Those Who Wear Clothes*, minus illustrations, is less than 30 pages in length. This slim volume nonetheless lives up to the promise of its tremendous title. As a collection of miscellaneous poetry, prose and anecdotes, it immediately sets the overall tone by opening with a seven-page lament titled "Man Has Gone to the Dogs!"[8] By the 10th century, Islam's days of rapid territorial expansion were a thing of the past, excepting future Ottoman conquests in eastern Europe, including that of Constantinople in 1453. To the contrary, this was more a period of material and academic enrichment, one in which, for many Muslims at least, the selfless military fervor of the 7th and 8th centuries had subsided in favor of a more pragmatic and worldly outlook. For the favorite poets of al-Marzubān, "real people" and "the reign of glory" were things of the past, replaced by (curiously enough) "wolves" and "dogs"—the only instance in which he quotes these terms in a pejorative sense—beings who figuratively devour each other when not behaving in a predatory manner.[9] By way of contrast, later in the text he recites a poem in which a Bedouin is insulted by a comrade with the slur of "dog" but chooses to take it as a compliment instead.[10] English commentator Haleem goes so far as to remind general readers that these differences in rural versus urban perceptions in the Arab sphere could have made courtly life for a naïve Bedouin awkward, in that (to him at least) positive dog-like qualities such as loyalty and friendship would be considered desirable in a leader but not necessarily taken as flattery by the leader himself.[11]

The heart of the work comes in the second half, titled "Man's Best Friend" and consisting of miscellaneous stories and poems in praise of dogs.[12] As in Pliny (see Chapter 3), a bereaved dog dies immediately after its deceased master; as in Plutarch (see Chapter 4), a helpless infant is weaned and saved by a she-wolf.[13] At least two stories are drawn from the *Arabian Nights*, both with canine heroes substituted for other members of the animal kingdom in the older collection, although the Persian and Indian sources for the original otherwise abound in canine imagery and motifs. Ibn al-Marzubān's tale of a king saved by the willing self-sacrifice of his faithful dog has a close parallel in the Persian story of King Sinbad being rescued by the suicidal death of his favorite hunting falcon.[14] The climactic scene in *The Superiority of Dogs* involves a variation on the timeless, borderless "faithful hound" theme in which a dog saves the child of his master by killing a snake, but then is killed by his later remorse-stricken master in a mistaken belief that the dog had murdered a yet-to-be discovered safe and sound child. Derived from the ancient Indian folktale of the Brahmin and the Mongoose, this tale, Professor Haleem is quick to point out, inspired subsequent European versions such as the 13th century Welsh legend of the faithful hound Gelert (see Chapter 8), a legend which appears to be a direct descendent of this same tradition, coming to Europe first via Persia and then later Arabia.[15] All in all, al-Marzubān repeatedly drives home his Persian-Bedouin pro-canine sentiments, although this repetitive, perhaps even strident, approach may have been necessary and appropriate given the stubbornly resistant cultural environment of his own urban milieu in 10th century Baghdad.

In effect, al-Marzubān was boldly challenging deeply ingrained, unfavorable cultural attitudes and social mores towards dogs. With the notable exception of the longstanding Arab love affair with the ancient Saluki breed (see Chapter 1), Middle Eastern popular sentiments towards canines have been traditionally ambivalent, if not wary, long predating the advent of Islam. This negative mindset is all the more curious since dogs were apparently first domesticated in the Middle East at the dawn of Western civilization. Nevertheless, Islam's deep concerns for ritual purity and cleanliness have created potential conflicts for interactions with canines in daily human life.[16]

The Qur'an is tactfully reticent on this controversial topic, although Sura V (*Al-Ma'ida*, The Feast) makes express allowances for consumption of certain meats gathered by "beasts of prey" (verse 3) provided the final killing, preparation, and proper blessings are supplied by the faithful observer.[17]

Bedouin tribesmen, among other Muslims, have eagerly interpreted this clause as allowing for necessary hunting and training activities by their prized Salukis. Indeed it is hardly conceivable that any human being with feelings or intellect could resist the irresistible Saluki charm. There is no indication, however, that al-Marzubān was writing for or near the precincts of a Bedouin nomadic society; more likely, he was consciously posing provocative questions for a literate elite on behalf of a foreign culture (Persia) where the ascendancy of Islam was a comparatively recent phenomenon, with impetus for these questions coming from an independent and (in many respects) more advanced Persian society.[18] Any entrenched, pre–Islamic prejudices from the Arabian Peninsula, Byzantine Empire, or anywhere else for that matter, had little resonance with Persian inheritors of the Zoroastrian tradition. Though writing or translating for a mainly non–Persian audience from the seat of the pro–Persian, Abbasid Caliphate in Baghdad, al-Marzubān appears to have been one of many literary voices actively engaged in this proactive educational process.

Somewhat surprisingly, Judaism (like Islam), is a belief system not particularly well-disposed, or at least highly ambivalent, towards canines. The Torah and Old Testament are sprinkled with negative dog references. In many respects this is to be expected, given that many of the ancient Hebrews' mortal enemies were dog worshippers in the literal or figurative religious sense. Some of the more prominent of these antagonists included the Assyrians and Babylonians of Mesopotamia (see Chapter 1), the Egyptians (see Chapter 2), and, perhaps most egregious of all, the Canaanites and Philistines of biblical infamy, both possibly descendants of the so-called Sea Peoples who once terrorized the eastern Mediterranean world in the days before the Hebrew Exodus.

A good example of Old Testament canine condemnation can be found in Deuteronomy 23:19, which proscribes "the earnings of a dog" as a temple offering, variously interpreted as the wages of a male prostitute or, more likely, the common pagan practice in the ancient Middle East of idolatrous dog worship as a healing or medicinal practice.[19] This same hostile attitude carries over into the New Testament, as exemplified by the extraordinary passage in Matthew 15:21–28, one in which Jesus publicly rebukes a Canaanite woman for her request (for her dying daughter) for healing with, "It is not fair to take the children's food and throw it to the dogs." Undeterred, the Canaanite woman responds with, "Ah yes, Lord; but even little dogs eat the scraps that fall from their masters' table," at which point Jesus praises her faith and heals her daughter without moving from the spot. The incident is striking on several levels, not only because Jesus (as a Jew) extends divine healing power to a widely despised gentile, but, even more scandalous, to a Canaanite whose ancestors worshipped dogs for this same specific purpose. Jewish religious skepticism towards dogs seemed to soften a bit by the late 11th century with the genius of Rabbi Shlomo Yitzhaki, aka Rashi (1040–1105), whose commentaries on Exodus 11:7 noted that dogs assisted the Israelites in their escape from Egypt by not barking, thereby earning their future domestic upkeep.[20] The 20th century horrors of the Holocaust, however, did little to improve a longstanding Jewish wariness towards canines, particularly in their formidable roles as guard and scenting patrol dogs.

Just when it seemed there was little hope for ever improving relations between devout Jews and specially trained security dogs, a remarkable individual by the name of Rudolphina Menzel (1891–1973) entered history. Dr. Menzel, a trained cynologist, escaped from the German-Austrian *Anschluss* of 1938 to British Palestine where before, during, and after World War II she began, nearly single-handedly, to rehabilitate the canine image in the eyes of her Israeli countrymen. Menzel found herself irresistibly drawn towards the feral street animals today popularly referred to as the Canaan Dog, also known in the more disapproving eyes of her Arab (and many Israeli) neighbors as the Palestinian Pariah Dog or Bedouin Sheepdog. Before Menzel's time, the Canaan Dog was widely considered a second class doggie citizen of the Middle East next to the venerated Saluki breed. Menzel proceeded, however, to train and domesticate these semi-wild creatures en masse, finding them to be highly intelligent, adaptable, and vigilant companions. By the early 1950s, thanks to the work of Menzel and her team, the Canaan Dog had become proficient in the very same security roles for Jews that had once been used against them in the old country, assuming the unofficial role of national dog for the fledgling Israeli state.[21]

During the 1960s, the breed was introduced into the UK and U.S., among other places, where it continues to thrive as a highly popular and much loved kennel club favorite. Unfortunately, back in the Holy Land, the same breed today is fighting for survival against encroaching civilization, warfare, and anachronistic attitudes, even as it continues to loyally serve in the roles of military working dogs for the Israeli armed forces.[22] Sha'ar Hagai Kennels, a direct descendent of Menzel's pioneering efforts to rescue the Canaan Dog from the deserts and streets of Israel, is currently facing legal eviction from government lands. Hopefully, the Canaan Dog will continue to survive against all odds, just as it has over the previous millennia. Evidence for their resilience can be found in the Lebanese city of Sidon with the "Alexander Sarcophagus" dating from the late 4th century BCE. Here a dramatic bas relief depicts Alexander the Great (see Chapter 5) and his local client king accompanied and assisted on a tumultuous lion hunt by what closely resembles a modern-day Canaan Dog, presumably the local king's very own hunting companion of choice.

The most startling evidence for the great antiquity of the Canaan Dog breed, however, comes from the city of Ashkelon located along the south Israeli coast. Detailed results of recent archeological digs on that historic site were published in July 2010 by the *Biblical Archeological Review* (BAR) under the unusual heading of "Why Were Hundreds of Dogs Buried at Ashkelon?" by Professor Lawrence Stager of Harvard University. Describing their find in BAR as "one of the strangest discoveries of the entire excavation," Stager's team unearthed over 700 dog skeletons in one concentrated area (with perhaps thousands more still uncovered) in what was pronounced as "by far the largest animal cemetery of any kind known in the ancient world." All of the skeletons bore a close anatomical similarity to the modern Canaan Dog breed.

Noting that the monumental pet cemetery dated from the period of Persian domination for that region (prior to Alexander the Great in the 4th century BCE), Stager hypothesized that "the best explanation seems to be that the Ashkelon dogs were revered as sacred animals." He adds that dogs, apart from their venerable standing within the pre–Islamic Zoroastrian tradition of Persia, were probably intimately associated with the pagan healing gods by non–Jewish Canaanite and Phoenician residents of that cosmopolitan city, much as they had been earlier by the Babylonians and Assyrians of Mesopotamia.[23] Stager concludes by stating that this hypothesis could be confirmed by the future discovery of a local pagan temple dedicated for this specific purpose, similar to the one identified in the Babylonian city of Isin for the healing goddess Gula (see Chapter 1). In either event, this amazing discovery seems to fly in the face of traditional perceived prejudices against canines in pre-modern Greek, Jewish and Islamic cultures.

As one might expect, there is a relative scarcity of sympathetically portrayed canines in Islamic art. Once again, however, the wonderful saluki breed proves to be an exception, as was Persian culture itself. One particular work viewed as a prime example, today housed within the famed David Museum in Copenhagen, Denmark, is *Man with a Saluki*, a miniature painted on cotton fabric, circa 1555, signed by Mulla Dust, aka Dust Muhammad (1490?–1565?), a well-known Persian artist of the period (or one of his students) employed by the shah. The image is a classic in the true sense of the word. Depicting a colorful but perturbed turbaned man holding a saluki on a leash, the supposed human master pulls vainly in one direction while the dog stands its ground with seeming effortlessness, facing in the opposite direction with an expression that could easily be described as a doggie smile. Any experienced dog owner will recognize the situation. It has been suggested that this composition might represent a metaphor for the subject matter's marital relations, but a literal interpretation carries just as much, if not more impact. To lead a saluki where it does not want to go requires much human willpower, not to mention physical strength. Al-Marzubān would have surely appreciated the sentiment of this image, even though it was painted over five centuries after his time.

Al-Marzubān probably wrote almost two centuries before one of the more momentous events in history, for better or worse, since the fall of the Western Roman Empire—namely the advent of the European Crusades into the Holy Land: for worse, because of the tremendous waste of life and incalculable destruction of property; for better, because many Europeans who survived the ordeal had their eyes opened to new (or forgotten) valuable ideas, as well as to the extensive, Islamic-preserved learning of the Greek and Roman ancients. The same temporary weaknesses of the Islamic political sphere so strongly hinted at by al-Marzubāin in his opening lament for *The Superiority of Dogs* may have also later provided the same initial opportunity for the Crusades to gain a foothold in the Holy Land. Persia, on the other hand, because of its remote geographic removal to the east, would be comparatively spared in terms of human casualties and financial expense, yet also relatively isolated from the profitable cultural exchange of ideas which followed.

By even greater contrast, the militant European nation bearing the overwhelming brunt of the Crusades, namely medieval France, would over the next several centuries be in the vanguard of world literary development, fueled in no small part by its futile and fanatical incursions into the Middle East. By the 12th century, the extensive Anglo-Norman kingdom, the great precursor to the English-speaking diaspora of modern times, would now become the focal point for a new kind of poetry and storytelling, leading to (among other things), the dissemination and widespread popularity of the Arthurian legends, as well as to other innovative and trendsetting artistic achievements. One of the more unlikely facets of this exciting, transformative era would involve a highly original, anonymous poetess, transplanted across the "English" Channel from France to versify (in French) on a wide variety of universal themes, including a rather unlikely one involving werewolves.

7

The Sensitive Werewolf

> *It is a certain thing, and within the knowledge of all, that many a christened man has suffered this change, and ran wild in woods, as a Were-Wolf. The Were-Wolf is a fearsome beast. He lurks within the thick forest, mad and horrible to see. All the evil that he may, he does.*—Marie de France, *Bisclavret*, 12th century[1]

To the considerable credit of Ibn al-Marzubān, he did not see fit to remark upon the alleged phenomenon of lycanthropy, a preoccupation fascinating to most western commentators on canine matters since the distant Greco-Roman era.[2] Perhaps he was too horrified by the openly predatory behavior of his fellow countrymen for any legends or mythologies to be prioritized within his not insubstantial critical radar on Middle Eastern political and cultural affairs. Whatever foibles or shallowness al-Marzubān may have been censoring in Baghdad during the early 10th century, however, this would prove to be minor in comparison to the materialist, pack-like aggressiveness of European Crusaders pouring into the Holy Land from the late 11th century and on. This destructive foreign invasion would be spearheaded, more often than not, by elite Norman nobility in search of land, wealth, and power not otherwise available in their homeland. These formidable warriors had previously lived among the wild wolves of northern Europe, the latter certainly regarded as the fiercest, or more precisely (in the words of Pliny the Elder), cruelest offshoots of their breed. By the time the First Crusade had succeeded in carving out a bloody, temporary foothold in and around the environs of Jerusalem, Western literature, particularly that written in the French language, was beginning to enter an exciting new phase in which extant myths of Arthurian military prowess were being intermingled with gentler notions of chivalric romance. In other words, humans (as well as wolves) in literature were now showing some signs of introspection and restraint, if not outright courtliness.

Almost nothing definite is known of the poet Marie de France, except that which can be deduced from the skilful texts attributed to her efforts. Her very moniker represents a presumed literal reading of lines from several of her own works. She was active in England during the latter half of the 12th century at the court of King Henry II (1133–1189) and his perhaps more famous queen, Eleanor of Aquitaine (1122?–1204). Marie wrote poetic short stories, or *lais*, for which she is best known. She translated or interpolated Aesop.[3] She wrote biographical sketches in verse on Saint Patrick and possibly Saint Aubrey as well. That is about all we know for certain.

Taking her at her word, her name was Marie and, like most Anglo-Norman nobility of the times, she had been born in France. This in turn has led to speculation identifying her with just about every French-born English noblewoman of the era named Marie, of which there were many, the most renowned probably being Marie d'Anjou (1140?–1216?), Abbess of Shaftesbury and illegitimate half-sister to King Henry, to whom she appears to have dedicated her lais.[4] Though certainly an attractive possibility, there is little to substantiate this theory. She was one of the pioneering medieval writers to incorporate elements of romantic chivalry into the Arthurian legends and, if she in fact wrote before the prolific bard of Champagne, Chrétien de Troyes, then she was likely the very first one to do so.[5] Her mostly literate audiences, comparatively limited in number, consisted mainly of other Anglo-French noblewomen, many of whose husbands had gone off crusading to the Middle East, leaving their bored and no doubt disenchanted wives back in England to keep the home fires burning.

For precise reasons that will probably forever remain a mystery, Marie opted to draw upon the ancient werewolf myth for one of her seventeen lais, titled *Bisclavret* (meaning literally "werewolf"), or The Lay of the Were-Wolf. Since the Dark Ages, lycanthropy had remained a popular subject in the vernacular (as it had during classical times), but serious European literature of any sort was scarcely to be found before the High Middle Ages. Marie may have heard of the legend that Saint Patrick (of whom she wrote) had punished the wicked King Vereticus of Wales by turning him into a wolf. This theory of association with Wales is bolstered by Marie's express attribution of *Bisclavret* to Breton tradition, since Breton and Welsh storytelling traditions were so strongly intertwined following the unequivocal and permanent Norman-Breton conquest of England in 1066.[6] To repeat, this same confluence was a major contributing factor to the simultaneous literary rise of the Arthurian legends.

As for legends and tales of lycanthropy, the alleged Greek origins of this tradition had been acerbically affirmed long before by Pliny the Elder (see Chapter 3), while the Greek-born Roman citizen Plutarch (see Chapter 4) noted that his shepherd-herdsmen fellow Greeks viewed wolves as natural enemies but also implied that the Romans were less hostile, especially given their religious belief that the infant founders of the Eternal City had been saved by a she-wolf.[7] By the time Marie was taking old Welsh warrior myths in the 12th century and transforming them into romance for female audiences at the English court, the moment was obviously ripe for the werewolf theme itself to undergo a new metamorphosis, if not a total shift in emphasis. Although there had been some hints of this more humane aspect in ancient accounts, it would now move to the unambiguous forefront of poetic concern, beginning with Marie. Modern sophisticates may laugh at the conceit, but for many audiences at the time the perceived reality of lycanthropy was no laughing matter. There is every indication that Marie's unusual invention was highly popular and had a number of French and Middle English imitators before sinking into comparative oblivion for nearly six centuries afterwards.[8]

Without spoiling too much for potential readers, the basic plot of *Bisclavret* can be briefly summarized. The unnamed hero is a baron in Brittany and close companion to the Breton king, but he also suffers from lycanthropy. Was Marie writing about one of King Henry's notoriously violent and uncouth barons?[9] When the nobleman's previously unaware wife decides to get to the bottom of her husband's mysterious disappearances, she uses feminine charm to draw out his closely guarded secrets, the most important of which is that putting back on his hidden human clothing is the key to bringing himself back to human form. "Thus, by the kiss of his wife, was Bisclavaret betrayed," writes Marie.[10] Disguising a reaction of horror to the revelation, the wife shuns her husband, takes a lover and the two conspire to steal and hide the husband's clothes while he is off in the woods, thereby trapping him into perpetual wolf-like form. A year later, the wolf Bisclavret is cornered by, ironically enough, the king's hunting hounds, but before being dispatched he unexpectedly flings himself on the mercy of the king in a very human, suppliant manner. Startled with instinctive recognition, the king adopts the wolf as a personal pet, while his court is astonished by the loyalty and gentleness of the beast as it clings to their monarch.

Later still, the miraculously peaceful behavior of Bisclavret is rudely interrupted when he encounters his unfaithful wife and her former lover, now her second husband. The wolf first attacks the husband and then, rather dramatically, bites off the nose of the wife. Punishment for these normally capital offenses is delayed, however, when a wise royal counselor advises the king to first interrogate the victims, presumably under torture ("their torment was very grievous"). The truth is revealed, the baron's clothes, along with his human form, are both restored, and everyone lives happily ever after except for the adulterous couple, who are forever banished from the kingdom. No mention is made of Bisclavret finding any new love interest. "The adventure that you have heard is no vain fable," Marie emphasizes in closing.

The multiple levels of implied meanings within this deceptively artless fable underscore Marie's unique achievement, even after considering the rich and longstanding traditions upon which she was expressly drawing.[11] Aside from the questionable propriety of using hounds to hunt a wolf (see Chapter 14), there is a repetitive emphasis in the moral of the story as to how all appearances and preconceptions can be deceiving. For one, betrayal in love can turn civilized human beings into beasts, and when this change occurs it is debatable whether they are completely responsible for their actions. Above all, no one is perfect, and mortal imperfections should be forgiven if at all possible.

Sometimes these same faults can be properly channeled into positive directions, and modern fiction writers would later pick up on this same idea. Like the Breton king in Marie's tale, who would not want a protecting werewolf at their side? Obviously, a loyal werewolf is better than a conniving spouse. The very fact that a werewolf can be faithful, or have any other redeeming qualities, is an unusual twist that went against the grain of established stereotypes. Such creatures may be bad, but they are not all bad, and perhaps in some cases might even be turned into something better with proper human care and compassion. Marie's unusual proposition almost has an evolutionary aspect to it, not only with respect to the behavior of barbaric husbands tempered by their gentle wives, but also to wild wolves being slowly bred into domesticated dogs by humans. This facet of the werewolf tradition has always been inherent in the legend, but insofar as we can tell, it was Marie de France who first pushed it front and center stage during the High Middle Ages. This was not accomplished through any arid literary theory or abstract university thesis, but as courtly entertainment provided by a groundbreaking poet, most likely as an enthusiastic hobby rather than any profession. In the same dedication of the lais, Marie herself states that she composed these works in order "to set evil from me, and to put away my grief."[12]

Marie's high reputation in world literature was not fully established until the 19th century, when interest in Arthurian legends and her prominent role in their development became first truly widespread. Often lost in the shuffle, however, was her charming and highly original detour into the realm of werewolf folklore. Victorian antiquarian Sabine Baring-Gould (1834–1924) acknowledged Marie's notable contribution to the obscure genre in his encyclopedic *The Book of Were-Wolves* from 1865, about the same period in which gothic horror fiction was beginning to establish itself as a reliable commercial entity.[13] *The Strange Case of Dr. Jekyll and Mr. Hyde* (1886) by Scottish novelist Robert Louis Stevenson (1850–1894) clearly has a werewolf subtext, but most fiction from this era dealing explicitly with lycanthropy is mediocre at best.[14]

The outstanding exception is *The Were-Wolf* (1896) by English suffragette-turned-novelist Clemence Housman (1861–1955), who bracingly presents the monster as a murderous femme fatale.[15] The apotheosis of Victorian horror novels came one year later in 1897 with Bram Stoker's *Dracula*, but this famous work mentions werewolves only in passing. Much later, journeyman American writer Guy Endore (1900–1970) produced his novel *The Werewolf of Paris* (1933), often considered to be the finest example of its type.[16] It would take the new 20th century medium of film, however, to vividly resurrect the old tradition in the popular imagination, and this would be accomplished far more effectively than previously achieved by any written or printed word. Nevertheless, Marie's uniquely romantic foray into the same realm also began to strangely manifest itself in a surprising manner after having remained seemingly dormant for centuries.

Perhaps the greatest testament to Marie's originality in preserving and amplifying this latent aspect of the werewolf tradition is to be found in the cinematic arts produced over the last eight decades, nearly eight centuries after her own works appeared. As early as 1913, a now lost silent film feature titled *The Werewolf* had been produced, but it was not until the late 1930s and early 1940s that this particular film genre was firmly established. Beginning in 1935 with Universal Picture's *Werewolf of London* starring Henry Hull and Warner Oland, the man-turns-into-wolf myth has pretty much continuously held the imagination of the movie-going public.[17] Here, the characters played both by Hull and Oland are portrayed sympathetically and tragically. Since that debut, the Anglo or Welsh setting of the story type on film has been a relative constant (with a few notable exceptions), perhaps an unconscious tribute to Marie de France's Anglo-Breton literary original. Six years later (in 1941) came arguably the most famous of all cinematic victims of lycanthropy, Lon Chaney, Jr., in *The Wolfman*, directed by George Waggner and featuring Béla Lugosi as the gypsy werewolf who infects Chaney's unwillingly tragic Welsh hero, Larry Talbot.[18] After this, the Hollywood floodgates opened, and the vast number of subsequent movies, books, comics, and video games featuring lycanthropy are too vast to catalogue; only selective highlights are practicable herein.

Following *The Wolfman*, other studios turned out a number of forgettable imitations, but soon Chaney reprised his dubious success by squaring off against Boris Karloff in the campy *Frankenstein Meets the Wolfman* in 1943. What is more interesting, *She-Wolf of London* (1946) starred June Lockhardt in a refreshing departure for the more typically male-dominated category.[19] As one might expect, Lockhardt's she-wolf is depicted less sympathetically than her male counterparts, if not in a more purely negative Shakespearean vein (see Chapter 4).[20] A werewolf makes perhaps its first appearance in children's fiction with *Prince Caspian* (1951) by C.S. Lewis, a writer always friendly towards the animal kingdom (see Chapter 18).[21] Hollywood 1950s-style low budget science fiction and horror were combined in *The Werewolf* (1956) to otherwise bland effect. In the wake of Elvis Presley and the advent of rock and roll came an opportunistic production from cult horror specialist Herb Cohen, *I Was A Teenage Werewolf* (1957) with a 21-year old, pre–*Bonanza* Michael Landon equating the more murderous and sexually aggressive aspects of lycanthropy with perceived widespread juvenile delinquency in late 1950s America.[22] The film was panned by critics even as it made a small fortune at the box office, doing little in the process to discourage future Hollywood exploitations of the same concept.

The next notable entry in this lengthy catalogue was *The Howling*, a 1981 loose adaptation of the 1977 Gary Brandner pulp fiction novel, which successfully sought to update the gothic horror aspect of the old story line, nonetheless sparking a series of forgettable sequels.[23] The most interesting facets of the original include a screenplay co-written by distinguished director John Sayles, and a journalistic plotline featuring both male and female werewolves, including one memorably portrayed by horror and sci-fi film icon Dee Wallace (aka Deanna Bowers), who was soon to land a leading role as the mother in Steven Spielberg's *E.T. the Extra-Terrestrial* (1982).

From almost the very same moment, however, a far more comedic view of the ancient superstition was being presented to delighted mass audiences via *An American Werewolf in London* (1981), directed by John Landis, which also took the trouble to restore the original Anglo or Welsh setting of the tale. Rick Baker won an Oscar Award for makeup. A 1997 follow-up with no involvement from the 1981 team, *An American Werewolf in Paris*, was far less successful; but despite this lack of quality, it still brought home a surprisingly large gross. In 1994 came *Wolf*, a freewheeling interpretation by Mike Nichols and Elaine May, featuring an all-star cast including Jack Nicholson, Michelle Pfeiffer, Christopher Plummer, and James Spader and graced with a soundtrack by the incomparable Ennio Morricone. The critics continued to be ambivalent (at best) but box office revenue once again was lucrative. More recently, in 2010, the inevitable update/remake for *The Wolfman* was produced, directed by former special-effects artist Joe Johnston and featuring both Anthony Hopkins and Benicio del Toro as father and son victims of lycanthropy. Emily Blunt played the love interest and atmospheric music was composed by Danny Elfman. Rick Baker won his second Oscar for werewolf makeup. Critics complained and profits continued to roll in.

Meanwhile, a new wave of printed fiction geared towards teenagers and young adults had come to dominate commercial bookshelves, then quickly translated into movies, most of which tapped into the werewolf tradition and often created new and sometimes startling variations. Beginning with the inescapable *Harry Potter* fantasy series by British mega-author J.K. Rowling (b. 1965), brand new riffs on the same old theme began to manifest themselves in the popular imagination, more often than not with pre-adult audiences, strongly suggesting that this entertainment trend is not about to go away anytime soon. Possibly taking a cue from the variable werewolf characters belonging to both sexes in the smash TV series *Buffy the Vampire Slayer* (1997–2003), Rowling's third consecutive blockbuster novel, *Harry Potter and the Prisoner of Azkaban* (1999), by 2004 had likewise become a blockbuster movie, introducing another very popular character, Professor Remus Lupin, one of 13-year-old Harry's several unconventional instructors.[24] Lupin, played as an adult in the series by accomplished British film star David Thewlis, also happens to be a recovering werewolf of sorts but is able to control and harness his inherent savagery towards achieving virtuous ends. Although the character of Lupin is killed off by Rowling in the final installment of the series, *Harry Potter and the Deathly Hollows* (2007), Harry at the conclusion of the saga becomes godfather to Lupin's orphaned son, who is not a werewolf like his late biological father.[25] In effect, Rowling popularized (if not outright invented) the notion that lycanthropy is a containable and controllable affliction.

Rowling's primary commercial rival (however unworthy in the imaginative sense) in recent years has been the American Mormon young adult novelist extraordinaire Stephenie Meyer (b. 1973), whose *Twilight* series has since 2005 become a self-contained franchise unto itself both in print and on film.[26] Although all of these efforts are primarily concerned with vampires, one of Meyer's more fascinating characters is Native American werewolf Jacob "Jake" Black, introduced as a friend, protector, and competing love interest for the story's heroine. It is revealed that not only is Black able to shapeshift himself at will into a werewolf, but so can his entire Quileute tribe (sometimes acting in pack unison). They carry this hereditary trait as a badge of tribal honor in their never ending struggle against evil vampires of the world. The real-life, highly resilient Quileute nation of Washington State and the Pacific coast, like other selective Native American tribes, indeed claim ancestral descent from wild wolves. It is unlikely that either they or, for that matter, Stephenie Meyer, have ever read the works of Marie de France. However, the sympathetic and even desirable melding of man and wolf in these traditions clearly demonstrate that this distinctive literary or religious conceit was not unique to European culture. Like Marie's nameless Bisclavret of the French Breton forests, the Quileute tribe has managed over the ages to survive against all odds while obtaining a small piece of literary fame in the process.

No sooner had the *Twilight* series appeared to have made werewolves as likeable as they could possibly become, romance novelist and Texas Anglophile Rachel Hawthorne, aka Lorraine Heath (b. 1954), unleashed her *Dark Guardian* series, beginning with *Moonlight* in 2009.[27] Simplistic titles disguise daring concepts gaining noticeable readership traction in a notoriously competitive field. Television adaptations are rumored to be in the works. The overarching plot involves a long-established society of werewolves living in peaceful solitude and harmony along the Canadian Rockies border with the United States. Much effort and planning by the werewolves goes into keeping out the intrusions of unwanted, evil human beings. Love and romance play out against this fantastical backdrop. In Hawthorne's supernatural universe, not only have werewolves become a desirable state of being, they are now physically and morally superior to their mere human counterparts. In the *Dark Guardian* saga, werewolves have finally transformed into the good guys. Thus the public image of lycanthropy seems to have come full circle since Marie de France first suggested during the 12th century that some werewolves were perhaps more good than bad. Given the recent, phenomenal success of *Harry Potter*, *Twilight*, and *Dark Guardian*, all utilizing similar conceits and exaggerating these devices even further, it would be quite difficult to say whether this accelerating trend of sensitive werewolves in fiction has yet peaked.[28]

In retrospect, it seems incredible that such a far-flung conceit from distant days of yore has achieved such widespread resonance on the big screen over the last mere 78 years. Something about it clearly is tapping into or touching a nerve in the public consciousness. Aside from providing considerable employment for Hollywood makeup artists, the all-pervasive werewolf theme in popular fiction and film would also seem to represent something that enthusiastic audiences either relate to or admire on a basic instinctual level: the human conflict between body and soul, the physical embodiment of male or female sex symbol, the ruthless administration of natural justice or selection—the list of possibilities is certainly extensive.

To Marie de France, however, must go the laurels and distinction of first shaping this peculiar genre into a viable storytelling mode combining all of the above elements and possibly other facets as well. Although she lived nearly eight centuries before motion pictures were invented, her talents at striking dramatization anticipated modern movie tastes, particularly for adolescents, in many respects. Part of this appeal was the mood of the times in which she wrote. During the early 13th century, not long after her lais had been widely disseminated throughout Europe, a great saint and visionary of the church emerged in Italy, one who would have many new and daring things to say regarding, among other controversial topics, the close ongoing relationship between humans and canines. His adopted Christian name of Francis, curiously enough, also would literally mean "Frenchman" or "of France."

8

Carnivores Forgiven

All the people being assembled, the saint got up to preach, saying, among other things, how for our sins God permits such calamities, and how much greater and more dangerous are the flames of hell, if the jaws of so small an animal as a wolf can make a whole city tremble through fear.—The Little Flowers of Saint Francis, Anonymous, 14th century[1]

If Marie de France achieved everlasting literary fame by retelling the tale of a benevolent werewolf, then it was Saint Francis of Assisi (1181?–1226) who would later earn eternal credit for demonstrating that real-life wild wolves had redeemable moral qualities, in the allegorical sense if nothing else. While Anglo-Norman Crusader widows and noblewomen at the English court of Henry II were being entertained by the highly original conceit of Marie's *Bisclavret*, a far more spiritual and effervescent voice was coming of age far to the south in Italy at the turn of the 13th century. Despite the fanatical fervor of those times, this voice would not particularly concern itself with the Crusades, with much-needed institutional reform of the Roman Catholic Church, or, for that matter, with any presumed inherent righteousness of Christianity. Book learning, not to mention the alleged superiority of humankind over the rest of creation, would have little or no place in his worldview.

In retrospect, there appears to have been no especially good reason why such an eccentric, uncompromising and unambitious individual should not have otherwise lived and died in happy obscurity, totally forgotten to history. Nevertheless, Saint Francis, almost in spite of himself, proved to be arguably the most influential figure of his age, as well as one of the most venerated religious personalities of all time both among Christians and non–Christians; moreover, his relevance today seems greater than ever, with no signs of abating anytime soon. Without any exaggeration, Franciscan English translator Raphael Brown has called Francis "the most popular figure in the history of Christianity after Jesus Himself and the Blessed Virgin."[2]

No justice of any sort can be done to the immeasurably powerful life and legend of Saint Francis in this small space. Northern Italy during the late 12th and early 13th centuries was more or less a hodge-podge of bickering, warring city-states in which wealth, power, and prerogative were concentrated into the hands of a tiny, elite segment of society. Preciously scarce resources and manpower were routinely consumed by waves of failed, ill-conceived Crusades on distant overseas shores. The church as an institution was in a widely acknowledged state of moral decline. Human life, in the words of one later philosopher, tended to be nasty, brutish, and short.[3] Into this violent, disordered world was born Giovanni Francesco di Bernadone, better known to the world as Francis, son of a wealthy textile merchant of Assisi and a mother with French Provençal family roots, according to tradition.

The adolescence of Francis was reportedly spent mainly in the enjoyment of all the sensual and aesthetic pleasures that his exceptionally privileged position in life afforded him. He was steeped in the courtly, poetic tradition of the French troubadours (as was Marie de France before him), and longed for military glory in imitation of King Arthur and his Knights of the Roundtable.[4] Traumatic experiences upon reaching adulthood, however, both as a P.O.W. and a convalescent from a life-threatening physical illness, profoundly changed him. After this, all he seemed capable of doing was giving away to the less fortunate anything material that his affluent father provided him with.[5] Furious that his sole male heir was showing monastic tendencies, the father dragged the son before the local bishop—himself reputed to be quite a rough customer—where he accused his son of owing him the very clothes off his back. Then, before the entire assembled town of Assisi, Francis renounced all worldly possessions and stripped off his clothing, which he threw at the feet of his father, who then stormed out of the proceedings in exasperation. After a dramatic moment of uncertainty, the bishop ordered the naked Francis to be covered with the first forerunner of a Franciscan habit, and the disinherited, disgraced son embarked upon his epoch-shaping ministry, not as a preacher but as a street beggar—socially scorned, physically beaten, and considered mad by most of his fellow townsmen. The year was about 1209 and Francis was approximately 28 years old.

According to biographers, Francis early in his pastoral career received initial kindness, not from the citizens of Assisi but from comparative strangers in the neighboring Umbrian town of Gubbio. Sometime later, when Gubbio found itself terrorized by a wolf that devoured both man and beast, Francis intervened, as recounted in chapter 21 of *The Little Flowers of Saint Francis*, an anonymous late 13th century collection of factually disputed Franciscan traditions from the life and times of the saint. Fearlessly confronting the man-killer on his own initiative, Francis blessed the beast as *Frate Lupo* (Brother

Wolf), attributed its past crimes to hunger, and then led the now miraculously docile animal back to Gubbio as if it were a domesticated dog. There, Francis brokered an agreement between beast and townsfolk in which the wolf would be fed at public expense while the wolf in return would no longer attack anyone or anything. As related in *The Little Flowers*, the wolf lived out the last two years of its life peacefully within the friendly confines of Gubbio, becoming a kind of town mascot. It remains a civic symbol to this very day.[6] Local residents have ever since revered the memory of the wolf as a tribute to the great Christian saint who once walked in their midst. Most Italians are angered by any suggestion that the story represents a fable or allegory. The Wolf of Gubbio also retains a central place within a much larger tradition evoking the legendary or actual powers of Francis over nature itself, making him the official patron saint of both animals and the environment—in other words, a very contemporary saint for the 21st century and well beyond.[7]

Slowly, many came to see Francis less as a madman and more as a visionary pointing towards a better way of life. Within his short lifetime, he not only attracted numerous followers, but he also lived to see the fashionable, papal-endorsed spread of his new order all across Europe and beyond—much to his own dismay since he apparently believed that true followers of "Lady Poverty" were relatively small in number.[8] Once again disillusioned with worldly affairs but retaining the old crusading fantasy of his youth, Francis, after several failed passages, finally made it to Egypt in 1219, only to witness the nightmarish siege of Damietta (along the Nile River) in full swing. One glance at the hellish military operation unfolding around him appears to have forever cured Francis of crusader fever, but he nonetheless intrepidly pressed forward to find an audience with Sultan al-Malik al-Kamil (1180–1238), nephew of Saladin, conqueror of Jerusalem, and absolutely determined to convert the sultan to Christianity or, more likely, obtain the glory of martyrdom in the attempt.

Astonishingly, he was admitted behind the lines during a brief truce and found himself standing before the sultan explaining the nature of his business there. Christian accounts of the words exchanged between Francis and al-Kamil (there are no Islamic ones) range from the humorous to the fantastical, but there is general agreement that the sultan was, if nothing else, fairly impressed with the undaunted courage of the saint.[9] On the other hand, it is a documented fact that the Franciscans have enjoyed a uninterrupted ministerial presence in the Holy Land officially or unofficially tolerated by the Muslims ever since the time of Francis, which may well in part be a tangible result of their founder's personal intervention.[10] After this extraordinary encounter, Francis was given safe passage back to the Christian lines and then promptly shipped back to Europe.

Once home in Italy, he found time, among other things, for staging the first live Christmas nativity scene utilizing both humans and animals, establishing yet another longstanding Christian tradition. Soon afterwards, as a sign of divine favor, he was mysteriously marked with the stigmata of Christ.[11] Not long after this he died at the approximate age of 45 from natural causes likely aggravated by his own austerity and self-mortification, for which he famously and humorously apologized to himself on his death bed.[12] Within two years he was canonized. It has been rightfully observed that Francis is the only saint over the last thousand years universally honored by all branches and denominations of the Christian faith. Even so, he was never officially ordained a priest.

Franciscan hagiography is a notoriously difficult field, even among medieval specialists. Regarding the Wolf of Gubbio, the bottom line is that the story does not make a surviving appearance in manuscript until the late 14th century, over 150 years after the death of Francis. Early biographers such as Thomas of Celano and Saint Bonaventure make no mention of the tale. Not until the Latin *Actus beati Francisci et sociorum eius* and its dynamic Italian interpolation, *Fioretti di Santo Francesco d' Ascesi* (Little Flowers), does the most famous wolf in all of medieval literature join the official paper trail of the Western tradition.[13] The ongoing popularity of the book is attested to by its being lavishly printed in 1476, not long after the invention of movable type. The first English translations were made during the 19th century and have been continuously updated ever since. Scholars now generally agree that most of the material for both the *Fioretti* and the *Actus* were largely compiled by an obscure monk known to history as Ugolino of Montegiorgio, who appears to have been active during the late 13th and early 14th centuries. Ugolino may have been writing to preserve certain questionable Franciscan traditions then under criticism from official church authorities, and he seems to have personally known at least some of those who knew Francis' first disciples, if not the disciples themselves, such as Brother Leo (d. 1270), secretary and confessor to the saint, as well as his conjectured very first biographer (*The Mirror of Perfection*).[14] *The Little Flowers*, despite a likelihood of having several subsequent glossing authors (in addition to Ugolino), is written in a consistent tone of humorous folklore, but with an underpinning serious message of spiritual hope and salvation. It is the product not of literary sophistication, but rather of faith and devotion.

Given that many, if not most, elemental forces in the universe appear to be hidden from frail and fallible human understanding, this writer is not prepared to deny the existence of miracles. Despite every rational indication that the Wolf of Gubbio is a fabrication or, at best, a symbolic representative of a reformed local criminal, a large part of us still wants to believe the story literally, and many of us still do in fact believe it. Raphael Brown has in fact given a convincing summary of how various tales were conflated to form the legend, nevertheless adding that some of the most respectable of academic historians are still reluctant to dismiss it as fiction.[15] Wild predators are not known to convert from man-killer to domesticated mascot with a mere sign of the cross; then again, Saint Francis of Assisi was certainly no ordinary individual. His alleged powers to tame or control otherwise hostile creatures of nature must be acknowledged to some degree, since similar talents in other individuals are documented in modern times. Plus, this is how wolves evolved into dogs at some point in the first place, though admittedly not within a single moment. Surely less believable than the powers of Francis to tame wild beasts is the Gubbio townsfolk subsequent forgiveness and benevolent attitude towards a creature that had previously harmed and terrorized them.

Perhaps the most impressive aspect of the old tradition is that several decades after the death of Francis there was clearly a concerted and sustained effort by the institutional church to suppress the story; it nonetheless continued not only to survive, but also to thrive even more than before.[16] Something about the parable—if it is a parable—touches us deeply, in spite of our rational doubts.[17] While it is Francis of Assisi the saint that we should try to imitate, it is in fact the Wolf of Gubbio that most of us relate to more on a personal level. Ultimately, we tend to impose our own humanity on the wolf, and is this not appropriate? Francis would have likely agreed. The wolf may be bad, but it does not necessarily enjoy being that way. In this case it happened to be looking for a better way to live, for which the empathy of the saint provided fortuitous opportunity. At its very core, the Wolf of Gubbio is a tale of divine grace, something that most, if not all, of us are in continual need of. Given that the wolf is permanently reconciled with the citizens of Gubbio, it is somewhat implied that his previous human victims were possibly not the most popular individuals in town. For them (with encouragement from the saint) reconciliation becomes more desirable than vengeance. In the final analysis, not only is a deadly carnivore forgiven, it is also subsequently and willingly accommodated, but within more reasonable and humane bounds.[18]

Nothing in the surviving written legacy of Francis diminishes his unimpeachable reputation for holiness or oneness with nature. His beautifully accomplished poetry offers us a glimpse into his legendary effectiveness as a preacher, as well as his adolescent love for the French troubadours of his mother's Provençal heritage. Like many nature lovers before and after him, Francis loved birds most of all (especially hooded larks), and *The Little Flowers* also recounts his ubiquitous preaching encounters with the alternatively noisy or attentive swallows of Umbria.[19] His sermons and poetry at times seem to verge on a kind of Christian pantheism, praising a certain unity of creation in which sun and fire are given prominent places of hierarchy within the natural chain of being.[20] He actively advocated for the humane treatment of all animals, and was the first notable historical figure in this regard, if not the very first.[21] Arguably the greatest tangible legacy of Francis' love for nature, however—apart from the ongoing commercial industry that has continually flourished by reproducing images of his likeness and legend—is the annual church Blessing of the Animals ceremony held on his feast day of October 4, a ritual enthusiastically observed by both Roman Catholic and Episcopalian denominations (among others), and still growing in popularity as this is being written.[22] After humans, dogs tend to be the dominant churchgoers at these events, followed by cats, birds, and any other tamable creature.

It was therefore no coincidence that in the immediate aftermath of Francis' life and legacy came a period in which animals, and dogs especially, began to gain places of honor and importance within European Christian literary tradition. The legend of the faithful hound Gelert (an alleged contemporary with Saint Francis), mistakenly killed by his master, Llywelyn, after saving the prince's child from a wolf, was probably derived originally from Asiatic sources and brought back to Wales by Crusaders returning from the Middle East (see Chapter 6). The tragic-heroic dog's namesake Welsh village of Beddgelert appears to have obtained this specific moniker sometime during the mid-13th century.[23] Taking this same motif to the extreme, the French have given us the Passion of Guinefort, the 13th century faithful hound of Lyon, achieving unofficial, albeit temporary veneration as a canine Christian saint with a similar act of heroism and undeserved punishment. Although continually censored by a strongly disapproving church establishment, this perceived doggie sainthood persisted much in the same manner that the Wolf of Gubbio resisted all official efforts to sever its close connection with Saint Francis. As late as 1930, official suppression of the Guinefort cult was deemed necessary by Roman authorities.

A dog also became the close symbolic companion of a canonized human saint (however dubious) around the same time period. The quasi-historical Saint Roch (1248?–1327?) in turn became the designated patron saint of dogs, apparently entitled to one of their own since Saint Francis, though patron saint of animals, had interacted with a wolf, strictly speaking.[24] Saint Roch, according to tradition, was a Franco-Italian Franciscan martyr who, while tending to plague victims, was himself brought back to health with assistance from a dog belonging to a local nobleman. The dog is said to have procured bread for Roch after the saint had fallen ill and was quarantined in the wilderness and abandoned by the rest of society. The healing association of Saint Roch linked with a canine companion calls to mind similar pagan traditions from ancient Mesopotamia (see Chapter 1). It almost goes without saying that all of these aforementioned saintly traditions involving dogs have found ample representation in medieval, Renaissance, and modern art.[25]

This brings us straight back to the Wolf of Gubbio and its seemingly limitless popularity as artistic subject matter. As one might expect, the town of Gubbio has several public shrines strategically placed for the benefit of tourists, including a gorgeously sentimental bronze statue of Saint Francis embracing a standing wolf in the central piazza, and, for those more esoteric in taste, a striking 1973 bas relief of a similar scene in a park setting by the distinguished Italian sculptor Farpi Vignoli (1902–1997). Over the centuries, artwork depicting the same episode has followed the Franciscan order wherever its ministry has traveled, which is to say worldwide. The United States is no exception in this regard and may well provide the greatest number of outstanding examples. Sculptures, paintings, mosaics, iconography, stained glass windows, medallions, religious jewelry, and even staged photographs have all received serious treatment on the same morally reformed wolfish theme. From the very moment *The Little Flowers of Saint Francis* became a book some seven centuries ago, illustrators have had a field day with the idea of a repentant wolf. Printing presses only accelerated this trend. Contemporary religious and children's literature never seems to grow tired of retelling and embellishing the old story. Recently this author found himself innocently browsing through Saint Francis statuettes at a remote central Wisconsin retail establishment and happened to stumble upon one with the Wolf of Gubbio tenaciously clinging for protection to the habit of the saint. This is a state in which wolf-hunting has been recently legalized after much controversy, even allowing dogs savagely to be used in the pursuit (see Chapter 14). Thus what should have been a purely innocuous, idle situation in an artwork emporium suddenly became unexpectedly poignant.

Any casual Internet search will reveal the staggering range of variety that artists in all mediums have discovered for this brief and possibly apocryphal chapter in the life of Saint Francis. Perusing these images (which number in the hundreds), a few of the more unusual ones deserve at least an honorable mention. *The Wolf of Gubbio* by Luc-Oliver Merson (1846–1920), an oil painted in 1877 at the outset of the French belle époque period and today housed at the Palais des Beaux Arts de Lille in suburban Paris, is unique in that Saint Francis is nowhere to be found in the scene. Instead viewers behold the aftermath of his miraculous intervention within the town itself. An oversized, collared and haloed wolf or dog—the level of domestication is intentionally left vague—receives sustenance from the affectionate and grateful townsfolk of Gubbio. The centerpiece is a smiling mother allowing her excited young daughter to pet the beast as it is fed raw meat by the local butcher. An unconcerned dog sleeps off to the side while a slightly more wary cat watches from the stoop.[26] The picture feels like a pleasant glimpse into some future better place.

At the other extreme end of the spectrum is a stunning series of 20th century woodcuts by German post–Expressionist artist Otto Schubert (1892–1970) of Dresden. His scenes from the life of the saint, including *Saint Francis and the Wolf of Gubbio* (among others), are today privately owned but on full public display as part of the eclectic Web site collection known as Sacred Art Pilgrim. Here, a monstrous wolf, physically bigger than the haloed Francis, crouches down accommodatingly on its hind legs as the two figures appear to joyfully dance hand in paw with each other near a church setting. There is nothing cuddly or domesticated about this purely Germanic wolf, but the fearsome creature is nonetheless quite happy to be in good saintly company. Interestingly, Schubert in 1937, along with some of the greatest creative names in Europe, found his work condemned by the Nazis as "Degenerate Art" and included in the infamous exhibition held in Munich of that same year. Schubert managed to outlast his persecutors, however, not to mention the Allied firebombing of Dresden in 1945, and continued working productively within the Soviet Eastern Bloc of Germany for several decades after the war.[27]

By the second half of the 13th century, and about fifty years after the death of Saint Francis, the endless futility and waste of the Crusades would finally begin to make an impression on the political decision makers of Europe, thus setting the stage for the somewhat more productive eras of the Renaissance and Reformation. The more pressing concerns of Francis with individual behavior back home in Europe (as opposed to taking back the Holy Land from infidels) in hindsight can be seen as a kind of forerunner to these broader events and trends. The legendary or factual Wolf of Gubbio represents only a single facet of a seemingly inexhaustible tradition, but nonetheless a highly effective one, to be sure. About three centuries later, however, Europe would find itself engulfed in its own internal, horrific and drawn-out Wars of Religion, with many of the worst atrocities occurring in France, the same country which had earlier lent its moniker to both the poet Marie and the holy man Francis. At the very epicenter of this remorseless conflict was a great humanist essayist, one neither poet nor saint, yet one whose boundless sagacity is still read today for comfort by those confused by the violent behavior surrounding them. This essayist was also a great reader of the classics and steeped in the ancient traditions of Pliny, Plutarch, and Diogenes Laërtius, as well as their pointed and sometimes unfashionable observations on canines. The essayist was Michel Eyquem de Montaigne.

9

Animal Intelligence and the Wars of Religion

The men who serve us do so more cheaply than our falcons, our horses or our hounds; and they are less carefully looked after—what menial tasks will we not bow to for the convenience of those animals! The most abject slaves, it seems to me, will not willingly do for their masters what princes are proud to do for such creatures. When Diogenes saw his parents striving to purchase his freedom he exclaimed: "They must be fools: My Master looks after me and feeds me; he is my servant!" So too those who keep animals can be said to serve them, not be served by them.—Michel Eyquem de Montaigne, *An Apology for Raymond Sebond*, 16th century[1]

All warfare by definition is ugly, hellish business, but civil war is unquestionably the ugliest, often openly pitting brother against brother, father against son, families against themselves. Add to this unsavory mix the inflammatory divisiveness of religious intolerance, and one begins to get a disturbing picture of military strife in pre–Enlightenment Europe, an epoch making a deep, lasting impression on the Founding Fathers of the United States, as well as on subsequent philosophers formulating theories of good government. While Saint Francis of Assisi, by the sheer force of his personal example and self-sacrifice, helped to inspire a much-needed reform and revitalization of the institutional church during the 13th century, by the 16th century, self-professed, fanatical Christians of the Western church were committing unspeakable atrocities against each other, all the while invoking the mantle of whatever they happened to define as the one and only true faith. As the Wars of Religion engulfed Europe during the Renaissance and Reformation, the phrase "Wars of Religion" itself came to be most closely associated with France, a country in which a good case can be made that the most appalling crimes were committed by all sides involved in a lengthy, remorseless struggle.

Fortunately for civilization, the same culture that had previously produced Marie the poet and inspired Francis the holy man now brought forth arguably the greatest sage of that troubled era, Michel Eyquem de Montaigne (1533–1592), writing eloquently for his own contemporaries as well as for all time, even as the French kingdom seemed to be crumbling all around him during the last four decades of the 1500s. Montaigne, like countless other wise men before and after him, observed that human standards of behavior often paled in comparison with the intelligence, adaptability, and even moral fortitude frequently exhibited by higher orders of the animal kingdom, particularly those of canines.

Although the Protestant Reformation had swept through Germany, England, and northern Europe well before the death of Martin Luther in 1545, France had resisted the new tide due in part to the solid Roman Catholic majority of its population combined with the firm political strength of its two mid-century monarchs, Francis I and Henry II.[2] When Henry was accidentally killed, however, during a recreational jousting tournament in 1559, a gaping power vacuum opened up, unleashing long-suppressed demons within the French realm which seemed to cut across every layer and segment of society.[3] By 1562, all-out war had commenced between French Catholics and French Protestants, continuing virtually unabated over the next 36 years.

One of the first official military engagements involved the successful Catholic siege of Protestant-held Rouen in 1562. Present at that memorable event as a courtier among the royalist forces of Charles IX was a 29-year-old Michel Eyquem. Ten years later, the low point of the extended conflict began in Paris on August 23, 1572, the eve of Saint Bartholomew's Day, when a premeditated Catholic massacre of leading French Protestants, or Huguenots, spontaneously cascaded into a holocaust, spreading first into the immediate countryside and then beyond to the provinces. Within a matter of days, tens of thousands had been murdered in cold blood. No one knows exactly how many died, but by August 24 the city of Paris seemed to have turned to the color red in the eyes of many survivors. Immediate Protestant reaction to the outrage was to strengthen themselves militarily under inspired leadership conveniently provided by Prince Henry of Navarre (later to become King Henry IV), himself narrowly surviving Saint Bartholomew's Day by pretending a speedy conversion to Catholicism after having married Princess Margaret of Valois.[4] After lapsing back into Protestantism, Henry later achieved mastery of stubbornly resistant Paris by converting yet again to the Church of Rome, adding his shrewd and tart declaration that *"Paris vaut bien une messe"* (Paris is well worth a mass). Such was the pragmatic and sanguine character of a much-beloved French king as he gradually put an end to the raging civil-religious wars of his homeland.[5]

9. Animal Intelligence and the Wars of Religion

In a country viewed by historians as the ultimate flashpoint for the 16th century European Wars of Religion, ground zero could well have been considered the prosperous region of Bordeaux in southwestern France, emanating from its dynamic capital port city. Though traditionally and persistently Catholic, Bordeaux was also proximate to the French Pyrenees district of Navarre, home province of Henry IV, and thus became the locus of constantly marauding, see-saw violence throughout the conflict, especially during its early years. It was to this volatile place on the map, situated in a rural district set amidst agriculture, nature and wildlife, outside the modest town of Saint-Michel-de-Montaigne, that its then-current namesake nobleman retired in 1571 at the relatively young age of 38 in hopes of finding some tranquility and peace of mind. He found neither, but soon learned that he could alleviate his depression by writing self-exploratory essays, a novel literary form of which he soon became the all-time master.

Montaigne had fled to this self-imposed exile after the death of his much-loved father, Pierre, in 1568, full inheritance of his estates, and the subsequent, overwhelming political upheavals in France made any further public life unbearable for him, though living a public life was what he had been specifically trained to do. Montaigne had in fact been brought up as a "gentlemen"— a category which, in the words of the late American essayist Gore Vidal, no longer exists. His fixed plan of quiet study and meditation, however, disagreeably turned into deep depression, especially since the early death of Montaigne's best and perhaps only close friend, the philosopher-poet Étienne de la Boétie (1530–1563), had by then left him no one to converse with on an equal plane. Dutifully complying with an arranged marriage, Montaigne produced a daughter (of whom he seems to have been fond) but no surviving male heirs. By 1578, he was suffering from kidney stones, a persistent, then-untreatable malaise eventually accelerating his demise. Finally, desperate to alleviate the relentless onslaught of melancholy, he turned to writing books, an activity that he never planned, desired, or considered himself particularly qualified to do.

It had helped Montaigne enormously that the first 13 years of his life had been spent (under the guidance of his humanist-influenced father) making Latin his first language with help from some of the best educators in Europe, thus enabling him to tap into vast resources offered by ancient literature, all contained within the extensive private library of his château.[6] These books included, among many other things, countless Greco-Roman observations on canines. The next 25 years of his life were spent as a lawyer, soldier, and courtier actively engaged at the highest levels of French political power. When civil war came, his family split right down the middle, beginning with his father (a Catholic) and his mother (a Protestant), then spreading down to his siblings.[7] He himself was moderately Catholic but maintained friendship with Protestant leaders, most notably Henry of Navarre. Montaigne's first two volumes of essays were published in 1580, making him somewhat of a laughingstock amongst his neighbors, but otherwise achieving immediate classic status. They have remained classics ever since.

His was one of the few public voices of those unsettled times highly esteemed by leaders of both sides during the civil war. In typical deadpan fashion, Montaigne attributed his own miraculous survival to a conspicuous lack of fortifications around his estate, which circumstance was less provocative to the repetitive military incursions throughout the countryside. The fact that he had no hand in the crimes of Saint Bartholomew's Day and that his own family was well known to be on both sides of the fight may have helped him to stay alive as well. During the early 1580s, he was drafted against his will to be mayor of Bordeaux, an appointment personally ratified by King Henry III. During his four-year tenure, Bordeaux enjoyed a short period of peace and relative calm, while Montaigne often found himself inclined to defend those with whose political opinions he otherwise disagreed, actions for which he was criticized at the time but later lauded. He traveled the European continent, including Italy, whenever he could find sufficient time and health to do so. A third volume of revised and expanded essays was published immediately after his death in 1592 at age 59. Montaigne did not live to see either Henry IV's triumphant entry into Paris in 1594 or Henry's Edict of Nantes in 1598 granting limited but official religious toleration to French Protestants.[8]

At 194 pages (in the English translation by M.A. Screech), by far the longest essay that Montaigne ever produced was *An Apology for Raymond Sebond*, written during the late 1570s and published in 1580 as the centerpiece of his second volume of essays from the first edition. Raymond Sebond (?–1436) had been a somewhat obscure, Spanish-born French professor of theology at Toulouse, France, whose Latin book *Theologia Naturalis*, though pre–Reformation, had become a sort of touchstone for French Catholic apologists despite its somewhat heretical and lowbrow reputation among both Catholic and Protestant scholars. Montaigne's very first published literary effort had in fact been a French translation of Sebond in 1569, commissioned by (and later dedicated to) Montaigne's father shortly before his death.

Montaigne's *Apology* picks up a few years later on the same theme as the French Wars of Religion raged all across the country, as well as around Montaigne's own estates. The work is addressed to an unnamed patroness, often surmised to be Margaret of Valois, wife of Henry of Navarre.[9] By that time, Sebond's once quaint ideas about simple faith, restraint, and, above all, intellectual humility, seemed desperately needed in order to halt the escalating violence. Montaigne, writing this time in the French vernacular, figuratively goes to town with his subject matter, bringing all of his classical learning to bear on bolstering and updating the arguments of Sebond's treatise.[10] On the topics of humility and the frequently overestimated powers of human reason, for a full 36 pages, or nearly 20 percent of the total, he muses on the natural world and animal kingdom—usually canine behavior specifically—anecdotes mostly drawn from classical antiquity which he, as a trained Latin scholar, had been familiar with since childhood. His main point in this section of the essay is driven home relentlessly: mankind's rational capabilities do not compare favorably with that of animals in general and dogs in particular.

Beginning with his own personal observation that French noblemen often treat their dogs better than they do their own fellow human beings and buttressed by the acerbic comment from the Greek cynic Diogenes (see Chapter 5) that this dynamic is a favorable arrangement for dogs (including Diogenes himself), Montaigne pulverizes the assumption that human intelligence and virtue are superior to those of the animal kingdom. Regarding canine capacity for deductive reasoning, he cites the Greek account of a dog charging down a third crossroad without hesitation after failing to detect the scent of its master (or prey) along the two other paths, slyly hinting in the process that some of his human contemporaries were not as quick in their mental ascertainment.[11] He also repeats Plutarch's observation of a hungry dog accessing oil at the bottom of a jar by filling the jar with pebbles, again implying that not all men would have been able to come up with a solution to a similar problem.[12]

Dogs prove capable of abstract thought as well, in the form of doggie dreams. Drawing a direct parallel between the Roman poet Lucretius and his own experience, Montaigne writes: "Guard dogs can be found growling in their sleep, then yapping and finally waking with a start as though they saw some stranger coming."[13] With respect to the virtue of fidelity, and drawing upon Plutarch and Pliny (see Chapters 3–4), Montaigne retells famous stories of ancient dogs choosing to be cremated alive with their dead masters, and of dogs who reacted to crimes of theft and murder by fearlessly pursuing and identifying the perpetrators.[14] Living in a time and place in which theft, rapine, and murder were commonplace, Montaigne clearly prefers canine behavior over that of many fellow humans. Drawing once again on his personal experience living in a rural area, he writes of local hunters breeding the pick of dog litters, not by their own choice, but by allowing the mother of the puppies to make the choice with a simulation of danger, thus forcing the mother to rescue the puppies one at a time in order of her own preference.[15] He cites the playacting abilities of trained canines by recalling Plutarch's amazing report of a dog's coordinated performance with human actors before the Roman Emperor Vespasian.[16]

Montaigne notes with interest that military working dogs continued to serve humans (the Spanish) efficiently in the New World: "Those animals displayed eagerness and fierceness but no less skill and judgement, whether in pursuing victory or in knowing when to stop, in charging or withdrawing as appropriate, and in telling friend from foe."[17] Most of all, however, he is impressed by the disciplined self-sacrifice of trained guide-dogs working in the vicinity of his own neighborhood. In complete contrast to the so-called beastly behavior of humans, these animals consistently displayed an impressive combination of skill, intelligence, and virtue, often disregarding their own personal convenience and comfort in order to serve the welfare of their handicapped masters.[18]

This pro-canine, almost antihuman interpretation of Montaigne's *Apology* is nothing new; there is every indication that the essayist intended this overt message to stick, especially given his repetitive, digressive approach to the issue. Montaigne's more recent English translator, M.A. Screech of Oxford University, commented at length on this conspicuous, unusual aspect of the *Apology*:

> Montaigne's attitude to the beasts became central to some of the great controversies among the most famous philosophers and theologians of the seventeenth century. In its own way it even had something of the appeal of Darwin. By a very different route it forced people to re-examine in anger or humility what place Man occupied in the Book of Nature among all other creatures. And Montaigne emphasizes that the common examples of ants, bees, and guide-dogs are just as persuasive as exotic rarities.[19]

Noting (as many others have) that Plutarch was obviously Montaigne's favorite author, Screech adds that this pro-canine attitude of humility becomes a central plank in his attempt to assay and come to grips with the endless public outrages of the times, as well as to defend the modest theology of Sebond against all extremist attacks: "Montaigne answers ... criticism of Sebond by first crushing human pride: no purely human reasons can show conclusively (as Sebond can) that Man—for all his 'reason'—is in any way higher than the other animals."[20] Thus any attempted human rationalization or justification—of which there were many—for the unrestrained violence then being inflicted on French society was both unfounded and presumptuous.[21] The same principle applied not only as encouragement for a cessation of hostilities, but also to discourage the unsavory type of theological ultimatums then so rampant in every corner of France and throughout Europe. Montaigne's other disturbing implication is clear: animals on their worst days, not even dogs, would ever commit such atrocities.

Nor was this unusually sympathetic view of canines and the animal kingdom an isolated occurrence within Montaigne's essays. A dog owner himself (as well as a cat owner), Montaigne asserts that human cruelty towards animals or other humans is essentially the by-product of concealed cowardice, intemperate anger, or both combined. The essays "On Cruelty" and "On Cowardice, the Mother of Cruelty" are long meditations on what seemed to be the reigning vice within late 16th century France. In the latter work, he makes a rare reference to wild wolves by unfavorably attributing some of their less admirable qualities to humans, particularly their tendency to gang up on weakness, quoting the Roman poet Ovid in a similar vein.[22] At one startling point, Montaigne even seems to condemn the then-exclusively aristocratic sport of hunting as a recreational activity mainly encouraging the baser human instincts. Speaking for himself, he admits to enjoying the chase but hating the kill. Quoting Seneca, Montaigne asserts that the ultimate cruelty is to kill anything purely for sport; and like English philosopher John Locke a century later (see Chapter 10), he suggests that such behavior will eventually lead to similar cruelty towards humans.[23] In contrast to this barbarity, Montaigne favorably cites customs among the ancient Egyptians and Sicilians for honorable burials of their favorite pet animals.[24] He also admits that he cannot resist feeding human food to his own dogs whenever they beg, at the same time finding highly disagreeable the sight of his hunting hounds tearing apart their prey after giving chase.[25]

As Montaigne himself would have been the first to acknowledge, these were not new ideas at the time, but it took someone of his high-caliber genius and unique background to rearticulate them in print for the benefit of anyone able to read and willing to learn. Around the same time that Montaigne and the better part of the civilized world was still reeling from the aftershock of Saint Bartholomew's Day in 1572, the first major artistic depiction of this appalling event was created by the Huguenot sympathizer François Dubois (1529–1584) as a 3' × 5' oil painting on wood, today housed in the Musée cantonal des Beaux-Arts in Lausanne, Switzerland. Dubois' grotesque landscape portrays the infamous moment at which the French queen mother, Catherine de' Medici, publicly emerges to approvingly inspect the carnage that is beginning (only somewhat) to wind down.[26] The dead and dying are strewn everywhere. Interestingly, at the forefront of the scene on either side of the painting are two dogs, neither depicted as aggressors, scavengers, or bystanders. The one on the left appears to be guarding the corpse of its dead mistress, while the other on the right seems to be chasing attackers rather than leading them. The message of the painting recalls the same Latin anecdotes repeated by Montaigne in the *Apology* with respect to canine fidelity, as well as his implied suggestion that such acts of mass murder were uniquely characteristic of human beings. The Dubois work was only the beginning of a steady stream of similar interpretations on the same event that continued to haunt artists in all mediums ever since. During the 20th century, the Saint Bartholomew's Day Massacre would continue to be a favorite cautionary tale in movies, beginning with D.W. Griffith's *Intolerance* (1916) and still going strong into the present day with French contemporary films such as *Queen Margot* (1994) and *The Princess of Montpensier* (2010).[27]

On a happier note, canine art from the earlier French milieu of Montaigne's youth can be found (somewhat surprisingly) in the great anonymous masterpiece from the School of Fontainebleau circa 1550–1560 titled *Diana the Huntress*, today on display in the Louvre. The centerpiece of this renowned painting is a nude figure reputedly modeled by Diane de Poitiers, mistress to King Henry II and a central figure in political intrigue at the French court before Henry's untimely death in 1559. Beside Diana in the same scene is a sleek hunting greyhound springing to the chase ahead of its mistress, almost as prominent in the image as its namesake.[28] The timing of this creation, for one, is noteworthy. The royally patronized School of Fontainebleau flourished during the final decade of relative peace in France before internal hostilities erupted all across the realm. Afterwards, the school was abandoned in wake of widespread civil disorder accompanying the Wars of Religion. During this comparatively tranquil period, Montaigne would have been a young aristocrat practicing law and rapidly advancing through the competitive ranks of the French nobility.

It was a relatively idyllic, happy time for him which he would years later, in his psychologically probing essays, sometimes nostalgically hark back to, although with a tone of caution, no doubt remembering the horrors that followed in its immediate wake. Regarding the painting itself, it is sobering to recall that Diane was a woman deeply hated by the king's widow, Queen Catherine, a formidable personage in her own right. Not long after her husband's death, Catherine would instigate unimaginable bloodletting in the name of Christianity, not unlike the hated predecessor and half-sister to Queen Elizabeth in England, Queen ("Bloody") Mary. Diana's hound (Diane's dog in real life?) is itself beautifully delineated, very similar to the goddess in its taut athleticism and single-minded focus—in other words, the epitome of youthful spirits in all of its admirable qualities and purity. Within a few short years, such ideals would have been completely shattered, replaced by a public mood of anger, despair and shame. It was partly in response to this drastic shift that Montaigne wrote his timeless essays.

While open, armed hostilities in France between Catholics and Protestants subsided to some degree with the turn of the 17th century, the Wars of Religion in Europe as a whole did not. Instead, the black and white theological allegiances of the 16th century were replaced by a complete blurring of ideological lines as national boundaries on the map seemed to crumble and shift, sometimes permanently, other times temporarily. The stupefying Thirty Years' War of 1618–1648 witnessed the dreadful spectacle of rotating Catholic-Protestant combines between central European powers (including France), often made openly for the opportunistic sake of territorial gains. The only positive thing to be said about these violent developments is that at least they displayed a certain pack-like mentality (in the canine sense) for savvy aggressors, as opposed to committing premeditated mass murder over religious doctrinal disputes.

Curiously enough, England would be comparatively spared during this lengthy ordeal, mainly because it was fighting its own internal Civil War during 1642–1648, a conflict fought less over religion or territory than the balance of power between economic interests aligned with either Crown or Parliament. In its aftermath would follow the philosophic underpinnings of modern democracy, leading in turn to the American and French revolutions. The seminal figure in this movement would have many new things to say about the inherent rights of mankind, as well as certain duties of man owed towards the animal kingdom. Radical, egalitarian notions such these would have been completely alien to the French aristocrat from Saint-Michel-de-Montaigne; but then again, he had probably been personal witness to an appalling side of human nature that the intellectual fathers of the Enlightenment had only read about in books or heard about secondhand through the traditions of their forebears.

10

Natural Rights of Animals

> *One thing I have frequently observed in children, that, when they have got possession of any poor creature, they are apt to use it ill; they often torment and treat very roughly young birds, butterflies, and such other poor animals, which fall into their hands, and that with a seeming kind of pleasure. This, I think, should be watched in them; and if they incline to any such cruelty, they should be taught the contrary usage; for the custom of tormenting and killing of beasts will, by degrees, harden their minds even towards men; and they who delight in suffering and destruction of inferior creatures, will not be apt to be very compassionate or benign to those of their own kind.*—John Locke, Some Thoughts Concerning Education, 17th century[1]

The peripheral and half-hearted involvement of England in the Thirty Years' War of Europe came to a grinding halt in 1642 as the homeland of our Puritan forefathers erupted into its own violent period of civil strife, ending temporarily with the victory of Parliamentarian forces over Royalists and the public execution of King Charles I in 1648.[2] In retrospect, England was probably better off for not having been fully engaged on the continent. Whereas during the previous century Montaigne had personally witnessed in France the worst horrors that a civil-religious upheaval could inflict on an otherwise civilized society, the English Civil Wars of 1642–1648 demonstrated, if nothing else, that armed struggles over the prerogatives of kings and parliaments tended to be somewhat less savage and prolonged than those fought exclusively over abstract religious doctrines.[3] In the long run, England also seemed to emerge stronger and more advanced as a constitutional monarchy after the Restoration of Charles II as English king in 1660. (Another fringe benefit of the aftermath was the highly visible and fashionable popularity of the delightful King Charles Spaniel dog breed.[4] But in this we digress.)

Emerging from the persistent turbulence of 17th century English history was a philosopher later proving to be the most singular influence on the Founding Fathers of the United States, namely John Locke (1632–1704). Locke's long distinguished career was largely shaped by three major political upheavals in England during his own lifetime—the English Civil Wars, the Restoration, and lastly, the Glorious Revolution of 1688, which established King William and Queen Mary as English monarchs. Locke had also been a survivor of London's last major plague epidemic and city fire that occurred during the years 1665–1666. Consequently, he tended to be a man who highly valued political and socioeconomic stability (despite his later strong influence on American and French revolutionaries), as one who had experienced very little of these things personally in life. His father had been a Puritan country lawyer and, briefly, an officer in the Parliamentarian army which later so dominated battlefields of the British Isles throughout the mid–17th century. But the son was cut from a different, more contemplative cloth.[5]

A first-rate education in philosophy and medicine at the renowned Westminster School of London and Christ College at Oxford University was immediately followed by membership in the Royal Society and aristocratic patronage, though Locke seems to have been dissatisfied with his own formal schooling. Through his first major sponsor, the Earl of Shaftesbury, Locke got a taste of English politics (via the Whig Party) and began his tentative forays as a political essayist. He suffered from inconsistent health and, until the autumn of his years, the variable fortunes of his patrons. He never married or had children. Travels on the continent and a five-year exile to the Low Countries (1683–1688) were the main results of being perceived to be on the wrong side of the aisle while an attempted coup was being made against King James II. Locke returned to England securely and permanently in 1688 when William of Orange ascended to the English throne.[6] It was during this final period that Locke produced some of his greatest and most influential writings, all the while simultaneously working, sometimes reluctantly, as an appointed civil servant for the new monarchy. The most renowned English literary and scientific figures of the period (such as Isaac Newton), viewed Locke as an intellectual peer. His high reputation quickly spread abroad, especially to France and America, and continued unabated long after his death.

Locke's major works for which he is still remembered followed in quick succession after his happy return to England in 1688. These included *Two Treatises on Government* (1689); *A Letter Concerning Toleration* (1689–1692); *An Essay Concerning Understanding* (1690); and *Some Thoughts Concerning Education* (1693). These treatises presented in clear expression bold new ideas on economics, the natural rights of man, religious toleration by governments, personal self-knowledge, and the central importance of education as a necessary foundation for any healthy commonwealth, all well written with convincing authority by one possessing both a privileged education and wide experience in life.[7]

None of these writings touch directly upon canine matters, but the heart of his widely admired essay on education, unexpectedly and without any prompting, swerves into the fledgling field of animal rights, virtually an unheard of concept before the Enlightenment. After observing accurately enough that cruelty to animals is usually followed in short order by cruelty to humans (as already quoted), Locke praises at length an unnamed mother of his acquaintance who was quick in allowing her daughters to have pets (beginning with dogs), but then also was ruthlessly vigilant in making sure they took proper care of the animals, with penalties attached if they did not. Locke adds, "for, if they were negligent in their care of them, it was counted a great fault, which often forfeited their possession; or at least they failed not to be rebuked by it, whereby they were early taught diligence and good nature."[8] Although nowhere does Locke say that animals have natural rights or rights similar to mankind, there can be no mistaking his link of animal welfare to that of humans; moreover, humane treatment of pets obviously plays a key role in his view as to how children should be properly educated. We are not aware of any firm evidence that Locke was himself a dog owner; on the other hand, his rural upbringing, as well as his rural retirement to Essex during his late, most productive period, all leave little doubt that his personal exposure to the animal kingdom, both domesticated and wild, was at the very least considerable.

The origins of Locke's *Some Thoughts Concerning Education* went back to the early days of his Dutch exile in 1684, when Mr. and Mrs. Edward Clarke of England solicited letters from Locke seeking his guidance on the upbringing of their children.[9] At first glance, the thought of a respectable married couple with children approaching a politically banished bachelor with no children for such advice may seem strange to modern readers, but Locke had previously been a tutor for Shaftesbury's son and his reputation for reliability and wisdom had been established early on. Although well-known treatises on education had earlier been published in England, most notably Henry Peacham's *The Compleat Gentleman* (1622) and before that—possibly most famously of all—Montaigne's essay *On the Education of Children* (1580), Locke's letters of advice to the Clarkes developed into something quite new and groundbreaking.[10] He was among the first, if not the very first, to produce a stand-alone work devoted exclusively to the subject of child education, to approach it in a systematic manner, and to directly link the importance of education with a healthy body politic.

While Locke had been deeply influenced by Montaigne (see Chapter 9), since he owned copies of the French essayist's works in both English and French, Montaigne himself had not delved into the unusual topic of animal rights or how cruelty towards animals could be harmful to children.[11] By contrast, Locke places this discussion in the direct center of his work, framed by the importance of instilling good moral values into children. He underscores his friendly views towards the natural world by repeatedly recommending Aesop's animal fables (many of which deal with canines) as preferred reading material for children, and particularly as a tool for developing multilingual literacy skills (as he himself possessed).[12] Locke was 58 years old when the finished essay was finally published in 1693. Within less than two decades, it had been translated into French, German, and several other languages.[13]

Though remaining silent on the direct applicability of natural rights to animals, proverbially speaking, Locke had opened the door for others to do so, particularly the French Enlightenment political theorists following in his immediate wake. First out of the block was none other than Jean-Jacques Rousseau (1712–1778), whose preface to *A Discourse on the Origin and Basis of Inequality Among Men* (1754) could hardly have been less equivocal in its justification of animal natural rights:

> By this method also we put an end to the time-honored disputes concerning the participation of animals in natural law: for it is clear that, being destitute of intelligence and liberty, they cannot recognize that law; as they partake, however, in some measure of our nature, in consequence of the sensibility with which they are endowed, they ought to partake of natural right; so that mankind is subjected to a kind of obligation even toward the brutes. It appears, in fact, that if I am bound to do no injury to my fellow-creatures, this is less because they are rational than because they are sentient beings: and this quality, being common to both men and beasts, ought to entitle the latter at least to the privilege of not being wantonly ill-treated by the former.[14]

Rousseau's direct mandate against animal cruelty was not a frivolous detour; the idea tied into his larger theme, namely that whatever was harmful to man (including animal cruelty) was in fact also something all of us had a right to be protected against—even our own misbehavior, in this instance. Rousseau, like Locke before him, later went so far as to produce his own treatise (in novelistic form) on the upbringing of children, titled *Émile: Or, On Education* (1762), considering it to be among his most important works. Here he even seems to flirt with the endorsement of a vegetarian lifestyle, or at least the proposition that meat-eating (especially in children) is merely a conditioned habit rather than any basic necessity for good health or practice to be encouraged.[15] All in all, Rousseau's literary and philosophic output taken as a whole leaves little doubt where he stood on the issue of animal rights, as well as his view of the dire consequences for anyone actively engaging in practices of animal cruelty.[16]

Far less diplomatic on the same subject matter (and in typical combative fashion for him), was another influential thinker of the French Enlightenment. Voltaire, aka François-Marie Arouet (1694–1778), under the heading of "Animals" in his widely read *Philosophical Dictionary* (1764), scornfully declared, "What a pitiful, what a sorry thing to have said that animals are machines bereft of understanding and feeling...." Then Voltaire launches into his celebrated praise of canine fidelity, contrasted with the inhuman, horrific practice of vivisection:

> Bring this same judgment to bear on this dog which has lost its master, which has sought him on every road with sorrowful cries, which enters the house agitated, uneasy, which goes down the stairs, up the stairs, from room to room, which at last finds in his study the master it loves, and which shows him its joy by its cries of delight, by its leaps, by its caresses. Barbarians seize this dog, which in friendship surpasses man so prodigiously; they nail it to a table, and they dissect it alive in order to show the mesenteric veins. You discover in it all the same organs of feeling that are in yourself. Answer me, machinist, has nature arranged all the means of feeling in this animal, so that it may not feel? Has it nerves in order to be impassable? Do not suppress this impertinent contradiction in nature.[17]

It is interesting that, of all animals, Voltaire chose dogs to forcefully illustrate his point. Obviously this was the most extreme (and brutal) example that he could think of. Then, as now, brutality towards test animals was often speciously justified by advances in the medical sciences. Voltaire's subtle implication is that if society attempts to justify such barbaric practices against dogs, then why not against humans as well? Thus within the space of a mere 71 years (1693–1764), we have traveled from Locke's basic yet stern admonition against animal cruelty to the affirmed natural rights of all animals in general and dogs specifically, a la Rousseau and Voltaire.

The new ideas of Locke, Rousseau, and Voltaire were soon imported into the New World where these became a rallying point for wealthy British colonialists feeling oppressed by rising taxation without legislative representation. Although Voltaire and Rousseau both died in 1778 while the outcome of the American Revolution was still in doubt, by this time unexpected, decisive colonial victories at Trenton and, more dramatically, at Saratoga, had made it clear to the rest of the world that the struggle for independence would be prolonged and, at the very least, highly expensive for the British.[18]

Natural rights of dogs or any other animals were never an issue in this conflict; in fact, it may have something that most of the antagonists agreed upon in that few on either side would have supported the idea. Locke's natural rights of man, however, became a central talking point for the Founding Fathers, as best articulated and popularized by Thomas Jefferson ("unalienable Rights") in the 1776 Declaration of Independence. Only a century earlier in England outmoded doctrines such as the divine right of kings, religious intolerance, and limited access to education were all still being seriously debated, spurring in many instances English migration to the New World where a fresh start, far removed from these arcane controversies, might be achieved for those willing to take the risk. It would take another two centuries for the concept of animal rights to gain widespread acceptance, even though Rousseau and Voltaire had pretty much endorsed a similar idea by the mid-18th century.

With European settlers came European dogs into the Americas. Canine capabilities with respect to hunting alone made them a desirable asset, especially among aristocrats—that is to say, especially among the Founding Fathers and particularly among Virginia planters. As in most other things, however, Thomas Jefferson proved to be an unusual and somewhat iconoclastic case. After American independence had been militarily achieved by 1781, the Francophile Jefferson traveled to France, where he saw with his own eyes the efficient utilitarian role of French shepherding dogs within the sheep-raising and lucrative wool-producing industry. He brought back with him in 1789–1790 to Monticello, Virginia, a shepherd dog named Bergère, and this female gave birth in route to two puppies, Armandy and Claremont (names probably Americanized from "Normandy" and "Clermont").[19]

These animals were well remembered by Jefferson's surviving slaves long after his death in 1826. By the early 1800s, in part imitating Jefferson's example, sheep-raising (with the help of specialized canine labor) had become a fixture of the agricultural economy throughout Virginia and the South. Subsequent importations of French herding dogs to Monticello (some more successfully bred than others) led to their widespread dispersion throughout the piedmont region by the 1820s, and no doubt their ancestors today are alive and well in the form of either slightly or substantially different breeds. Obviously Jefferson was not the only American colonialist engaged in these kinds of importation and breeding activities, but as a Founding Father he may well have been the most prominent figure of his generation in this regard. Though predatory wolves were a constant threat to these endeavors, when Jefferson's son-in-law brought a tame wolf to Monticello, the scientifically inclined father-in-law appears to have been fascinated, and the interbreeding of the wolf with domesticated dogs elsewhere was proposed, though the results of this idea (if any) were never reported.[20]

Lest the wrong impression be given, it should be emphasized that Jefferson appears to have possessed a very complex, paternalistic attitude towards canines, not unlike the manner in which he seems to have viewed his own slaves. Whenever dogs proved unruly, violent or untrainable, he had them ruthlessly destroyed. There is no hard evidence to suggest that he viewed them as anything less or more than agricultural labor or personal property. When attacks on livestock by wild or irresponsibly owned dogs had become a problem in several states by 1810–1811, Jefferson wrote an infamous letter to a neighbor in which he hyperbolized (?) a "hostility to dogs" and more incredibly, a willingness to "readily join in any plan of exterminating the whole race."[21] But then Jefferson softened as he continued: "I consider them as the most afflicting of all the follies for which men tax themselves." In this sentiment he seemed to echo Montaigne from two centuries before (see Chapter 9). Jefferson concludes his missive by recommending only partial extermination (through law), use of dog collars for identification, and making dog owners legally liable for the misbehavior of their animals. In this last remark he profoundly harks back to the ancient dog control laws of Mesopotamia (see Chapter 1).

It may well have been that Jefferson the consummate politician knew quite well that he was dealing with a rural neighbor who did not want to hear anything about the natural rights of dogs while livestock was being destroyed. Jefferson's own figures of speech sometimes reflected his obsession with dogs, "canine appetite" being one of these, used both in reference to himself and (more humorously) the Marquis de Lafayette.[22] Another example occurred when Jefferson's young grandson showed a general fear of dogs when the grandfather had one brought into the house as a pet while he was acting as babysitter. These were not the actions of a dog-hater, as some have tried to portray Jefferson based on one single letter written in a delicate political situation. All of this of course may seem a long way removed from John Locke's eloquent condemnation of animal cruelty. Yet in hindsight it was revealed that Locke, like Jefferson after him, profited as an investor in the African slave trade. It would appear that great voices in favor of liberty and freedom are sometimes intertwined with personal behavior directly at odds with these same lofty goals being sought by others.

By the late 17th and early 18th centuries, it was becoming apparent in British society (among many others) than domesticated dogs were far more than household working assets, especially for the expanding, affluent middle and upper classes. Nowhere was this better reflected than in art. Possibly the greatest exponent of this trend was the finest English painter and engraver of his generation, William Hogarth (1697–1764), following in the immediate aftermath of Locke and approximate contemporary with both Rousseau and Voltaire.

One of Hogarth's most famous works is his 1745 self-portrait, titled *Painter and His Pug* with prominent inclusion of Hogarth's beloved dog Trump, a depiction in which artist and artist's pet seem to bear a remote facial resemblance to each another.[23] This striking production, however, was hardly an isolated example in the prolific output of Hogarth. His brilliant 1742 color portrait of Mary Edwards (today in the Frick Collection in New

York City) features a beautiful shepherd breed gazing adoringly at its mistress, an ornament then becoming a standard device in European portraiture.[24] More daringly, Hogarth's outrageous *Marriage A la Mode* satire series of six painted panels from 1743 to 1745 (on view at the National Gallery) includes three with more sympathetic domestic dogs as part of a larger and far more troubling human landscape. On a more somber and disturbing note, Hogarth's series of paintings and engravings for *A Rake's Progress* (1733–1735) prominently feature a number of dog characters, as do his later engravings for *The Four Stages of Cruelty* (1751). This latter social commentary begins with the inhumane torture of dog for sport but ends with another dog, somewhat fittingly, scavenging human remains from a crude medical experiment. These represent but a sampler of Hogarth's deep artistic interest in canine symbolism as a reference point for the everyday vanities and foibles of mankind. This doggy symbolism in fact became a kind of trademark or calling card for most of his pioneering visual work.[25]

Not too surprisingly then, with the mid–18th century British Enlightenment came the first golden age in canine portraiture, as well as human. With respect to both, surely the two most outstanding figures of the era were Joshua Reynolds (1723–1792) and Thomas Gainsborough (1727–1788). Reynolds especially excelled at pairing up dogs with young girls, as exemplified by his *Princess Sophia Matilda of Gloucester* (1774), *Miss Jane Bowles* (1775), *Lady Elizabeth Delm and Her Children* (1779), *A Young Girl and Her Dog* (1780), and the sumptuous *Portrait of Miss Anna Ward with Her Dog* (1787). Reynolds also produced a string of masterworks between 1759 and 1780 featuring English noblewomen or aspiring noblewomen using their canine pets as fashionable accessories, symbolic companions, or both. These included portraits of Caroline, Duchess of Marlborough, Lady Charles Spencer, Mrs. Elisha Mathew, The Honorable Miss Monckton, and Mary Amelia, first Marchioness of Salisbury.

The prolific output of Thomas Gainsborough was even more varied, beginning with incorporation of canines within diverse landscape settings and culminating in dog portraiture itself.[26] One of Gainsborough's earliest major efforts was *Portrait of the Artist with His Wife and Daughter* (1748) with obligatory inclusion of the family dog. Like Reynolds, he portrayed children with dogs, such as the masterful *Cottage Girl with Dog and Pitcher* (1785) and *The Marsham Children* (1787). Rather than depicting noblewomen with dogs as Reynolds did, Gainsborough aimed socially both higher and lower with *Queen Charlotte* and *Mrs. Mary Robinson*, both from 1781. He also painted noblemen with their dogs, sometimes framed in a semi-hunting mode, such as *John Plampin* (1755), *William Poyntz of Midgham and His Dog Amber* (1762), *George Lord Vernon* (1767), *Carl Friedrich Abel* (1777), and *Por-

trait of Colonel John Bullock (1780). Gainsborough portrayed couples with their dogs as well, including portraits *Mr. and Mrs. Andrews* (1750), and, more spectacular, *Mr. and Mrs. William Hallett* (1785). Then came the dogs by themselves. *Spitz Dog* from 1765 is considered a classic of its genre, while *Pomeranian Bitch and Pup* (1777) portrays same female canine posing for Gainsborough at the foot of Carl Friedrich Abel, a London-based German composer known to Mozart. On a more brutal plane, anticipating the naturalistic tendencies of the 19th century, Gainsborough during this same period produced *Two Shepherd Boys with Dogs Fighting* (1783) and *Greyhounds Coursing a Fox* (1785). Both of these vivid canvasses break from the prevalent cutesiness of dog painting that both Gainsborough and Reynolds profited from and loved to indulge in, reminding viewers that all dogs, no matter how domesticated, are capable of behaving more like wild wolves from which (we now know) all are descended.

One cannot help but wonder what Locke's reaction would have been to this rather high artistic prioritization of dogs, not to mention the earth-shaing American and French revolutions, all of which came to pass less than a century after his death. Canine fine art had been comparatively scarce during his lifetime, a period in which England was mainly preoccupied with and distracted by prolonged, complex struggles between its monarchy and Parliament, while American colonists, mostly from England, were primarily concerned with surviving in the new and frequently hostile environment to which they had fled or been coerced into going to.[27] At the close of the 18th century, however, much of this uncertain dynamic had been permanently altered, if not stabilized in a narrow sense.

By the time that Thomas Jefferson, acting as third president of the United States, effectively doubled the size of the country in 1803 with the Louisiana Purchase from France—money that was used to finance its ongoing wars against England—a completely different intellectual and cultural climate had spread more or less over all of Western civilization, replacing the era of Enlightenment which had preceded it.[28] Arguably the greatest literary figure of this age hailed from neither America nor England, nor France, for that matter, but rather from Germany, a nation that bore the full brunt of the Napoleonic Wars then raging. This artistic leader of the bold transition to the new sensibility of Romanticism was, curiously enough, not particularly fond of dogs, yet saw fit to make a dog the protagonist of his greatest and most famous work. If Jefferson's attitude towards dogs could occasionally be ambiguous, then there was nothing ambiguous whatsoever regarding the express distaste for canines of Johann Wolfgang von Goethe. Up until this point in history, the thousands-of-years-old love affair between Western man and canines had come in fits and starts, culminating in a philosophic, if not popular, mandate for humane treatment of Man's Best Friend and all animals in general. Now, with the dawning of the United States, the next two centuries and beyond would see a significant intensification of this argument over the precise scope of animal rights, the proper relationship between dog and man, and (rather surprisingly) the genetic relationship between dog and wolf.

11

Devil Dogs

Dog! Abominable monster!—Change him, oh infinite spirit! Change back this worm into his dog-shape, as he used to amuse himself in the night when he trotted along before me, rolled in front of the feet of the harmless wanderer and, when he stumbled, clung to his shoulders. Change him again to his favorite form that he may crawl on his belly in the sand before me and I may trample on him with my feet, the caitiff!—Johann Wolfgang von Goethe, *Faust*, 19th century[1]

In late 1775, not long after the American Revolution began to unfold in the aftermath of Bunker Hill, a crucial though far less celebrated event in the annals of Western literature transpired in German-speaking central Europe, far removed from the rapidly escalating conflict between the British and their dissatisfied colonial subjects of the New World. At the independent city-state of Weimar, the recently invested and newly married 18-year-old Duke Karl August (1757–1828) invited to the lucrative patronage of his court a financially struggling 26-year-old lawyer-turned-novelist by the name of Johann Wolfgang Goethe (1749–1832), based on the somewhat disreputable popular success of one book and one play, along with a single face-to-face interview between the two men the previous year in Frankfurt. Their personal and professional relationship, give or take a few ups and downs, would last nearly 53 years, ending only with the duke's death.

Though few if any could have guessed it at the time, this rather casually begun association would in hindsight prove to one of the most productive and beneficial of its kind in the history of letters. Long before it concluded, Goethe himself had been officially ennobled ("von Goethe") and, what was more important, been given the money, time, and freedom to produce some of the world's greatest literary masterpieces in several different genres. The most renowned of all these works, the stage drama *Faust*, also happened to introduce its formidable antagonist, Mephistopheles (or Mephisto), in the corporal form of a black poodle, though this unusual and obscure aspect of the play is rarely remarked upon and almost always glossed over in subsequent interpretations.

Many people simply do not like dogs and are more afraid than fond of them. This writer is of the opinion (and it is only an opinion) that such attitudes are more the result of environment and conditioning than any preconceived disposition or inherent personal nature. Those people not well disposed towards canines, however, can point to Goethe as arguably their greatest literary representative, and he is a great one indeed. In no fewer than three of his mature published works (including *Faust*) he takes a gratuitous swipe at Man's Best Friend, and nowhere, to the best of our knowledge, does he offer praise. There is some evidence to indicate that the childhood and adolescence of young Goethe in Frankfurt was spent in comparative isolation, somewhat sheltered from the messy world surrounding him, as his striving middle class father sought to carefully educate his son and prepare him for the social advancement that he accurately believed would eventually come his way.[2]

Despite the suggestive connotations of his given middle name (Wolfgang), it rather appears that Goethe, during the course of a long and productive life, never willingly interacted with canines, and whenever he was forced to, did so reluctantly and resentfully.[3] By the time he was 22 years old, having completed his legal and humanist studies at Leipzig and Strasbourg, the mold had been cast for Goethe; the world literary stage was now set for one of its most gifted and rarified geniuses to make his dramatic entrance and to firmly hold international audience attention for over the next six decades. On full display would be Goethe's many virtues and shortcomings as a person, and in these many, sometimes contradictory, qualities we, the enthralled audience, would immediately recognize our own deficiencies.[4]

Goethe's father believed that law was the best path for his son's future success, but the son had other ideas. Having dabbled in writing throughout his school days, the young Goethe again turned to literature as a pastime when conventional work proved unbearably boring. In 1773, his first play, *Götz von Berlichingen*, was a surprise hit in no small part because of the irreverent attitude and scatological lines of its hero. Next, in 1774, came Goethe's first novel, *Die Leidden des jungen Werther* (The Sorrows of Young Werther). *Werther* appears to have been written on a lark. Telling (allegedly tongue-in-cheek) the tragic story of suicide committed over love, the novel reputedly did in fact inspire real-life suicides as it made its way to best-seller lists in several different languages. Goethe's own love affairs with the fair sex were frequent, varied, and lifelong.

Now suddenly (and without design), he found himself at the forefront of a new artistic movement, later coined Sturm und Drang (Storm and Stress), a harbinger of 19th century Romanticism and emotional reaction to the rational subjectivity of the 18th century Enlightenment, especially reflected in literature, music, and all of the performing arts.[5] One tiny facet of this new trend was that canines were now often openly portrayed in a more sinister light. When Goethe and Karl August were introduced to each other in 1774, it no doubt occurred to the soon-to-be Duke of Weimar that a person of Goethe's caliber could be of multiple uses, not only as artist in residence happily flaunting the stuffy old guard traditions, but as one who could also competently hold down a day job as a useful government bureaucrat and agent. As for Goethe, he needed the money and craved the status. Although he had already achieved fame of sorts, 18th century copyright law was nonexistent, and artistic popularity did not automatically translate into a livelihood, as many of his talented but less fortunate contemporaries would learn to their grief and frustration.[6] Therefore, in 1775 Goethe gladly accepted an invitation from the Weimar ducal court to effectively become its resident provocateur, and the rest is literary history. Fifty-seven years later, Goethe and Karl August would be fittingly buried side by side in Weimar, and the Duke deserves far more credit than he is usually given for enabling Goethe's spectacular accomplishments, culminating with his two powerful *Faust* plays of 1808 and 1832. A small price that Goethe would have to pay for this patronage, however, was the Duke's unabashed love of dogs, and to this interesting subject we shall soon return.

Goethe worked on the Faust theme for most of his life. The German version of the tale of a man selling his soul to the Devil in return for youthful pleasures and worldly knowledge stretched back to at least the 16th century and appears to have been loosely based on an actual historical figure by that name. By the 1590s the legend had been imported to England where it enjoyed notable stage success in a play by Christopher Marlowe (*Doctor Faustus*). Goethe's beginning primary source, however, was an anonymous 1587 German chapbook, or pamphlet, which happens to include an evil, magical dog as Faust's constant companion.[7] It is generally accepted that this is where Goethe got the idea to incorporate a dog into the story (not found in Marlowe), although it is quite possible that he witnessed a similar device used in a retelling of the legend for the puppet theaters with which he was enthralled as a child. Goethe's semiautobiographical second novel, *Wilhelm Meisters lehrjahre* (Wilhelm Meister's Apprenticeship), from 1795 to 1796 describes both youthful puppet theater experiences and then later an annoying incident in which a play performance is disrupted by the unruly dogs of irresponsible pet owners.

Notwithstanding Plutarch's account, famously repeated by Montaigne, of talented playacting dogs in ancient Rome (see Chapter 9) or Shakespeare's use of a dog onstage for comic effect in *Two Gentlemen of Verona*, Goethe the dramatist seems to have had no use for them except in a negative context. During his Sturm und Drang period of the 1770s, Goethe made a foray into the Faust legend, known to scholars as the *Urfaust*, but this version never made it to publication and he set it aside. Later, during the late 1790s, at the urging of the poet Friedrich Schiller, Goethe returned to his old manuscript. This time he had more resources to draw upon, including the old German chapbook from the Weimar library.[8] Interestingly, around the same period in 1801 that he was writing new opening scenes incorporating "den schwarzen Hund" into the drama, Goethe found himself traveling with the duke's entourage through Göttingen, where they were kept awake at night by incessantly barking street dogs.[9] The problem was forcefully, if not meanly, solved by the party throwing objects at the animals from the windows of their rooms.

Later, in 1817, Goethe published his relatively unknown short story *Die guten weiber* (The Good Women), including a sniping, secretive exchange between the main characters admitting to their dislike of dogs and recalling an incident almost identical to the one earlier experienced by Goethe at Göttingen in 1801. Even as Goethe spent much of his remaining years working on a posthumously published (and much lesser known) part two of *Faust*, he did not deign this second time around to include a dog as the embodiment of Mephisto or as a generic symbol of evil and foreboding. By this time he may well have taken too much flak for what he had already written against Man's Best Friend.

The year 1817 also saw another biographical incident for Goethe that did not do anything to improve his attitude towards canines.[10] Goethe's artistic duties at Weimar included supervision of the ducal theatre (which had seen the premier of *Faust*, part one, in 1806), and over a long tenure his good taste brought in distinguished productions from the likes of Shakespeare, Schiller and Voltaire. Unfortunately, however, not all of the stage troops were happy with Goethe's iron-fisted control of the venue, including star actress Caroline Heygendorf-Jagemann, who concocted an elaborate, effective scheme for driving a wedge between the good relations of Goethe and Duke Karl August.

When the insipid but popular adaptation of the play *Dog of Aubry* (*Dog of Montargis* in the French original) came to Weimar that same year featuring a live performing poodle, probably not unlike the one representing Mephisto in *Faust*, Goethe balked at allowing the spectacle in his theatre. Jagemann intervened with the Duke, an avid dog-lover surely appreciative of the old tale in which a loyal canine identifies and bravely fights a murderer, and Goethe was overruled accordingly. Goethe left town in a huff and was promptly relieved of his theatre management duties by the duke, in essence being told that he could stay or leave but the dog was going to stay. Relations between the two men otherwise remained cordial; by this point their fruitful association had lasted over 40 years and was not about to be destroyed by the isolated intrusion of a single pooch. Nevertheless, *Dog of Aubry* hit the boards at Weimar that season and audiences were no doubt delighted.

Unlike the poodle that relieved Goethe of his responsibilities as theatre manager, it seems improbable that the one he envisioned for *Faust* was a live, trained animal. This is a topic that deserves its own research and study, but a more likely scenario in the case of Goethe is that he conceived the poodle role as a puppet prop that could be easily controlled and precisely choreographed. More important, a live dog, no matter how well trained, would probably lessen the intended gravitas of the dramatic scene. Given that Goethe may well have been introduced to the story through the puppet theaters of his youth, as well as his repeated disdain for live dogs on the stage, this seems to be the most probable scenario. This is not to say that a live trained poodle could not play the role; it merely suggests that is what Goethe's own personal preference was likely to have been.

It is also noteworthy that the many subsequent stage and operatic variations of *Faust* produced in the 19th and 20th centuries, without exception, opted to dispense with Mephisto's canine introduction to the audience altogether.[11] An obvious alteration such as this from Goethe's idiosyncratic original was both a simplification of stage traffic and possibly a concession to audience pro-canine sentiments as well. On the other hand, anyone seeing the potential power and subtlety of a skillfully executed puppet show—even when otherwise surrounded by human actors—must admit this approach to be a viable if not preferable option as well. It is a shame, in fact, that Goethe's original vision of the *Faust* legend is not performed more often in this precise fashion.

There is evidence in the text to suggest that Goethe was aware of the dog aspect of the legend at a very early stage. After a lengthy prelude and introduction, Faust first encounters the devil in dog form (as a stray) while publicly strolling with Wagner, his friend and confidant. Described specifically as a black "Pudel" (line 1150), the animal ingratiates itself with the two men even as they make disparaging remarks, commenting on its alleged stupidity and lack of spirit (lines 1167–1173). After following Faust home to his study, the poodle annoys his new master with its persistent barking, commotion, snarling, moaning, and whining (lines 1186–1209, 1238–1243), conspicuous traits likely to offend a presumed non-lover of dogs. After the poodle transforms itself into Mephisto posing as a university student, Faust famously exclaims in verse (line 1323), "Das also war des Pudels Kern!" (Then this was our poodle's core!), thereby suggesting that many other (if not all) canines are true devils at heart. This portion of the play was written in 1801.

Later in the drama, however, in a prose section composed for the *Urfaust* of the 1770s, Goethe makes overt references to Mephisto's dog-like character and appearance likely derived from the old traditions of Faust being accompanied by a black dog, with which he had somehow been previously familiar. In the scene leading up to Gretchen's execution, subtitled "Dreary Day: A Field," Faust attacks Mephisto's callousness with "Hund!" (see header quote), demanding that he resume his former dog incarnation ("Hundsgestalt"), and when this does not happen, he still flings insulting canine metaphors at his tormentor ("Don't bare your greedy teeth at me like that!"). Thus it appears that Goethe as a young man was well aware of this aspect of the tale, long before taking up residence in Weimar under the patronage of Duke Karl August.

Use of canines as overt symbols of evil or satanic forces was nothing new in Western literature. Both Greek and German mythology used the device long before the Faust legend came into being. During the 20th century, folklorist Barbara Allen Woods indicated that, especially within the German tradition, these satanic dogs were often black in color, poodles by breed, and sometimes both combined.[12] Other distinctive, supernatural features seized upon by Goethe for *Faust* included the animal's ability to grow in size, to ride its victim piggyback, and to represent the guise of the devil himself.[13] Given that the Napoleonic Wars were raging throughout Europe by 1801, and that Goethe's Germany for many years bore the brunt of French territorial expansion, there may have also been an element of German Francophobia involved in Mephisto's poodle guise—poodles being a breed often specifically associated with the French.[14] What was more important, however, as Woods pointed out in her oft-cited "The Devil in Dog Form" article from 1954, the symbolic satanic image of a "Black Dog" or "Hellhound" stalking its victims runs throughout modern Western cultural tradition, from the Flying Dutchman legend to American blues music.[15]

This is all a far cry from earlier, more typical Enlightenment-era idealizations of dogs, carrying over for some of Goethe's Romantic contemporaries and represented by highly contrasting examples such as Lord Byron's moving and majestic 1808 poem "Epitaph to a Dog" in homage to Boatswain, his beloved, recently deceased Newfoundland.[16] Within the context of *Faust*, use of a black poodle for Mephisto's dramatic stage entrance, in tandem with his costume of a traveling university student, all seem to convey Goethe's stern message to audiences that even the most benign or harmless appearances can sometimes conceal lethal, diabolical intentions.

In fairness to Goethe, his unfavorable attitude towards canines was moderate and restrained in comparison to many of his contemporaries, even in Germany. In 1812, for example, Jacob and Wilhelm Grimm released their seminal collection *Rotkäppchen* (better known in English as *Children's and Household Tales*), with inclusion of perhaps the best-known modern version of the Little Red Riding Hood fable. Here, arguably the ultimate incarnation of the "Big Bad Wolf" archetype makes its most notorious appearance, although in the Grimm retelling of the old tale, good triumphs over evil and the wolf is destroyed.[17] This particular wolf is neither particularly magical nor the embodiment of satanic power like the Black Dog symbol of Goethe's *Faust*. It is simply a savage natural creature hell-bent on human destruction, and capable of using subterfuge to accomplish its goals.

The Brothers Grimm had in fact adapted the same tale from a much earlier French version titled *Le Petit Chaperon Rouge* by Charles Perrault in 1697, around the same time that English philosopher John Locke had been advocating against animal cruelty (see Chapter 10).[18] In Perrault's dark, Hobbesian rendering, there is no happy ending, the Big Bad Wolf devours all of its prey, and the entire story is expressly made to be an allegory for predatory human, rather than animal, behavior. Later during the 19th century, the Big Bad Wolf made a distinctive entry into English folklore with the fable of the "Three Little Pigs." These prevalent anti-wolf cautionary tales of the Romantic era seem to have distant roots in the ancient Hellenic traditions of Aesop, including "The Boy Who Cried Wolf," "The Wolf and the Lamb," "The Dog and the Wolf," and "The Wolf and the Crane."[19] All may reflect a popular resurgence of long-engrained human hostilities against wolves, as natural enemies to both mankind and agricultural livestock. For a sharp difference in attitude, one need only turn to the medieval traditions of Saint Francis miraculously taming and reforming the Wolf of Gubbio (see Chapter 8).

Artwork touching upon the subject matter of the satanic Black Dog or its more worldly canine cousin, the Big Bad Wolf, is so extensive and diverse that any attempt to reiterate them within these pages would seem superfluous. By way of contrast, however, German pictorial representations of poodles from the era of Goethe can tell a different story as to how these animals were viewed by their fawning, proud owners. For example, in 1817—the same year Goethe and his duke had a temporary falling out over the issue of a trained poodle dominating the stage at Weimar—artist Johann Adam Klein (1792–1875) executed a sensitive pencil etching of a Viennese poodle named Schwalerl for its wine merchant owner. Today the British Museum's reproduction of the original may be conveniently viewed in former curator Catherine John's magnificent anthology.[20]

Closer to home for the Weimar court known to Goethe is an 1805 formal portrait of his patron, Duke Karl August, in the prime of life at 48 years of age, casually reclining next to a favorite mastiff asleep at its master's side during the sitting process. The image speaks volumes about the duke's reputation as a dog-lover, and his mastiff obviously felt the same way about the duke. This would have been only one year before part one of Goethe's *Faust* premiered on the Weimar stage. More revealing still is a 1780s engraving of Goethe, Duke Karl August, and the singing actress Corona Schröter (1751–1802), all going for a stroll together in a Weimar park with two greyhounds in attendance, presumably pets of the duke. One of the greyhounds ignores the entire group as it scents the trail ahead while the other glances back directly at Goethe with what can only be described as a look of suspicion and wariness.[21]

Most telling of all is that, in age where portraiture often featured Man's Best Friend as a faithful companion, there are no instances of this popular device being used for Goethe himself, despite many opportunities presented over the course of a long and celebrated career. It may even have been that Duke Karl August, who surely did more than anyone in Europe to subsidize Goethe's greatness, made tolerance of his beloved hounds an express condition of employment for anyone and everyone under his protection, Johann Wolfgang von Goethe not excepted. Then again, the duke may have simply just loved his dogs. All that Goethe had to fight back with would have been his literary works, and even these were prudently used in a relatively discreet manner.

The high drama of Goethe's *Faust* will live on in the minds of serious readers as long as great books continue to be read. His achievements in this and many other works transcend all languages, times and places. Like many other writers of genius throughout the ages, Goethe engages us less because of his personal shortcomings than in spite of them. Even to dog lovers, beginning with Karl August and continuing down through the ages, he entertains and edifies. Indeed, it would be difficult to name a literary figure more important or central to the founding of the Romantic tradition, which, in many respects, continues to be strong into the 21st century. And yet, Goethe was also a scientist and product of the Enlightenment, although this is rarely remarked upon either. Had he not been so fortunate as to have found a base in Weimar, it is possible that this side of his genius would have eventually become more pronounced. Interestingly enough, in late 1831, less than three months before Goethe's death, Charles Darwin, a 22-year-old yet-to-be-famous English prodigy, boarded a sea vessel named (appropriately enough) HMS *Beagle* to begin his own rapid trajectory towards world literary and scientific renown. This remarkable individual, however, often showed less fear of animals than of his own human species.

12

Everything Is Connected

> *Even in the case of the breeds of the domestic dog throughout the world, which I admit are descended from several wild species, it cannot be doubted that there has been an immense amount of inherited variation; for who will believe that animals closely resembling the Italian greyhound, the bloodhound, the bull-dog, pug-dog, or Blenheim spaniel, &c.—so unlike all wild Canidæ—ever existed in a state of nature?*[1]—Charles Darwin, *The Origin of Species*, 19th century

> *Our domestic dogs are descended from wolves and jackals, and though they may not have gained in cunning, and may have lost in wariness and suspicion, yet they have progressed in certain moral qualities, such as in affection, trust-worthiness, temper, and probably in general intelligence.*[2]—Charles Darwin, *The Descent of Man*, 19th century

It would perhaps be more accurate to assert that 19th century Romanticism supplemented the rationalism of the 18th century Enlightenment rather than simply opposed it. One of the great paradoxes of the latter period is that, despite its unabashed embrace of subjective emotionalism, the 1800s witnessed many of the greatest intuitive and scientific breakthroughs achieved up until that point in human history, a number of which would find full flower in the 20th and 21st centuries, even as large numbers of the general population continued to resist and even reject these same ideas. No individual better symbolizes this ongoing conflict between technological progress and populist opinion than Charles Robert Darwin (1809–1882), whose immeasurably influential theory of evolution via natural selection is to this day, over 150 years after the fact, widely and stubbornly resisted within the American educational system. Among countless controversial new insights, Darwin was also among the first to publicly insist that dogs, wolves, and humans all had far more in common biologically with each other than was (and remains) typically recognized or commonly acknowledged.

An original Shropshire lad of the West Midlands, Darwin was born in the historic medieval town of Shrewsbury during the height of the Napoleonic Wars. His family roots were strictly English middle class but culturally refined nonetheless. The parents were ostensibly Unitarian but their second son, Charles, was baptized into the Anglican Church, probably for political convenience. His father, Robert, was a successful physician with little use for conventional religion, and this freethinking tendency was clearly instilled into the son at a tender age. His mother, Susannah, was the granddaughter of Josiah Wedgwood, founder of the famed English pottery manufacturing company. A painted portrait of the seven-year-old Charles depicts a bright-eyed boy affectionately holding a potted plant, an image rather prophetic of the child's tremendous future. Then at age eight, his mother suddenly died, the first in a long series of personal blows that seemed to gradually extinguish Darwin's belief, to whatever extent ever held, in a benevolent sky-god.

As an adolescent, he enjoyed escaping into nature and outdoor sports, especially hunting. The elder Darwin wanted his son to follow in the family footsteps as a doctor, and Charles was sent off to the University of Edinburgh, the alma mater of both his father and grandfather, to study medicine, but the preordained plan went awry when young Darwin showed little interest in surgery, let alone people in general. His first loves were botany, birds, and taxidermy. To the credit of Darwin's father, he quickly recognized that he was outmatched and had Charles transferred to Christ College, Cambridge, hoping that his son would eventually find refuge in the Anglican ministry.

It was at Cambridge that Charles met his first intellectual guru, noted botanist John Stevens Henslow, onto whom Darwin glommed as a disciple. After an extremely shaky and unpromising academic start, Darwin graduated in 1831 with a B.A., finishing strongly within the upper 10 percent of his class. Shortly after graduation, and still with little inkling on what to do with his life, Darwin learned that he had been recommended by Henslow to Captain Robert FitzRoy, surveyor, meteorologist, and future British royal governor of New Zealand, to be FitzRoy's companion as a "gentleman naturalist" on a projected five-year circumnavigation of the globe. Darwin was 22 years old and unabashedly eager as his life's work now began to unfold before him.

The problem with the bold proposal was that it offered only an unpaid position. Darwin's father was dead set against the venture and refused to pony up. At this crucial moment, Charles' maternal uncle Josiah Wedgwood (II) came to the financial rescue.[3] Thus, on December 27, 1831, Darwin joined the captain and crew of HMS *Beagle*—never was a ship more appropriately named—as it left port at Plymouth.[4] The *Beagle* was a not a big ship; basically it was a light-armed sloop, designed more for speed and endurance than for pitched fighting or heavy cargo transport. Originally launched in 1820, it was still a relatively new vessel when Darwin set foot aboard in 1831. After Darwin returned to England, it would go on to make several more successful worldwide voyages before being obscurely sold off as obsolete and dismantled for scrap in 1870. This was a Dickensian time and place with little sense of historic preservation, even as Darwin was making final preparations for publication of *The Descent of Man* in 1871.[5]

The story of Darwin's five years at sea are best told elsewhere, especially in the treasure trove of his own prolific and elegant writings. Suffice it here to say that by the time the *Beagle* returned to Cornwall in 1836, the now 27-year-old Darwin had become an almost legendary figure and was immediately accepted as a peer by the English scientific elite. By this time his father had come around as well, relishing his son's fame and organizing considerable financial support for Charles' subsequent career.

In the year 2013, the 1831–1836 voyage of HMS *Beagle* comes across as only a slightly less amazing journey than the fictional one portrayed in the 2012 Oscar Award–winning 3D film by Ang Lee, *Life of Pi*.[6]

For Darwin, there was no shipwreck, starvation, or depredation, but instead a breathtaking journey of the mind in which old, outmoded paradigms were cast aside and exciting new ones formulated. Over the long term, these new formulations would challenge rigid religious beliefs that had been in place for several millennia, including some previously held by Darwin himself. As a person, he seems to have had little fear of death or the natural world; his fellow humankind, on the other hand, clearly made him very nervous. Then again, as the American evangelist Sherwood Eddy (1871-1963) once quipped, faith itself is reason grown courageous, an observation Darwin would have likely appreciated.

The man who survived a five-year circumnavigation of the globe, however, had trouble navigating the competitive intellectual world of the 19th century London scientific publishing industry. Though given as much work as he cared to take on (typically a lot), Darwin did not perform well under publishing deadlines and, for the first time in his life, began to suffer from bad health, a handicap that plagued him for the remainder of his career. The great book that everyone expected from him did not immediately appear. Instead, it slowly gestated as Darwin collaborated with fellow scientists, churned out articles, and studied the doomsday philosophy of Thomas Malthus (1766–1834). In 1848, Darwin's father died, never living to see fulfilled the promising destiny of his son. He finally seems to have been spurred into action as younger contemporaries such as Alfred Russel Wallace began to openly support a theory of evolution.

In general terms, the theory itself had been around a long time but consistently derided as irreligious and heretical. Darwin, though possessing a first-rate education, had not heard anyone speak favorably of it until his student days at Cambridge. The paper trail clearly shows that Darwin was the first to develop a logical expression of natural selection in the wake of his voyage on the *Beagle* but chose not rush to publication with it. During the long interim of 23 years, and after much hesitation, he married his first cousin Emma Wedgwood (daughter of his Uncle Josiah) in 1839, knowing all too well the biological risks involved. Ten children followed, including five sons who went on to distinguished careers of their own; two other children died in infancy. Tragically, one included a favorite daughter, Annie, who died at age 10 in 1851, an event which seemed to blast any remainder of Darwin's conventional religious faith. For eight more years he waited, reevaluated, and reconsidered while gathering additional corroborating evidence and organizing that which he had already amassed. Then, at age 50, he hurled his first thunderbolt.

In 1859, *The Origin of Species* was published and the earth shook. Articulate, beautifully written, and presented with steel trap logic buttressed by unimpeachable personal experience and professional credentials, the book made a lot of people angry and continues to do so into the present day. An enduring, misleading public image of Darwin formed that could not have been more at odds with the actual personality. Stung and saddened by a firestorm of criticism and false accusations, including persistent caricatures of him as an ape man, Darwin withdrew from the spotlight and did his best to keep a low profile, even as he continued his research and writing while *The Origin of Species* sold like hotcakes. (He would have been deeply hurt by today's use of the popular expression "Darwin Award" and horrified by the atrocities and holocausts that have been committed in the name of his evolutionary theory.)[7] Between his first and second most famous works came the American Civil War, a fact worth remembering given that both the Darwin and Wedgwood families were passionately active in abolitionist circles long before it became a fashionable thing to do. In 1871 came Darwin's *The Descent of Man*, with an interesting word choice in the title (as opposed to "Ascent"), in which the famed author, instead of making apologies for himself, took the theories of evolution and natural selection to even more profound and controversial heights, effectively erasing the already blurring lines allegedly separating humankind not only from each other but from the animal kingdom as well.[8] Suffering from chronic heart disease, Charles Darwin died quietly at his suburban London home in 1882, surrounded by loved ones. At the immediate petition of the Royal Society, he was entombed in Westminster Abbey, not far from Isaac Newton.

Although Darwin's revolutionary theories are most often (and rightfully) associated with his observations on multifarious bird species, his enthusiasm for canines—an outgrowth of his youthful hunting days—is readily apparent to any reader browsing through his major works. As almost a deliberate contrast to canine behavior being widely perceived as vicious, Darwin prefers to dwell on the extraordinary viciousness of male birds in mating season (which he repeatedly characterized as "pugnacious") and hummingbirds in particular, which he categorizes as "one of the most quarrelsome."[9] In citing the prodigious powers of canine memory, Darwin later wrote of his own dog, who immediately recognized him upon his return home after a five-year absence during the *Beagle* voyage, not unlike Ulysses being recognized by his dog Argos after an even longer separation (see Chapter 5).[10]

In *The Origin of Species*, as a common-sense example of evolution, Darwin dwells upon the everyday activities of dog breeders and the manner in which natural instincts, as well as physical traits, can be easily manipulated by them from one generation of animal to the next. He then summarizes by citing a documented case of a domesticated dog being bred with a wild wolf, thus producing domesticated offspring with selective wolfish traits.[11] In his original journals, an impressed Darwin recalled how in Argentina professional sheep herding dogs were trained by being taken away from their natural mothers as pups and then placed with ewes, where they were raised as one of the flock and grew to maturity believing themselves its designated protectors.[12] More amazing still, while traveling through the Patagonian Shelf, Darwin stumbled upon the rapidly disappearing Falkland Islands, a breed which he accurately predicted would soon become extinct, as it did by the 1870s.[13] Situated almost 300 miles from the Argentine mainland, the presence of these animals proved an unaided ability to travel long distances over the ocean by hopping island keys with the assistance of icebergs.[14] Their natural curiosity and lack of fear, however, ultimately proved fatal when they came into prolonged contact with European explorers.

The Descent of Man in many respects picked up where *The Origin of Species* left off. Darwin appears to have been annoyed and offended by a growing, shrill chorus of critics insisting that humankind was physically and morally superior to the animal kingdom, almost in direct opposition to the stance taken by Saint Francis of Assisi many centuries before (see Chapter 8). The various reasons spouted for this alleged superiority became Darwin's new target, and his responses still have the power to offend and anger anyone not prepared to cope with the evidence he presents. At one disconcerting point in the narrative, the respective embryos of a human and a dog are accurately illustrated side by side, and one needs captions to tell the difference.[15] The close similarities are almost comical, if not scary.

Canine powers of imagination and abstract thought are demonstrated by their dreams, as noted long before by Montaigne and, long before him, ancient observers (see Chapter 9).[16] Canine capacity for deductive reasoning proves a favorite for Darwin, just as for countless other perceptive human observers before him. He cites the irrefutable examples of artic sled dogs intentionally spreading the distribution of their weight on thin ice with no human prompting (see Chapter 15), as well as that of wolf packs attacking their prey in looser formation whenever in a similar situation.[17] Perhaps more astounding are his examples of British hunting retrievers, as Darwin stayed in contact with hunters and gamekeepers (as reliable sources) long after he himself had given up the sport. In separate reported instances, two ducks were brought down with a single shot, one killed and one wounded. In both cases the retrievers, though trained not to kill, dispatched the wounded bird before separately bringing back both to the respective hunters, prompting Darwin to note in wonderment "this was the only known instance of her [the retriever] ever having willfully injured any game."[18] As with the Argentine sheep dogs, Darwin underscores unique canine abilities to assimilate and adapt and remarks upon puppies raised with cats and adopting feline mannerisms.[19] Canines, asserts Darwin, not only recognize human vocabulary but likely have something akin to their kind of language not understood by humans.[20]

Then Darwin kicks into high gear, no doubt for the benefit or aggravation of those critics adopting religious justifications for their own mulish views on alleged human superiority. Dogs, he asserts, are not only unmatched in their positive social tendencies and unwavering fidelity towards humans, but very likely have "something very like a conscience" as well.[21] They too (like humankind), possess free will ("self-command") quite apart from any instilled fear of disobedience, and, more controversial still, have attitudes towards their masters and mistresses highly suggestive of human religious feelings.[22] If this were not enough to send his unsuspecting Victorian readers over the edge, Darwin concludes by musing on the many close similarities between human sexual courtships and those of dogs.[23] Obviously, none of these explosive arguments were designed to be politically correct, pander to ignorance, or, for that matter, win friends and influence people. Nevertheless, *The Descent of Man* sold well and only enhanced Darwin's already considerable fame and notoriety. At this point in his long career he had little left to gain; after the abuse he had suffered to date, he probably did not care a fig how people reacted. In spite of any real or imagined indifference to public relations, however, Darwin continued to profoundly influence large numbers of people, especially within the scientific community, even as conservative establishment voices continued to pillory and anathematize his name over the next century and a half.

In the immediate wake of Darwin's most famous books, literary artists working in the Romantic idiom began softening their attitude towards canines. The famed Danish children's author Hans Christian Andersen (1850–

1894) published the traditional Scandinavian fable *The Tinderbox* (1875), in which three monstrous, magical dogs like something out of a Goethe nightmare (see Chapter 11) turn out in the end to be indispensable saviors of the story's hero. A few years later, Scottish popular novelist Robert Louis Stevenson (1850–1894) published his unusually thoughtful essay, *The Character of Dogs* (1883), in which the superior moral status of Man's Best Friend is once again emphatically reaffirmed, despite all that species' surface shortcomings often cited by its critics. Stevenson even goes so far as to suggest that blame for most of these canine faults are more attributable to human masters than to any inherent qualities of nature. The interesting thing about writers like Stevenson and Andersen making such commentary is that both were, by anyone's standards, considered highly mainstream in their own day, unlike, say, Darwin. Had the author of *The Origin of Species* and *The Descent of Man* made similar arguments, he would have likely been ridiculed and mocked for it. Darwin's message—quite apart from his theories of evolution and natural selection—was apparently already being accepted by large numbers of people, even as the messenger himself continued to be scorned.

Progressive scientists and writers were not the only ones influenced by Darwin. The artistic community took note as well. Immediately prior to the publication of *The Origin of Species* in 1859, canine art in Great Britain was dominated by the poignant work of Edwin Landseer (1802–1873), whose 1848 painting *Alexander and Diogenes* has been previously discussed (see Chapter 5), and was known to have been mildly criticized by Darwin for portraying an anatomically incorrect, albeit symbolic, bulldog as Alexander the Great. After 1859, the subjective excesses of Romanticism began to be gradually tempered and reigned in by a new awareness of empirical realism, but this trend did not diminish the attractiveness (or mass popularity) of Landseer's sentimental and often humorous works. Canine allegories such as *Trial by Jury* (1840) or *Dignity and Impudence* (1839) are classics by any measure, and sympathetic portrayals of white and black mastiffs in *Saved* (1845) as well as other paintings have led to this particular breed being officially dubbed with the moniker "Landseer." *Attachment* (1829) takes the old British school of depicting dogs with children (see Chapter 10) to new levels of emotionalism. Many of Landseer's portraits were made for the royal family (all including their beloved dogs), such as *Queen Victoria on Horseback* (1840), *Queen Victoria at Osborne House* (1865), and *Windsor Castle in Modern Times* (1841–1845). But he also had an eye for the impoverished side of life, as exemplified by *A Highland Breakfast* (1834), in which a poor Scottish woman attentively prepares a humble meal for her expectant and exclusively canine household. Doggy dependence on human kindness has never been more lovingly portrayed than in Landseer's *There's No Place Like Home* (1842). These represent but a small sampling of Landseer's prodigious output utilizing dogs as ornaments or primary subject matter.

In direct contrast to the unrestrained subjectivity of Landseer followed the blunt camera-like eye of Briton Rivière (1840–1920), a gifted British-born artist of French Huguenot ancestry who loved dogs no less than his predecessor but often painted them in a somewhat grittier light. Rivière also had the distinction of being one of the illustrators employed by Darwin himself for *The Expression of the Emotions in Man and Animals*, his emphatic 1872 follow-up to *The Descent of Man*. Rivière's vivid depiction therein of "Dog approaching another dog with hostile intentions" is memorable for its unromantic lack of cuteness. The undated *Dog Chasing a Rat* likewise shows an unpleasant side of canine behavior that one almost never encounters in art prior to Darwin. *Watching Dog* (1875) depicts a sleeping house pet that, as every dog owner knows, is still quietly on the job nonetheless. Much of Rivière's early work that incorporates dogs had a classical theme attached, such as *The Dog, Whom Late Had Granted to Behold His Lord* (1873) and, on a more majestic plane, *Pallas Athena and the Herdsman's Dogs* (1876). His takes on the timeless motif of canine loyalty, even in death, can be viewed in *Faithful to the Last* (1869) and, more famously, *Resquiescat* (1888).

With respect to dog companions of children and adolescents, works such as *Sympathy* (1878) and *Fidelity* (1869) are unsurpassed in their emotional impact, either because of or in spite of their heightened sense of realism and detail. As in the case of Landseer, these examples represent the mere tip of the iceberg in terms of Rivière's lifetime accomplishments. By the time he died shortly after World War I, his style had come to be viewed by some as almost passé, a stance that overlooked that he had been a bold pioneer, or that even his later work possesses a peculiar, unmistakable power when accepted on its own terms. One could easily say that, by the 1920s, the adjective "Darwinian" had firmly planted itself into the English vocabulary, either as a compliment or (more frequently) in the pejorative sense.

Darwin's astounding feats of deductive reasoning in linking the ancestral familial relationships of dogs and wolves—not to mention those of both with that of humankind—would much later in another century be sensationally vindicated by genetic science (see Chapter 20). The inseparable interconnectedness of all life forms may well be viewed as the great insight Darwin bestowed upon the world, even as this achievement came at the devastatingly high cost of widespread public scorn combined with damaged religious faith. By the time Darwin's turbulent personal journey through life had come to a surprisingly peaceful and tranquil end in 1882, Western civilization had become a much different place than it had been eight decades earlier when Napoleon Bonaparte was vying for control of the Old World.

Only three years after this (in 1886), in the Midwestern heartland of the New World, a nomadic and financially struggling performance artist published his very first book, on the rather unpromising subject matter of successfully breeding prairie chickens, an obscure, offbeat topic that nonetheless would have probably fascinated Darwin had he still been alive. In less than two decades following this inauspicious debut, this oddball writer would achieve literary immortality by utilizing the same aphorism used as a title for the aforementioned painting by Edwin Landseer, *There's No Place Like Home*. L. Frank Baum's primary audience of early 20th century American children, however, could not have been more unlike the readers of the controversial author who eventually became synonymous with the brutal expression "survival of the fittest."

13

Toto Speaks

He [the magician] must be the most cruel person in all the world, for to prevent a dog from growling when it is his nature to growl is just as wicked, in my opinion, as stealing all the magic in Oz.—L. Frank Baum, *The Lost Princess of Oz*, 20th century[1]

It has been written that Charles Darwin exerted a particularly strong influence on American writers who followed in his immediate wake during the latter half of the 19th century, even on those otherwise viewed by conventional society at large as being perhaps less fit for survival than many of their literary competitors in the dog-eat-dog world of Anglo-American book publishing.[2] Darwinian ideas or common American misperceptions thereof widely resonated in the aftermath of an era wholeheartedly embracing, or apologizing for, crimes committed in the name of Manifest Destiny and westward expansion into a hostile and previously untamed environment. Less noticed was the incontrovertible reality that Darwin had effectively blurred established lines by insisting upon the mutability, unity, and interconnectedness of all things, especially of all life forms.

In turn, it was the irrepressible imagination of Lyman Frank Baum (1856–1919) who promptly imported these same new controversial concepts into the realm of children's fantasy fiction. As a storyteller, Baum loved to blur lines—child versus adult, male versus female, human versus animal, animal versus vegetable, living versus inanimate, and so forth. Therein lies a great deal of his unique power and appeal. It naturally followed as a matter of course that Baum's fertile imagination created one of the most famous and cherished canines in all of film and literature (and certainly the most famous terrier), Toto from the *Oz* books.

Baum has always been viewed with a degree of suspicion by establishment critics due to a number of factors, all traceable to his highly unusual background as a writer. These included personal religious and political beliefs that appeared a bit out of step for his times (in particular, an alarming indifference to political correctness), his highly privileged childhood, a total, childlike lack of business acumen, a marked preference for female characters (beginning with the eponymous Dorothy Gale), and a somewhat unconventional but blissfully happy marital relationship, which all of us probably have to thank for Baum's later creation of the immortal *Oz* fantasy series.

Born in upstate New York (Chittenango near Syracuse) to a wealthy family of German-American immigrants, Baum as an early adolescent had clearly demonstrated his misfit tendencies by recoiling from the imposed disciplines of military school. Afterwards, his cultured, affluent parents opted to home-school their painfully sensitive son and indulge his youthful passions for journalism and theater, particularly the latter. By the early 1880s, Baum was allowed to comanage a family-owned chain of small-town opera houses while writing, directing, and acting in his own plays, the most successful of which was a musical melodrama, *The Maid of Arran*. In 1882, Baum made perhaps his first, and certainly greatest, sensible choice in life by courting and marrying Maud Gage, daughter of radical suffragette Matilda Joslyn Gage. Soon after this, however, the Baum family fortune began to dramatically fail on all fronts (including the theater business), being caught up in the turbulent American economy of the mid–1880s, the same events that helped destroy the fortune of Baum's older contemporary, Ulysses S. Grant, a writer with whom Baum shared some surprising commonalities.

Displaying more pluck than savvy, Baum unsuccessfully tried his hand at being a retailer, a salesman, and a breeder of chickens, writing his first published book in 1886 on this last unlikely subject, *The Book of the Hamburgs*. Caught up in the zeitgeist of his times, Baum moved his growing family west in 1888 to the frontier town of Aberdeen, Dakota Territory, where he attempted to run an upscale retail business while writing columns for the local newspaper. The store failed, however (along with the entire local economy), and today Baum is mainly remembered during this period for penning opinion pieces advocating the heartless extermination of Sioux Native Americans in the Dakotas, unsuccessfully walking the fine line between producing ironic hyperbole and xenophobia for hire, with the irony being lost on less perceptive readers, which comprised the majority.[3]

At the end of their ropes by 1891, the struggling Baum family made a crucial decision to retreat from the western frontier of the Dakota Territory back eastward to the explosively growing urban center of Chicago, anticipating the Columbian Exposition, where the future author of the *Oz* books eked out a living as a traveling salesman when not otherwise at home improvising bedtime stories for his delighted children.[4] Whatever Baum lacked as a provider he made up for by being a devoted parent and husband. Eventually settling into an old German immigrant neighborhood at 1667 North Humboldt Boulevard, he once again began toying with the idea of creative writing as a means for producing extra earnings. At the urging of both his liberated wife and his formidable mother-in-law, Baum began tentatively by finding a publisher for his *Mother Goose in Prose* (1897), an Americanized version of the French original. To his amazement, it turned a profit. Then in 1899 came a follow-up, *Father Goose, His Book*, consisting of original verse and proving even more financially successful than *Mother Goose*. Both volumes were skillfully illustrated, which considerably helped sales.

Finally, in 1900, the George M. Hill Company published *The Wonderful Wizard of Oz*, dedicated to Baum's wife and featuring lavish color illustrations by W.W. Denslow.[5] It was a runaway bestseller from the moment it hit the shelves at the Palmer House Summer Book Fair and has never since been out of print.[6] From the very beginning, Baum envisioned a musical production based on the book, and between 1902 and 1904 he personally mounted a profitable touring production of a musical stage play titled *The Wizard of Oz*. It was during his 19 years in Chicago that Baum transformed his working situation from total obscurity to literary greatness (and not without considerable controversy over the true extent of that greatness) within the space of a mere three years—again, not unlike Ulysses S. Grant before him. In the original *Oz* books, the Emerald City becomes a clear symbol for Chicago, the first and only large metropolis Baum ever lived in.[7]

Having rather suddenly transformed himself into the country's most popular children's author, and a wealthy one at that, Baum unfortunately proceeded to squander a good part of his new fortune with failed theater ventures. Then in 1910 he did what so many writers would later do after him: he relocated to a then relatively unknown Hollywood, California, in order to pursue his ambitions there in the fledgling motion picture industry. This was an early era, however, long before Hollywood came to be dominated by big profits and big business, although Baum obviously saw in his mind's eye the huge phenomenon it would one day (soon) become. Forming his own film company for the specific purpose of bringing Oz to the silent screen, Baum once again fell prey to his own natural lack of business sagacity and overextended himself badly. He and his wife also had a pronounced taste for the high life, which accelerated the fall even faster.

Between 1914 and 1915 he completed three *Oz* films, none of which were commercially successful, and his movie venture quickly folded. Baum resentfully returned to churning out *Oz* books for a living (as well as his family's upkeep), completing no fewer than 14 of these (plus six short stories) over a tight space of 20 years, plus a staggering 48 additional non–Oz novels written under his own name or various pseudonyms.[8] Around 1917, his health began to fail, even as his last Oz works revealed a more introspective and appealingly philosophical side to his genius. By the time he finally died of heart disease in 1919 (a watershed year in American history), approximately one-quarter of his prolific output had been devoted to Oz-related themes.

As nearly every filmgoer and fan of Baum knows, animals in the Land of Oz can talk, with the exception of Toto, at least in the first seven novels of the series. From the opening pages of the first edition in *The Wonderful Wizard of Oz*, Toto's prominence in the story is made clear. Denslow illustrates him on the first page of the introduction (before he does Dorothy), as well as the first page of the first chapter (with Dorothy) and the last page of the last chapter (again, with Dorothy)—and just about everywhere else in between. Baum immediately emphasizes that "it was Toto that made Dorothy laugh, and saved her from growing as gray as her other surroundings."[9] From that point forward, Dorothy's dog plays a key role in her adventures. He helps her fall asleep as a cyclone carries away their house and helps her awake with a cold nose after it has landed; Toto helps to expose the temerity of the Cowardly Lion by barking at him and likewise ultimately assists in exposing the Wizard as a humbug. Like his mortal flesh-and-blood comrades, Toto falls asleep in the field of scarlet poppies; in the Emerald City, he is required, like everyone else, to wear green spectacles. In a rough parallel to the 1939 film version, Toto bites the Wicked Witch of the West (after she strikes him), eventually leading to the first culmination of the plot.[10] In the original book, citizens of Oz are genuinely surprised to learn that Toto cannot speak human language like other animals. Another event in the original book almost never remarked upon (at least until some 95 years later) is an unusually brutal scene in which the Tin Woodman slaughters with his axe a wolf pack sent by the Witch to attack Dorothy's approaching party.[11] Obviously Baum's sentimentality did not extend to wild wolves, an attitude common for his time and place, as well as for his audiences.

There is every indication that, following the unqualified success of *The Wonderful Wizard of Oz*, Baum intended to branch out into other Oz and non–Oz related themes that had little if anything to do with Dorothy and Toto. Reading audiences, however, would have none of it and demanded more of the same, especially of Toto. Baum at first clearly resisted the notion. In *Dorothy and the Wizard in Oz* (1908), he attempted to replace Toto with a pet cat named Eureka, but the public responded to this and other changes with lower sales figures. Toto returned emphatically to his role of lovable doggie companion in *The Road to Oz* (1909), even being featured in the distinctive cover art by John R. Neill. But by now Baum's readership was beginning to repeatedly ask why he could not speak like all of the other animals in Oz.

In his 1913 short story "Little Dorothy and Toto" (from the *Little Wizard*

Stories of Oz), Baum explained that Toto, though he could clearly understand human language, and even read signs, was "just a common Kansas dog" and therefore could not speak. However, earlier Baum had made a mistake in *Ozma of Oz* (1907) by introducing Billina (feminine of "Bill"), a Kansas Yellow Hen who could speak quite articulately almost from the moment of her first arrival in Oz.[12] By the time that Baum had permanently relocated Dorothy, Toto, Aunt Em, and Uncle Henry to the Land of Oz in *The Emerald City of Oz* (1910), there no longer appeared to be any barriers or logical justification for keeping Toto silent, and audiences were now in suspense, no doubt much to Baum's chagrin as a storyteller.[13]

Finally, during the early summer of 1914, just as Baum embarked on his ill-fated movie-making career and right before the world exploded into prolonged conflict, he grudgingly relented in *Tik-Tok of Oz* by giving Toto a single line to speak. After Dorothy reiterates to Princess Ozma her mistaken and mildly insulting belief that Toto cannot speak due to his Kansas heritage, Ozma informs a startled and somewhat betrayed Dorothy that "the same spell has affected Toto, I assure you; but he's a wise little dog and while he knows everything that is said to him he prefers not to talk."[14] Immediately summoning Toto into her presence, Dorothy demands that he speak, but his first replies are only "Bow-wow" and "Woof!"[15] Finally, she has had enough: "'Just one word, Toto—and then you may run away.' He looked at her steadily for a moment. 'All right. Here I go!' he said, and darted away as swift as an arrow."[16] That was it.

In Baum's next book of the series, *The Scarecrow of Oz* (1915), the stubborn children's author merely informs readers that "a fuzzy little terrier dog, named Toto, lay at Dorothy's feet but seldom took part in the conversation, although he listened to every word that was said."[17] At this late date, with only four years left to live and his film-making career in ruins, it is difficult to say whether Baum actually believed that he had put the matter of Toto's speaking to bed (so to speak) or he wanted more time to contemplate exactly what would be said in terms of human language by Dorothy's canine companion (if anything) when the proper occasion presented itself.

The proper occasion came soon indeed with *The Lost Princess of Oz* (1917), arguably the finest book in the Oz series after *The Wonderful Wizard of Oz*, although everyone of course has their own favorites. By this time Baum knew that his days were numbered, and once again like Ulysses S. Grant before him, he seems to have been inspired rather than crushed by the thought. After 17 years in print and limiting himself to one single line, Toto now becomes quite talkative, at times loquacious and in the end, yes, even eloquent—but at a price. Concurrent with the lost Princess Ozma, Toto discovers midway through the tale that, rather symbolically, he has lost his cherished ability to growl as well. Insistently, Baum maintains this "lost growl" riff for over a hundred pages, with the storyteller (and Toto) obviously far more concerned about this sudden deficiency than the dog's rapidly expanding powers of verbal expression. Before the sinister magical arts of Ugu the Shoemaker deprive him of his growl, Toto is best described as a laconic dog ("although he could speak, he seldom said anything"), mainly concerned with Dorothy's whereabouts, his own stealthiness, physical comfort, and (most of all) food sources.[18]

As Baum reflected, "He [Toto] was a wise little dog, in his way, and didn't intend to worry when there was something much better to do."[19] Then, without warning, Toto announces to his best animal friend, the Cowardly Lion, "I've lost my growl!... What do you suppose has become of it?... It's an awful thing to lose one's growl...."[20] Toto's disinterested animal companions keep trying to change the subject to no avail. But Toto persists: "But none of you has answered my question: Where is my growl?"[21] Toto is momentarily distracted by an argument with the Cowardly Lion, over personal vanity, as to which of them is more beautiful. The inanimate Sawhorse, acting as appointed judge, declares that he, as a perfect work of art, is more beautiful than either of them. This prompts the Cowardly Lion to make one of the more famous speeches in all of Oz literature, concluding with "variety is the spice of life and we are various enough to enjoy one another's society; so let us be content."[22]

Immediately after Princess Ozma is rescued by Dorothy and the Wizard, Toto recovers his lost growl in almost anticlimactic fashion. Having realized that an evil magician is responsible for all of these mishaps—Toto rhetorically asks, "He has stolen about everything else of value in Oz, hasn't he?")—once the power of Ugu the Shoemaker is broken then all other lost things are at once restored.[23] Upon sniffing out a mouse in a corner, Toto lets loose with a fearsome "Gr-r-r-r-r-r!"[24] Baum had likely learned from personal experience that children were typically delighted by sudden turns of events such as these.

It is impressive, if not amazing, how Baum was so adept at incorporating simple life lessons for children into his animal parables, both canine and otherwise. Many elaborate theories by critics have been put forth to suggest that hidden within these charming fables are various complex political and economic allegories on America at the turn of the 20th century. As for Baum, he always insisted that he just wanted to please kids and earn a living while doing it. We see no reason to disagree with this. Another part of Baum's considerable appeal as a storyteller derives from his glorious lack of pretense or logical consistency, very much like any beleaguered parent struggling to improvise a bedtime tale for an impatient child. Recently, during an NPR interview, Baum scholar Michael Patrick Hearn recalled how one of the first questions children still like to ask is why Toto does not speak like the other animals in Oz.[25] Leaving aside the fact that Toto does in fact speak in the later Oz books less well known to readers, Baum (were he still alive) would surely assert that a dog's real-life ability to growl was more wondrous than human speech (see opening quote).

On the surface, Toto has nothing profound to say; below the surface, however, a lot appears to be going on. Although Baum was one of the greatest all-time masters of irony, there is nothing ironic in Toto's distress and determination to regain his growl. It also noteworthy that after Toto succeeds in this quest, he has nothing left to say in *The Lost Princess of Oz* or any of the subsequent Oz sequels. Baum's suggestion that a canine growl is superior to human language has proven hard for many audiences to swallow, even among children, but then again, close textual reading of Baum has always gone against popular, more simplified conceptions of his work as presented on the big screen. Another example of this dichotomy is Toto's close relationships with Dorothy, the Cowardly Lion, the Tin Woodman, and the Scarecrow. Toto, a mature male dog, is ultimately Dorothy's pet, not her equal. The same goes for Toto's varied interactions with Baum's wide universe of mostly female antagonists and protagonists. It would not be too much of an exaggeration to say that Toto's total subservience, his obstinate refusal to speak in the first seven Oz books, and his low assessment of that ability after it is revealed are all only a notch less controversial than Baum's supreme, ongoing popularity with scores of adult readers living alternative lifestyles.[26] Strict conventional moralists have always been made uncomfortable by many aspects of Baum's unconventional fantasy world, especially in its original and undiluted format.

Baum's achievement did not go unnoticed among his contemporaries. Mark Twain, aka Samuel Clemens (1835–1910), to whom Baum at his best moments was favorably compared as a writer and lecturer, published in 1903 his anticruelty short story, "A Dog's Tale," a mere three years after *The Wonderful Wizard of Oz* had begun to dominate best-seller lists. O. Henry, aka William Sydney Porter (1862–1910), published in 1906 his witty short story "Memoirs of a Yellow Dog," thus effectively beating Baum and Toto to the punch in terms of providing the reading public with an eloquently articulate canine. Both of these works, however, were geared strictly towards adults. It is possible that Baum decided to let Toto speak after becoming aware O. Henry had used the same device. The conceit has been a regular part of adult and non-adult fiction ever since.

Things seemingly came full circle in 1995 with Gregory McGuire's astonishing novel *Wicked*, in which Toto is unfavorably portrayed as a spoiled, bratty, and meddlesome mutt.[27] Near the climax of the story, McGuire drags back into the harsh light of day Baum's unseemly killing of the witch's wolves by the Tin Woodman, presenting the disturbing episode as a wanton, ignorant act of prejudice when in fact the wolves had been sent as a friendly greeting party. *Wicked* goes even further by making the doomed Killyjoy, leader of the wolf pack, one of the Witch's favorite and quite sympathetic pets. This rewriting of fantasy history appeared around the same period that genetic researchers were in the process of scientifically proving what most of us have intuitively known all along—namely that the dog Toto and the wolf Killyjoy both had common wolfish ancestors (see Chapter 20).

Although most of our visions of Oz are defined by the classic 1939 musical (in which MGM assembled an all-star creative team), *The Wizard of Oz* had been made into a silent film as early as 1910, which Baum sanctioned in order to pay off debts as he moved to California. Fragments of this work survive and include Toto as a cast member. After Baum's death, another silent version of *The Wizard of Oz* was made in 1925, freely combining plot elements from several Baum books, omitting Toto completely, and egregiously turning the tale into a young adult romance, thus ignoring one of Baum's first maxims of children's storytelling. Toto has more or less been a fixture in movie versions ever since. The 1939 sound version was one of the first Technicolor films released (in dramatic manner) and is often cited as the most frequently viewed work in motion picture history, as well as one of the best.

Infrequently remarked upon is MGM's innovation of taking the late 19th century Kansas that Baum had only read about and effectively converting it into a contemporary depression-era tale on the plight of Dust Bowl refugees. The bold contrast between hyper-realism and fantasy still resonates today. In 1974, *The Wiz* by Charlie Smalls brought Baum's imagination (including Toto) to a new more urbanized, African American audience. More recently, the 2005 television special *The Muppets' Wizard of Oz* unforgivably converts Toto into a talking prawn and was predictably panned by critics and shunned by audiences. The year 2013 brought the highly publicized release of Sam Raimi's prequel, *Oz the Great and Powerful,* which includes a bevy of Darwinian monkeys and baboons with wings and dispenses with canines altogether but has reportedly not suffered too much at the box office for it. Perhaps it is fitting that there be none attempting to upstage the world's most beloved fictional terrier.

Baum's inexhaustible powers of invention allowed him to become America's first, and perhaps greatest, author of children's books despite the offbeat (and occasionally offensive) nature of his work. It is especially interesting that right before he comfortably settled into the upper echelons of the Chicago book publishing industry Baum and his family had made an unsuccessful foray into the American western frontier, a sojourn they managed to endure for a full three years before retreating back to civilization, one might say. For a dreamy, overly sensitive child of privilege, the experience must have been harsh. And yet Baum managed to transform that trauma into material that made his fantasy tales far more effective than they would otherwise be. This was a trait he shared with most literary greats.

It is also striking that around the same time a struggling and misfit Baum attempted to put down stakes in the Dakota Territory, Ernest Thompson Seton, a quite different kind of personality, one with an opposite family background, was in the process of transforming himself into one of the most renowned wild animal bounty hunters in North America. More remarkable still is that this iconoclastic individual, a future founder of the Boy Scouts of America, would soon become a best-selling author in his own right almost at the exact moment Baum finally realized writing books would be his own true life's work.

14

Empathy for Wolves

Since, then, the animals are creatures with wants and feelings differing in degree only from our own, they surely have their rights. —Ernest Thompson Seton, *Wild Animals I Have Known*, 19th century[1]

The excessive fear of and prejudice against wild wolves displayed by L. Frank Baum in the *Oz* books were typical of his milieu on several different levels. First and foremost, as a children's storyteller, phobia of wolves was a useful tradition inherited from his literary predecessors (see Chapter 11). Second, he was a city dweller who once briefly and unsuccessfully ventured into the American western frontier, and this wary or hostile attitude towards one of nature's most stigmatized creatures would have been especially pronounced in that environment. Third, it was certainly a mindset prevalent among anyone born before the late 19th century, as well as one that continues quite strongly into present times.

Nevertheless, by the end of that same century, incremental changes in public perceptions were detectable. The first decade of the new one (1900–1910), which saw Baum achieve the status of literary celebrity, also witnessed the presidency of Theodore Roosevelt (1901–1909), a man who, whatever his shortcomings were, could never have been accused of not taking an intense personal interest in the animal kingdom and its realistic portrayal in print. Despite his proud reputation as a big game hunter, however, Roosevelt had another close contemporary with unassailable hunting credentials, plus those of an artist, writer, organizer, and conservation activist, making nearly everyone else of his generation pale by comparison, even though he has failed to become a household name to the same extent. It is to the life and work of this remarkable individual that we now must turn our full attention.[2]

Ernest Thompson Seton (1860–1946) was born Ernest Evan Thompson in South Shields, County Durham, England (near the Scottish border and River Tyne), thus making him technically a Geordie by birth hailing from a region that has produced more than its fair share of outstanding personalities throughout history.[3] His improbable life story and staggering professional achievements have been best and most recently told by biographer David Witt, curator of the Seton Legacy Project in Santa Fe, New Mexico, but herein we shall present a mere condensed summary. By the time Seton was school-aged the Thompson family had immigrated to Ontario, Canada, and eventually settled in the Toronto area. However, his career-frustrated father was abusive and sadistic, often driving the unhappy boy into the rural outskirts of town where he found solace by communing with nature.

Having demonstrated considerable raw artistic talent from an early age, Seton won a scholarship to the London Royal Academy of Art in 1879, but poverty, isolation, and the sudden shock of urban life all conspired to break his already fragile health, and by 1881 he was back in Canada, once again suffering the harangues of a resentful, uncomprehending paternal figure. Upon reaching majority age, the son wasted no time in permanently breaking with his father and never spoke to him again. Ernest later changed his own last name to Seton, after an admired Scottish ancestor.[4] Seton then pushed out into the wilds of neighboring Manitoba (near Carberry) to join his brothers already farming there.

Though failing as a farmer, Seton fully immersed himself in riding, hiking, camping, shooting, hunting, trapping, taxidermy, and Native American culture. Over the next four years, he transformed himself into a world-class outdoorsman (and an expert on wolf hunting in particular), all the while maintaining his burgeoning artistic skills through a compulsive need to constantly draw and sketch the live game he regularly pursued or defended himself against out of necessity.

In 1885, Seton got his first big break by winning a major commission to do wildlife illustrations for the Century Dictionary Company. For the next five years he divided his time between Manitoba, Toronto, and New York City, meeting important artistic and naturalist colleagues while dabbling in writing by producing in 1886 a catalogue of mammals indigenous to Manitoba, which helped him to win a lifelong honorary appointment as official naturalist for the province. A late bloomer in most respects, Seton by age 30 finally managed to get himself to Paris, France, in order to seriously hone his artistic craft. Here he rubbed shoulders with some of the greatest intellectuals of the belle époque and his serious original paintings, such as *Awaiting in Vain* (or Triumph of the Wolves), were met with both admiration and revulsion for going against Impressionist fashion. It was also probably in Paris where Seton first encountered the longstanding French traditions of Courtaud, the King Wolf of France, and Le Bete, the Beast Wolf of Gevaudan, both of which he would later write about.[5]

Suffering from severe eye strain, Seton was ordered by doctors to take six months off and he returned to America in 1893. While in Paris and New York City, however, he had met the daughters of Lewis V. Fitz Randolph, a wealthy investor in the New Mexico cattle and sheep ranching industry. Then he met Fitz Randolph himself, in New Jersey, who was impressed by the 33-year-old Seton's unusual combination of cultural refinement and authoritative firsthand knowledge of the North American wilderness.[6] As fate would have it, Fitz Randolph's profits were then in the process of being seriously diminished by wolf attacks against his livestock and surprisingly ineffectual attempts by Southwestern specialists to kill the predators. Fitz Randolph convinced Seton to use his downtime away from the art world to hire himself out as an animal bounty hunter for a then extraordinary potential sum of $1,000 plus all expenses paid. By late that same year, Seton was in remote northern New Mexico (near Clayton) preparing himself for what he would later frankly describe as a life-changing adventure.

What transpired over the next three months in and around the environs of the Currumpaw Valley has been recently dramatized in the popular 2009 PBS *Nature* episode (narrated by F. Murray Abraham) "The Wolf That Changed America."[7] Although Seton had killed scores of wolves in Canada, and succeeded in making short work of scavenging coyotes in the vicinity of Clayton, he soon realized that he was dealing with no ordinary wolf pack. Its leader had developed a legendary name and reputation among locals even before Seton arrived on the scene. In short, a projected two-week wolf hunt turned into months of frustration as "Old Lobo," a 150-pound, six-year-old dark grey timber wolf and leader of the pack, not only repeatedly thwarted Seton's sophisticated poisons and traps but contemptuously defecated on these devices after identifying them.[8]

Then, on the verge of admitting defeat, Seton noticed what no one before him had, specifically, that Lobo's tracks were often accompanied by a female companion, also well known to the locals as "Blanca," a rare white wolf. The overall strategy was immediately shifted to target Blanca, using smaller, less obvious baiting and traps. The new plan quickly succeeded, and in late January, 1894, after a tumultuous chase, Seton and his comrades cornered the crippled white wolf and brutally strangled her with lassos, hoping not to spoil the pelt or spook the rest of the pack with any use of firearms. "She was the handsomest wolf I had ever seen," Seton later wrote.[9] As the bounty hunters triumphantly carried the corpse home, Lobo followed at a safe distance, wailing throughout the following night in a distinctive howl that no one who heard it ever forgot. Using Blanca's body as a lure, more snares were set, and within a matter of days, Seton, while pursuing a bear, stumbled upon the helpless Lobo firmly secured in no fewer than four of the traps that had been laid for him. Hoping to take the famed beast alive, Seton's posse carefully transported Lobo back to their ranch, where he refused to take food and water, or even to acknowledge his captors, then quietly and unexpectedly expired overnight, according to Seton, dying of a "broken heart."[10] His body was laid next to that of Blanca's, where the hardened cowboys of the mesa marveled over both of them. Seton carefully recorded the date as January 31, 1894.

Seton's days as a bounty hunter were finished. The rest of his long life, spanning an additional half century, would be devoted to conservation, and in particular, to the conservation of wolves. By the time his "Lobo, King of the Currumpaw" had appeared as the opening feature in Seton's classic, self-illustrated collection, *Wild Animals I Have Known* (1898), he had become a best-selling author, and would go on to write over 60 books, many with canine-related themes. In 1896 he married his first wife, noted suffragette and wealthy socialite Grace Gallatin, to whom *Wild Animals* was dedicated. (Their daughter, Anya Seton [1904–1990], went on to have her own successful writing career as a historical romance novelist.)

In 1902, during the first flush of his success, Seton responded to vandalism and juvenile delinquency in his own neighborhood of Cos Cob, Connecticut, by organizing the Woodcraft Indians, which is extant. Later he became a central figure in the formation of the both the Girl Scouts (Brownies) and Boy Scouts of America (BSA), being named first Chief Scout of the latter despite not having yet achieved American citizenship.[11] During the 1930s, Seton became an American citizen and moved to Santa Fe, New Mexico, with his second wife (and secretary), Julia Buttree. In Santa Fe he was immediately accepted into the elite ranks of American artists in residence there such as Wisconsin native Georgia O'Keefe and Iowa-born Raymond Jonson. Although his historic last house, Seton Castle, was destroyed by fire in 2005, its contents were fortuitously saved and today the Seton Legacy Project and Academy for the Love of Learning in Santa Fe, along with the Seton Memorial Library and Museum at the BSA Philmont Scout Ranch in Cimarron, New Mexico, all admirably preserve everything that he worked and stood for.[12] This seems only fitting, since it was in New Mexico that Seton's epic encounter with Lobo and Blanca had transformed his own personal beliefs on wild wolves, and eventually much of society's views on them as well. During his final years he returned to his true spiritual roots there, although these had been discovered relatively late, in mid-life.

The most controversial period in Seton's eventful and productive career came with the so-called Nature Fakers Controversy of 1903–1907. Respected naturalist John Burroughs (1837–1921) published a high-profile article in which he took great exception to the prevalent trend of animal behavior being fictionalized into human-like sentiment and then presented as fact for the sake of generating more sales. Among a group of accused second-tier writers, Burroughs made the mistake of naming Seton, whose *Wild Animals I Have Known* he singled out as the odious prototype for the entire genre. Within three weeks of the article, Seton was confronting Burroughs face-to-face at a Carnegie-sponsored dinner at which both were invitees. No one can agree on what exactly was said, but over the ensuing four years of the controversy, Burroughs never openly attacked Seton again.

Seton, for his part, devoted the next two years to producing a scientific tome titled *Life Histories of Northern Animals* (1909), whose later expanded edition (*Lives of Game Animals*) would, after Burroughs' death, win an achievement award named after Burroughs himself.[13] Seton also made his only public response to the incident in an article the following year in 1904. The article was disguised as a moralistic fable, in which Seton humorously referred to the unnamed Burroughs as "Little Mucky." Burroughs' earlier attack had done nothing to hinder Jack London's *The Call of the Wild* (1903) from becoming a runaway blockbuster that same year, though London did eventually get caught up in the same controversy as an alleged offender (see Chapter 15).

In *Wild Animals*, Seton, while insisting on the literal truth of his animal characters and stories, also admitted having "left the strict line of historical truth in many places." For example, in his "Wully, the Story of a Yaller Dog," he conflated two actual dogs into one character.[14] Viewed in retrospect, the verdict on Seton as an author is that, yes, he slightly embellished on occasion and, yes, he sometimes conflated—as do all great writers, for that matter, of both fact and fiction. As for the controversy itself, it effectively ended in 1907 when big game hunter and president Teddy Roosevelt publicly interjected his opinion on the matter (as he was compulsively inclined to do on almost everything) in favor of Burroughs.[15] Animal literature in all of its various shades between fact and fiction continued to be as marketable as ever, although some individual writing careers were unnecessarily diminished as a result. Seton's, however, was not one of the ones slowed down, for all intents and purposes, as he released no fewer than 10 books over the course of those five years.

In point of fact, it had been unfair to lay the accusation at Seton's doorstep in the first place, even had it been true. Popular animal stories and fables are as old as Western literature itself. The very same year (1894) that Seton vanquished Lobo in the Currumpaw Valley, widely admired British-Indian author Rudyard Kipling (1865–1936), published in serial form *The Jungle Book*, perhaps his best-known and most enduring work, and then, in 1895, its sequel, *The Second Jungle Book*. There can be little doubt that Seton's publisher, Scribner, was encouraged to take a chance on his unique work by Kipling's recent and resounding success as an animal fabulist. Both Kipling volumes include a number of canine-related tales and often draw upon the rich, non–Western traditions with which he had been raised and was so well acquainted.

Both writers appear to have had a mutual admiration for the other's work, and they are known to have corresponded with each other. Unlike Kipling, however, Seton was not selling fairy tales. He was careful to emphasize this in his introduction: "The fact that these stories are true is the reason why all are tragic. The life of a wild animal *always has a tragic end*."[16] Indeed, the pathos and fragility in Seton's animal lives are unmistakable, hitting directly home for readers having any exposure to the brutal and cruel realities of the natural world. Great writers always write about what they know from firsthand, personal experience, and Seton is no exception in this regard. As a result, Kipling entertains; Seton entertains, instructs, and inspires.

Seton was more or less self-educated; his writing style is arguably raw and unpolished. These qualities only seem to increase his authenticity and power. Whereas Mark Twain had a gift for creating the voices of unschooled but eloquent and intelligent characters, Seton seemed to be one of those characters himself, or at least ably assumed the persona of one. In addition to his opening account of Lobo and Blanca, *Wild Animals I Have Known* includes engrossing personality sketches of a mustang, a crow, a partridge, a rabbit, a fox, and two dogs. Almost every other page is graced with Seton's own sensitive and striking illustrations. In short, it is an ideal and exemplary book for children transitioning into adults, which for Seton himself had been a very painful and long-drawn-out process.[17]

His two separate character studies of seemingly domesticated dogs are both fascinating and disturbing. Wully is a composite of two sheep herding collies known to Seton during his early childhood in rural Durham-Northumberland. By day in public, Wully is the ideal working dog, good at his job and faithful to his human family. By night, in secret, however, thanks in part to a traumatic upbringing, Wully is a vicious serial killer of the same sheep that he protects during the day. When exposed, he shockingly turns on his human family and must be put down. Seton convincingly insists that such "Jekyl-Hyde" dogs are a real phenomenon, with at least six cases on record and two personally known to him.[18]

Perhaps more remarkable still is Seton's affectionate portrait of Bingo ("Bing" for short), his loyal canine companion during his years spent in the Manitoba wilderness. Bingo, despite his indeterminate mixed breed, is a courageous and savage wolf-hunter descended from an illustrious line of wolf-hunters—that is, until he finds a she-wolf that strikes his fancy. When the she-wolf is thoughtlessly killed by a hunter, Bingo holds as much of a grudge against the hunter as against male wolves. Climactically, Bingo saves

Seton's life from wolves with his ferociousness when Seton is temporarily disabled by one of his own traps. Thus we all probably have Bingo to thank for Seton's monumental accomplishments later in life. Eventually and sadly, however, Bingo is undone by a tragic, persistent weakness for wolf poison. Taken as a whole, there seems to be a very fine and porous line between wildness and domestication in Seton's insistently real-life canines. Bingo and Wully both have dual personalities, for better and for worse, just like a few human beings we all know.

More extraordinary still is the famous case of Lobo and Blanca, two wild killer bandits if there ever were, and yet their poignant attachment to each other, as well as their noble demise, wolf intelligence, aplomb, skill, and daring, all struck a deep chord not only in those who hunted them down, but to a general reading public and fledgling American conservation movement as well. Although coming to Seton's books comparatively late in life, this writer was jarringly reminded by his account of Lobo and Blanca as to why I personally gave up hunting long ago at the age of 22.

During the spring of 1978 (while giving a demonstration to school friends), I took a careless shot at a bird in a tree mistaken for a member of an odious grackle flock regularly stealing produce from our farm. The bird falling dead at my feet proved to be a far less destructive catbird, and this tragedy was almost immediately followed by the prolonged, mournful song of the bird's mate, still in the tree, which had refused to flee at the sound of gunfire. I have never gotten over it, despite having previously killed hundreds of other birds and animals with hardly a second thought. Such things, and such epiphanies, really do happen.[19] Seton's great 19th century predecessor Charles Darwin (see Chapter 12), who highly valued the observations of hunters and had himself been a hunter in his youth, related an almost identical anecdote in *The Descent of Man* as an example of some wildlife emotions closely paralleling those of humans.[20] Seton, writing well over a decade after Darwin had died, came to pretty much the same conclusion while bounty hunting in a part of the world that the well-traveled and eloquent Darwin never saw or wrote about. The New Mexico experience instantly and understandably converted him into perhaps the first truly modern animal rights activist.

Lastly, it would be remiss not to mention within these pages that Seton's visual artistic accomplishments were almost as influential (if not more so) than his literary art. *Wild Animals* taken by itself, quite apart from Seton's other substantial output, is a treasure trove of canine artwork, with Lobo, Blanca, Wully, and Bingo all depicted with immediacy and verve that only an eyewitness could draw upon. The three full-page illustrative plates of Lobo's wolf pack are an especial treat, and have become classics in their own right.[21] Viewers are happy to get to know these creatures—but only at a safe distance. The three plates of Bingo (one with his she-wolf) are unforgettable as well.

Seton's turn-of-the-century oil painting *Black Wolf of the Currumpaw*, today in the Philmont Museum in Santa Fe, is a fittingly majestic and unsentimental homage to the animal than changed his life. His 1896 pen and ink watercolor "Wolf Study" shows the beast at a full breakneck run, an unforgettable sight for anyone seeing such a wonder. His first known oil painting, *Sleeping Wolf*, painted in Paris circa 1891 when the artist was 31 years old and two years before he encountered Lobo, clearly demonstrates the greatness that was yet to come. Limited space does not permit any worthy discussion of Seton's other extensive and bracing animal artwork. Summarizing his visual achievements, suffice it here to say that he was among the first to bring a deeply informed sense of anatomy and taxidermy into his canine art, combined with an unflinching acknowledgement of danger and wildness. In the wake of Darwin, the time was right for such a style to resonate, and Seton was the ideal talent (however unlikely), to effectively bring it to the masses. His breakthrough enabled 20th century artists working in a similar vein to be successful, artists such as Wisconsin's Owen J. Gromme (1896–1991), whose highly original work nonetheless owes much to Seton's legacy.[22]

Arguably, the most striking quality in Seton's work, both visual and literary, is the manner in which previously rigid evolutionary lines become blurred and fluid. When does a wolf become a dog? And when does a dog turn into wolf? For that matter, what does it really mean to be "human" or to have a human "soul?" One walks away from Seton's unconventional observations on animal behavior naturally asking such questions. Even more discomfiting is the fact that these works were not produced in an ivory tower or by a personality especially impressed by ivory towers. On the contrary, these were the products of a daring outdoor lifestyle that could not have been further removed from the comforts of civilization and all of its supposed advantages. It is therefore no coincidence that within the long span of Seton's career there lived another, even more talented, writer, who learned early during his relatively short lifetime about the untamed savagery of the North American wilderness and felt a need to pose similar questions, but more in the guise of unapologetic, allegorical fiction.

15

Canine Heroes

> *His cunning was wolf cunning, and wild cunning; his intelligence, shepherd intelligence and St. Bernard intelligence; and all this, plus an experience gained in the fiercest of schools, made him as formidable a creature as any that roamed the wild.*[1]—Jack London, The Call of the Wild, 20th century

> *It was the beginning of the end for White Fang—the ending of the old life and the reign of hate. A new and incomprehensibly fairer life was dawning. It required much thinking and endless patience on the part of Weedon Scott to accomplish this. And on the part of White Fang it required nothing less than a revolution.*[2]—Jack London, White Fang, 20th century

During the early 1990s this writer found himself traveling on business through Anchorage, Alaska, on a cold, snowy February morning. Awoken early from my hotel room off Fourth Street by the excited din of howling, yipping canines, I looked out of the window realizing that I had stumbled into the ceremonial start of the annual Iditarod Trail Sled Dog Race, or as it is currently promoted without too much hyperbole, The Last Great Race. Although I had heard of this event, seeing it suddenly close up without warning left several immediate, permanent impressions. The first was the smallness of the dogs themselves—most were under 100 pounds and many less than 50 pounds. Second (and more vivid), the dogs were clearly having a blast. In short, they loved it. Doggie overcoats and booties were common paraphernalia. Others were decked out in their best, most colorful harnesses and collars. The mushers themselves were closely attentive to the needs of their teams and rather oblivious or even standoffish to the gathering crowd of human spectators. Ernest Thompson Seton, had he still been alive, would have certainly been gladdened by the sight. Then again, Seton was no stranger to dog sleds in the Canadian wilderness of his formative years.

Another writer no stranger to dog sleds (or canines) was Jack London

(1876–1916), born John Griffith Chaney in San Francisco during the centenary year of the United States, the son of a mentally unstable woman descended from one of the earliest Puritan families of Massachusetts Bay Colony and whose biological father and legitimacy status have always been in dispute. Later that same year, the mother married disabled Civil War veteran John London, after whom the boy took his adopted name. But the writer was largely raised by an African American freedwoman nanny with whom he remained close for the rest of his life. Although London had limited formal schooling, he became addicted to reading at an early age and was, fortunately, taken under the protective wing of Oakland public librarian (and future California poet laureate) Ina Coolbirth.

London's adolescence and young manhood were then spent living a dangerous, adventurous life of sea sailing and railroad tramping that he was lucky to have survived. In 1896, at age 20, he talked and tested his way into the University of California at Berkeley; but he had to drop out almost immediately because of nonexistent financial support. Then, in 1897, he left for the Klondike Gold Rush centered around Dawson City in the Canadian Yukon Territory. It proved to be the most vivid experience of his life; however, within a year his health was completely broken. Returning to San Francisco, a recuperating London discovered a secure place as a feature writer in the burgeoning print magazine industry, and by 1900 (at age 24) was, for the first time in his life, earning a decent living. That same year he married his first wife, Elizabeth Maddern, and began raising a family. Still, at this point, no one could have predicted that he was destined soon to become America's most popular writer and the first true celebrity author of the 20th century.

London, a canine lover from childhood, had written a magazine short story titled "Bâtard," about a dog that justifiably turns against and kills its evil French Canadian master. London then took careful note of the profuse praise he received for writing it.[3] In 1903, at age 27, his first novel, *The Call of the Wild*, was published and promoted through installments by the *Saturday Evening Post*. It was an instantaneous worldwide success—and, after 110 years, still a joy to read. The next 13 years would see a torrent of short stories, novels, plays, poetry, and essays issue from his pen, soon making London a wealthy man, although an early casualty of this celebrity was his first marriage. In 1906, he released *White Fang*, an eagerly anticipated, canine-themed follow-up to his maiden effort. Ten years later, in 1916, London would be dead at age 40 of an intentional or unintentional overdose of morphine, complicated by alcoholism, a fast lifestyle, and (no doubt) various untamed demons from his early years. His death, like his birth, has been a continuous subject of debate and controversy.

Long before that, however, in 1905 London married his second wife,

Charmian Kittredge, who appears to have been the true love of his life. The couple relocated to Beauty Ranch in Sonoma County, where they lived an extravagant lifestyle, all the while espousing Socialist political views. Mainly because of his phenomenal wealth and highly visible use of it, London was a constant target of plagiarism charges, including for *The Call of the Wild* itself.[4] London's usual habit of dealing with such charges was to plead guilty to borrowing ideas (as a voracious reader) and then go on doing his own unique thing, knowing full well that his writing style always was superior to that which he was accused of stealing.

More serious was the Nature Fakers Controversy of 1903–1907 (see Chapter 14), in which London found himself automatically embroiled because of his tremendous stature as an author of popular fiction with wildlife as favorite subject matter for his books. While other, far less talented writers of animal and canine fiction fought against the likes of President Teddy Roosevelt to preserve their reputations and livelihoods, London remained steadfastly silent in the face of withering criticism until after the storm had seemingly subsided. Then in 1908, when everyone thought the matter had been put to rest, London struck back hard with an eloquent, high-profile article, aimed at Roosevelt in particular, whom he basically accused of being shallow and somewhat of a sissy to boot.[5]

Whether Roosevelt's decision not to run for reelection that year and instead go off big game hunting on an African safari was in any way influenced by London's stinging accusations is a matter for more able historians than this one to further investigate. Next in the article, London defended his work, which, as any modern reader can quickly ascertain, has a large allegorical element to it, combined with a rigorous realism that has always been the foundation of its widespread popularity. London was surely amazed that he, of all people, had been publicly accused of over-sentimentalizing nature. In any event, the notoriety only seemed to increase his already hefty market value as a writer. By 1910 he was enthusiastically reporting on the boxing defeat of the Great White Hope by African American prize fighter Jack Johnson in Reno, Nevada. After that, he retired back to his Sonoma ranch, attempted to build (and then rebuild after fire) his grandiose, never-completed "Wolf House," while effortlessly churning out commercial fluff on demand until his untimely death in 1916. Today the vast estate has been converted into the Jack London Historic State Park, where he and his second wife lie buried.

The Call of the Wild defies criticism. London's poetic, emotional tale of Buck, a pampered, domesticated St. Bernard shepherd mix born and raised in California but stolen and sold into slavery as a Yukon sled dog, has been making an indelible impression on at least six generations of adult and young adult readers since it first appeared in print over a century ago.⁶ After unspeakable cruelties and hardships transform Buck into the toughest working dog of the Klondike Gold Rush, he at last is rescued and nursed back to health by a kindly and appreciative master in the heroic figure of gold prospector John Thornton. In a famous exchange, Thornton and his sidekick, Pete, converse: "'Never was there such a dog,' said John Thornton one day, as the partners watched Buck marching out of camp. 'When he was made, the mould was broke,' said Pete."⁷ Buck proves his worth when he saves Thornton's life by pulling him out of the water. But then the larger-than-life dog begins to socialize with his canine cousins, the wild wolves of the Yukon wilderness. While Buck is away frolicking, however, Thornton and his companions are senselessly murdered during a raid by a marauding band of Yeehat tribesmen. Upon his return to camp, an enraged Buck first proceeds to wreak terrible vengeance on Thornton's killers, then he opts (rather fittingly) to permanently join the wild wolf pack of the Canadian wilderness where, in the end, he at last metamorphoses into a Native American legend and myth.⁸

Three years after this literary and commercial triumph, London produced *White Fang*, a touching, poignant story with an opposite trajectory from savagery to domestication. The namesake canine hero is born in the wilds of the Yukon with lineage three-quarters wolf and one-quarter dog. When the pup's parents are killed, he is raised by Native Americans and then later trained by white men as a fighting wolf-dog, a horrible fate from which White Fang is rescued by Weedon Scott, a young American gold prospector from California. Slowly, incrementally, the wild creature is domesticated into a working sled dog by Scott. "I always insisted that wolf was a dog," exclaims Scott's previously skeptical hired musher.⁹ Upon his pending return to California, Scott cannot bear to part with White Fang after the two have bonded so closely with each other. Even when Scott tries to man up and leave White Fang in the Yukon where he thinks his beloved pet will be better off, the wolf-dog determinedly pursues him right up to the point of embarkation. The novel concludes with the "Blessed Wolf" (as he has been dubbed by Scott's family) mating and having pups with the collie of the estate, after repeatedly proving his courage, mettle, and discretion as a guard and rescue dog.¹⁰ Thus *White Fang* geographically and culturally concludes exactly where *Call of the Wild* began, namely in the idyllic country life of California to which London and his second wife had been drawn after financial success allowed them to purchase it.

London's unique brand of gritty, wolf-dog heroism harks back to the great canines of Western antiquity, from the she-wolf of Romulus and Remus (see Chapter 4) to Pliny's anecdotes on the fidelity and courage of domesticated dogs (see Chapter 3). In this sense, London was exploiting a very ancient literary tradition. He was also, like Ernest Thompson Seton before him (see Chapter 14), highly influenced by both the populism of Rudyard Kipling and the scientific breakthroughs of Charles Darwin (see Chapter 12). On the other hand, London takes the old device to new, unprecedented levels, in part by effectively exploiting the inherent evolutionary tension between the behavior of dogs and wolves, as well as the lack of a true divide between canine behavior and human behavior.[11] As critic Abraham Rothberg perceptively noted in his introduction to the Bantam edition, "London was not only treating animals like human beings, but treating human beings like animals, recognizing no essential difference between man and animal."[12]

Taking this further, one could easily argue that London's wolf-dogs are more intelligent and capable than many of his human characters. For example, in his short story tour de force, "To Build a Fire" (1908), the dog has more common sense than its foolish human master and, indeed, out-survives him in the end. As to loyalty, in 1906 (the same year in which a fictional White Fang is civilized from beast to pet), London released his collection *Love of Life and Other Stories*, featuring an intriguing vignette titled "Brown Wolf," in which a rescued Yukon wolf-dog is brought happily back to California by its new owners, only to instinctively and enthusiastically return north after fortuitously encountering its first, beloved and long-lost, sled-dog master. Thus London's evolutionary–de-evolutionary cycle for canines runs from domestication to the wild, back to domestication, then back to the wild, and so on indefinitely.[13] It is also noteworthy that within the space of a mere five years, from the publication of Seton's *Wild Animals I Have Known* (1898) to London's *The Call of the Wild* (1903), wolves and dogs progressed from creatures with human-like feelings to unequivocal canine heroes in the truest literary human sense.

By some strange coincidence of fate or roundabout series of related events, less than a decade after London's early and untimely death in 1916, a motley team of North American sled dogs performed a prodigious, true-to-life feat of heroism worthy of any novel or short story. During the fierce winter of 1924–1925, the remote and isolated city of Nome, Alaska, with a population extensively both white and Native American, began succumbing to a lethal diphtheria epidemic. It was discovered with alarm that the nearest serum supply in Seward (more than 900 miles away) could not be flown in because of severe weather combined with the primitive state of aviation in those years.[14]

To this very day, normal roads fail to connect Nome with Anchorage, as trails pass through some of the most intimidating mountains on the continent even in good weather. Sea travel through the Bering Straits was out of the question because of icebergs and limited time. At this point in the crisis (and with hope waning), the mushers and their intrepid teams stepped forward. With no options left, the territorial governor approved the desperate endeavor and wished the serum carriers Godspeed. The first relay team for "The Great Race of Mercy" departed from Nenana (near Fairbanks) on January 27. Astonishingly, a mere six days later, on February 2, the antitoxin arrived in Nome and the city was saved. The exploit deservedly became a media event. Norwegian musher Gunnar Kaasen and his dog-team leader, Balto (a Siberian Husky), who ran the home stretch in blizzard conditions, became national heroes, although it was a statute of Balto, not Kaasen, that was erected in New York City's Central Park shortly thereafter.[15]

Dog sledding aficionados, however, were more impressed by the performance of Norwegian-born Alaskan transplant Leonhard Seppala and his lead dog, Togo (a smaller, older Siberian Husky), who ran the longest, most difficult leg over treacherous mountains and the shifting ice of Norton Sound despite zero visibility, whiteouts, and deadly wind chill factors.[16] Togo had in fact developed quite a reputation even before the serum run as a 12-year-old veteran of the trails. Almost as an act of doggie one-upmanship, shortly after the handoff Togo broke free of Seppala's team to chase reindeer, disappeared into the wilderness, and was presumed lost or dead. However, a week later he sauntered solo into Nome, some 100 miles from where he had last been seen, as if to upbraid the newspapers for not giving him his proper due in the exploit.[17] The bigger-than-life account of the first Iditarod run has most recently been retold with eloquence by Gay and Laney Salisbury in their fine account, *The Cruelest Miles: The Heroic Story of Dogs and Men in a Race Against an Epidemic* (2003).[18]

Although professional dog sledding was nearly driven out of business by the dubious postwar invention of the snowmobile, the skill, endurance, and legend of the northland mushers was resurrected with aplomb by the first annual Iditarod Trail Sled Dog Race in 1973. After tentative beginnings during the 1960s, a semblance of the original trail route was assembled, largely thanks to the visionary and pioneering efforts of Dorothy G. Page and Joe Redington, Sr., the respective "Mother" and "Father" of the Iditarod, as they have come to be known—although neither was an Alaskan by birth.

The race has today grown into an international sporting event, which in 2013 saw 30 qualifiers divide up a $600,000 purse. The closely contested 2013 race also saw, at age 53, the oldest human winner (Martin Seavey) in the event's history, with a lead dog (Tanner) who, when not ferociously competing, could best be described as cute and cuddly. The 2013 Iditarod also witnessed an incident reminiscent of the original 1925 serum run. During mid-race, May, a blond female veteran sled dog, became separated from her team led by Jamaican musher Newton Marshall, creating a social media frenzy and prompting an intensive regional search effort. May was finally rescued a week later on the trail, having traveled at least 150 miles and probably more as she attempted to return to her distant starting point.[19] The episode had definite echoes of Leonard Sappala's dog Togo, who found his way to Nome a week after the antitoxin had been delivered there in 1925 and a week after being cut off from Seppala's team. None of these phenomena, incidentally, would have come as any surprise to Jack London, who as a young man during the Klondike Gold Rush had personally observed the indomitable spirit of the northland mushers and the faithful canines who served them.

Dogs have of course always been heroes throughout history in the human sense. But after the masterful fiction of London and the new medium of film which followed immediately in his wake, far more people became aware of the fact, especially in Anglo-American popular culture. *The Call of the Wild* has itself been loosely adapted for both movies and television on numerous occasions, attracting leading actors the caliber of which have included Clark Gable (1935), Charlton Heston (1972), and Christopher Lloyd (2009), among many others. Perhaps the rendition most faithful to London's original was a 1997 Canadian TV production starring Rutger Hauer and narrated by Richard Dreyfus. In an effort notable for the sheer wealth of detail, the popular television franchise *Animal Planet* presented a 13-episode series of the novel in 2000.

White Fang had been a feature film (now lost) as early as 1925, during the silent era, showcasing the early canine movie star Strongheart (see below). A sensitive remake of *White Fang*, starring a young Ethan Hawke, was presented on the big screen by Disney in 1991. This in turn segued into a 26-episode TV series based on *White Fang* in 1993 and 1994. Even London's heavily romanticized (and sanitized) 1943 screen biography was careful to give the sled dogs of the Yukon an honorable mention. Other examples of dog and wolf heroism in literature and film over the last century are too numerous to catalogue. Even Balto, the media darling of the 1925 serum run to Nome, has become the namesake for a successful franchise of animated films (1995–2004) produced by Steven Spielberg.

Almost immediately following London's death in 1916, World War I led to the recognition and subsequent immortalization of arguably the two best-known real-life canine heroes in modern Western culture, Lassie and Rin Tin Tin. In 1915, when a British battleship was sunk by a German submarine off the English coast, the sole survivor was identified and rescued by a Dorset collie-mix named Lassie.[20] This factual tradition had picked up enough steam in the popular imagination that by 1938, British author Eric Knight produced a short story on the subject for the same *Saturday Evening Post* that had first published London's *Call of the Wild* some 35 years earlier. In 1940, the short story was expanded into a novel, *Lassie Come-Home*. In 1943, during the height of the Second World War, a feature film was produced starring a young Roddy McDowall and a much lesser known, but future megastar, Elizabeth Taylor.

During the postwar era of television, *Lassie* was one of its first hit series, beginning in 1954 and lasting until 1973. By contrast, the historical Rin Tin Tin (1918–1932) was a French-born German shepherd puppy rescued by an American doughboy during World War I and brought back to the States as a pet. The animal was destined to become a household name thanks to Hollywood. With the 1921 breakthrough of another German shepherd performer from the old country, Strongheart (1917–1929), Rin Tin Tin made his silent film debut in 1922 (as a wolf) and never looked backed.[21] By the time of his death a decade later, the dog's film celebrity rivaled that of any human actor, and his final resting place in one of the most renowned pet cemeteries of Paris paid homage to the land of his birth. His extensive progeny continued the dog family acting tradition for decades, culminating in *The Adventures of Rin Tin Tin*, a successful 1954 competitor television series to *Lassie*. One may even go so far as to say that Lassie and Rin Tin Tin established the two basic doggie acting types: Lassie, the cutesy, protective female dog nurturing type, and Rin Tin Tin, the rugged, sturdy, somewhat wolfish male dog of action.[22]

The enduring appeal of Jack London's fictional adventures, as well as the nonfictional adventures of Ernest Thompson Seton, was indicative of a new outlook by society towards canines, more or less dating from the first quarter of the 20th century. Dogs and wolves—whether they be heroes, bandits, or something in between that was difficult to categorize—were far more often being personified into human stereotypes. This was a literary development that had been rare or nonexistent during the previous century. The shift had in fact been so sudden and dramatic that many people took exception, even among professed naturalists and preservationists. Were humans and animals really so alike? Perhaps a more probing question at this point in history, however, was to ask how we as human beings intended to behave towards the animal kingdom, and canines in particular, now that there appeared to be fewer differences between us than previously thought? As circumstances would have it, a little over a decade after the Alaskan serum run and only one year after the character of London's Buck made it to Hollywood with Clark Gable, one of the greatest Russian composers of the century was asked by a friend to create a musical tale for children utilizing the old "Big Bad Wolf" motif.

16

Justified Predators

> *But Peter paid no attention to his grandfather's words.*
> *Boys like Peter aren't afraid of wolves!*
> —Sergei Prokofiev, *Peter and the Wolf*, 20th century[1]

The era of the Great War (1914–1918) that saw the all-too-early death of Jack London in 1916 also saw the fall of corrupt old czarist Russia, and American foreign relations with that country have never really recovered since, notwithstanding the official demise of the Marxist Soviet Union in 1991. Fortunately, Russian-American cultural exchange over the last century has remained vigorous and healthy despite ongoing political and military tensions.[2] One of the most delightful, universally acclaimed by-products of this interaction has proven to be the children's musical drama *Petya i Volk* (Peter and the Wolf), Opus 67, by Sergei Sergeyevich Prokofiev (1891–1953), a top-ranked Russian creative artist who managed to survive during the Soviet era. Certainly he was also among the more dynamic composers of the 20th century by anyone's measure. Unlike his older Russian contemporary Igor Stravinsky (1882–1971), who left his homeland early in life to build a prosperous international career for himself, and unlike his younger Russian contemporary Demitri Shostakovich (1906–1975), who remained in Russia to hone his formidable art in the face of potentially lethal Soviet opposition, Prokofiev had a considerable taste for (and comfort level in) both creative worlds, Russian and international. In spite of this dichotomy, or perhaps because of it, his bracing work frequently had the potential to reach the broadest possible mass audiences while still occasionally baffling or confusing even the most sophisticated of music critics. Into the former category squarely falls *Peter and the Wolf*, by far and away the most popular and beloved piece for children in the entire classical music repertoire.[3]

Prokofiev was born in the remote regions of the Ukraine during the late 19th century totalitarian regime of Czar Alexander III.[4] His middle class parents were a fortunate combination of a professional father more than willing and able to financially support his son's artistic pursuits and an attentive, cultured mother who recognized and encouraged the boy's talent from an early age. It is more than likely that Prokofiev's lifelong interest in the musical education of children stemmed from the highly nurturing environment he himself had experienced as a child. By the time Prokofiev reached 13 years of age, he was accepted into the prestigious Saint Petersburg Conservatory through the influence of composer Alexander Glazunov (1865–1936), after the composer was particularly impressed by the child prodigy's fluent literacy in musical notation.

Upon reaching majority age, Prokofiev traveled to Paris and London, where he discovered Stravinsky's revolutionary musical idiom through the *Ballets Russe* of Sergei Diaghilev (1872–1929). When world war came in 1914, Prokofiev quickly found himself despising its senseless futility and the remorseless pursuit of a faltering government threatening to conscript him. He fled back to the conservatory for a master's degree in order to avoid the draft and meanwhile fell into understandable sympathy with the Bolshevik Revolution, which officially began in October 1917 only a few months after the abdication of disgraced Czar Nicholas II. By the end of that same year, Russia's disastrous war with Germany had effectively ended, but for the next five years the country would be engulfed by spreading civil strife and violence that proved to be just as destructive, if not more so, as the Eastern Front.

By 1918, with World War I winding down and Bolshevik leader Vladimir Lenin (1870–1924) effectively in power, Prokofiev decided to begin his international career as a performer and composer in earnest, using Paris as base and hobnobbing with the intellectual cutting edge of the European avant-garde. His decision to travel abroad was probably also influenced by the bitter Russian civil war then raging across the country between Whites and Reds, as well a basic need to earn a living and to see the world. In 1923 Prokofiev married the Spanish-born opera singer Lina Llubera and started a family.[5] For the next 13 years, he traveled widely in Europe and North America, wrote all kinds of music (especially for the ballet), conducted, and developed a formidable, if not iconoclastic, reputation as both composer and concert pianist rivaling that of his older touring compatriot Sergei Rachmaninoff (1873–1943).

Then, in 1936 at age 45, Prokofiev made the surprising, fateful decision to return home with his family to Mother Russia, by then known as the Union of Soviet Socialist Republics under the iron-fisted dictatorship of Joseph Stalin (1878–1953). It is possible, if not likely, that Prokofiev's middle-aged homesickness was compounded by a pressing need to support his family at the height of a worldwide economic depression. Thus he fled to the protective umbrella of a socialist state, which he had always openly supported since its inception. It should have welcomed him with open arms but instead it spent the next 17 years forcing the composer to prove and prove again his loyalty to the government, often with distasteful consequences while doing little to alleviate his financial hardships.

Soviet Russia, despite a lot of window dressing, was not a friendly place for creative artists of originality or genius. Stalin and the Soviet bureaucracy, fully cognizant of artistic power to sway public opinion, took an active, energetic role in its intense censorship and regulation. Dissident opinion was routinely met with firing squads or Siberian exile or was simply made to vanish. In 1936, the very same year that Prokofiev returned home, his famed composer colleague Demitri Shostakovich had narrowly escaped the wrath of Stalin and *Pravda* for his controversial, adults-only operatic opus, *Lady Macbeth of the Mtsensk District*. Prokofiev had to have known what he was walking into, but he also seems to have had a strategy of sorts.

His immediate focus would be on music for children, patriotic works, and strict cooperation with Soviet authorities. During the early 1930s, Prokofiev had already proven his abilities in both genres, and upon his arrival on Russian soil in 1936 he was invited by his friend Natayla Sats (1903–1993) to compose a musical tale for children to be premiered at the newly opened Moscow Central Children's Theatre.[6] He immediately committed his first unwitting act of defiance against Soviet authority by rejecting a libretto presented to him, declaring it hackneyed (no doubt to the astonishment of some technocrat) while confidently assuring his possibly by then frightened employer that he could write a better one himself. Prokofiev proceeded to casually complete a new libretto and all accompanying music within the jaw-dropping time span of one week. The work debuted on May 2, 1936, according to Prokofiev's journal, to a nearly empty theatre, with audiences possibly shying away because of the composer's assertive reputation, a quality most of them were certainly not used to encountering. After that, the entire episode seemed to be forgotten, including *Peter and the Wolf* itself, as Prokofiev tried to adjust the cocky and self-assured working habits he had cultivated outside of Russia during the previous 15 years. By 1937, Sats, the very same woman commissioning Prokofiev's masterpiece for the Children's Theatre, had been sentenced to hard labor in Siberia for, among other transgressions, being the mistress of one of Stalin's prominently purged victims within the Russian military.[7]

For nearly the next two years Prokofiev floundered as he tried to get a professional footing in his homeland, churning out one high-quality Soviet propaganda musical work after another for a system that did not properly reward quality or reacted to it with jealously and suspicion.[8] In 1938, Prokofiev's patience and perseverance was finally rewarded by his being allowed to score the movie soundtrack for Serge Eisenstein's classic war film, *Alexander Nevsky*. It has often been called, with considerable justification, the greatest film soundtrack ever composed. Moreover, no work of propaganda, artistic or otherwise, ever did more to psychologically prepare the Russian people for the firestorm that would soon come their way in the form of the 1941 German Nazi invasion.

The defeat of the Teutonic Knights Templar by Prince Alexander at the winter battle of Lake Peipus (near Novgorod) in 1242 proved prophetic in its subject matter, and indeed many of the Red Army extras used in the film would in fact perish within a few short years while defending their country. By 1939, Prokofiev's already considerable international stature had been further enhanced, and his old friend Serge Koussevitzky, always a champion of the composer's music and now conductor for the Boston Symphony Orchestra, persuaded RCA Victor to finance a 78-rpm recording of *Peter and the Wolf* with well-known American singing actor Richard Hale as the narrator.[9] The production was one of the early big hits of the classical recording era and remains a treasured collector's item. This success in turn set the stage for a postwar Walt Disney animated short film in 1946, and the widespread popularity of the piece has continued unabated ever since.

Unfortunately, Prokofiev now lived in a society in which commercial success did not automatically translate to personal financial gain or official government approval—more often the opposite, in fact. When all-out war came in 1941, Prokofiev, like millions of his countrymen, moved west to the Caucasus and continued working. But his wife and children stayed behind in Moscow, she being angered by his ongoing affair with a Ukrainian Jewish librettist, Mira Mendelson, who later became Prokofiev's second wife.[10]

Despite huge prestige shared by few of his peers and a continuously growing popularity outside of the Soviet Union, Prokofiev lived in relative poverty and after the war began to suffer seriously declining health. Both he and Shostakovich, though widely acknowledged as Russia's two greatest living home-based composers, were regularly persecuted and harassed by Stalin's bureaucracy for their resistance to convention and their openness to new ideas.[11] In late 1952, Prokofiev's ethereal Seventh Symphony premiered, originally designed as a children's piece for television. But as the mood of the piece turned darker and more complex, censoring authorities insisted on a more upbeat ending for the work, which the composer then dutifully provided. It was the last premier that Prokofiev ever attended. On March 5, 1953, he passed away in Moscow at age 61, approximately one hour before the death of Stalin on that same day. Incredibly, as a result of this misfortunate (but ironic) coincidence, the composer's death went virtually unnoticed and unremarked upon within the Soviet Union.

Prokofiev's borderless, timeless music for *Peter and the Wolf* speaks for itself and is best discussed elsewhere by those more qualified to do so. The striking original text, however, is often overlooked and will be given some needed attention herein. The English translation of the work has been an evolving affair since the late 1930s; that which is most often performed today closely resembles the edition prepared by Russian musicologist Vladimir Blok during the Khrushchev era. What one would not give to see the original proposed libretto rejected by Prokofiev in 1936. It is a safe bet that considerable inspiration for Prokofiev's own text came in direct reaction to the mediocrity with which he was first presented.

Most everyone knows the story line, wherein a young Peter captures a ravenous wolf using only a rope and fearless cunning wit, with some assistance from a friendly bird as a lure.[12] Most of Prokofiev's more unusual twists come near the end of the fable. When hunters appear only after the wolf has already been captured, Peter surprisingly exhorts them not to kill a predator that has just devoured a harmless duck, but rather to help transport the wolf alive to the local zoo.[13] Peter's grumpy, unimaginative grandfather, a naysayer to the very end, warns everyone that the moral of the story could be a bad one: "Grandfather shook his head discontentedly. 'Well, and if Peter hadn't caught the wolf, what then?'"[14] The final line to the tale offers another big twist. The lovable duck, though eaten by the wolf, is in fact still alive: "And if one listened very carefully, they could hear the duck quacking inside the wolf, because the wolf, in his hurry, had swallowed her *alive!*"[15] In some productions, the indigestible, living duck is at some point vomited out by the wolf. No one, not even Soviet authorities, could therefore accuse Prokofiev of killing off any of his animal characters, because the hapless duck is still, strictly speaking, alive at the end of the story, while the villainous captured wolf is carted off to the zoo.

Or is Prokofiev's wolf really that villainous? A wolf, after all, is only a wolf. It attacks every living thing in sight because it is hungry, and a carnivore by natural design. In this sense, it is a justified predator, similar to the legendary Wolf of Gubbio tamed by Saint Francis of Assisi (see Chapter 8). Even more unsettling for conventional moralists (or apologists for the Soviet regime) was Prokofiev's insistence on giving all of his characters, both animal and human, various shades of good and evil traits, rather than strictly black or white. Peter is clearly a misfit and rebel, despite his heroic status, not unlike his obvious namesake, Czar Peter I ("Peter the Great"). Never mind that the Bolshevik Revolution was itself the ultimate rebellious act against a traditional established authority.

Even more troubling for Soviet censors, Peter's supposedly wise grandfather is presented as a comically ridiculous and overly conservative figure.

Prokofiev himself was well known for his natural resistance to all authority, from his school days at the Saint Petersburg Conservatory to his later clashes with shallow Soviet autocrats. The duck is likable but stupid, leading to its quick demise. The bird is fast, agile and mouthy but, left to its own devices, ineffectual. Even the female cat, though highly intelligent and adept, is also self-centered, antisocial and ultimately disruptive; in the end she is closely and rather fittingly aligned with the grandfather. All of these stereotypes are somewhat alarming from a human perspective. Perhaps most troubling of all are the hunters, who make a lot of noise, accomplish nothing, and at their very core are—well (for lack of better descriptors), fearful and insecure. Stealthily, Prokofiev takes the traditional Big Bad Wolf of ancient European folklore and gives it a slightly modern twist, adding a sly and humorous human allegory to the animal kingdom worthy of Aesop and the ancient mythmakers.

Usually performed with a full orchestra and narrator, *Peter and the Wolf* has proven itself over the years to be highly adaptable to all forms of visual art, including film and dance. This writer recently saw one such live ballet version performed in Stevens Point, Wisconsin, in which a highly competent regional orchestra (the Central Wisconsin Symphony) combined with a local PBS radio personality (Jim Fleming), and supported by a team of teenage and preadolescent dancers, treated audiences to a uniquely compelling performance.[16] Earlier the same program had reportedly been presented to an enthusiastic capacity crowd of Portage County fourth-grade students. Among many high points, the chiefly adult audience on the final day seemed to respond most approvingly to three girl dancers portraying Prokofiev's loose-cannon hunters with more than a hint of cowardice and trepidation.

Wisconsin is currently in the throes of a political controversy over newly enacted wolf-hunting laws that, unlike similar laws in several other states, specifically allow for dogs to be used in tracking and pursuit.[17] Those in the audience mentioned above with a sense of distant history could not help but be reminded of Joseph Stalin's well-founded fears and concerns over the power of art being effectively used to sway public opinion over hotly contested political issues. We would heavily wager that the same Wisconsin fourth graders who attended this production will one day become adult voters for the most part opposed to the current state laws.[18] The pre-hunting law controversy history of indigenous timber wolves in the Badger State, from the near extinction of those animals due to unrestricted bounty hunting during the 1950s, to their tentative reintroduction and gradual comeback over the last half-century, has been ably documented by conservationist Richard P. Thiel in his two excellent books, *The Timber Wolf in Wisconsin: The Death and Life of a Majestic Predator* (1993) and *Keepers of the Wolves: The Early Years of Wolf Recovery in Wisconsin* (2001).

Meanwhile, as American hunters and conservationists spar over the propriety and proper place of recreational wolf hunting, art and art's most powerful populist exponent, motion pictures, continue to forcefully march on. As previously noted, the first film entry for *Peter and the Wolf* came dramatically in 1946 with a Walt Disney short feature that, while taking many liberties with Prokofiev's story line, made a memorable impression on a lot of viewers, as Disney's early works were known to have frequently done. *Peter and the Wolf* came in the wake of Disney's animated classical music masterpiece *Fantasia* (1940) and exhibited a similar impeccable level of artistry.[19]

Since that time, countless studio recordings and video productions of *Peter and the Wolf* have followed, too numerous to catalogue, but a few deserve at least passing mention. In 1958, a marionette version for early television narrated by the deceptively cerebral comedian Art Carney (*Art Carney Meets Peter and the Wolf*) was Emmy-nominated for its overall excellence. Some four decades later, in 1995, *Peter* did win an Emmy Award for an ABC production combining live action with animation and celebrity voice-overs. For the new millennium, National Public Radio (NPR) got into the act by putting together *Peter and the Wolf: A Special Report*, in which a compelling rendition of the work by the Virginia Chamber Players under the baton of JoAnn Falletta was interspersed with tongue-in-cheek news commentary from hosts of the innovative feature program *All Things Considered*. NPR followed this up over a decade later in 2011 with an honorary nod to Prokofiev's achievement titled *"Peter and the Wolf" Turns 75*.

Within the last decade, a multinational production team led by talented British director-animator Suzie Templeton deservedly won a 2008 Oscar Award for Best-Animated Short Film for her stunning 2006 feature, boosted considerably by the musical participation of the Philharmonia Orchestra conducted by Mark Stephenson. In this stylish interpretation, a format without text or narrator is utilized in which the story is effectively conveyed solely by the music and visuals, as well as an ending in which Peter bonds with the captured wolf and releases it back into the wild. Templeton's striking creativity succeeded in introducing Prokofiev's masterpiece to an entire new generation of children (and adults) for the 21st century.

In the meantime, almost every major conductor and story narrator of note have jumped at the chance to participate in similar projects. Recorded narrators alone have included the composer's surviving widow, Lina (1987), son Oleg and grandson Gabriel (1991), as well as everyone from Shakespearean actors to pop music and TV celebrities. The work's translation into other languages (besides English) is too extensive to detail.

In 2012, *Peter and the Wolf* once again came to the forefront of current events with the U.S. Supreme Court decision in *Golan v. Holder*. Since 2001 (when the action was first filed with the courts) expired copyrights for a number of popular classical works had resulted in those works entering the public domain. The court's final decision, however, legally restored this copyright protection to legitimate owners renewing these rights, and one of the most prominently affected was Prokofiev's celebrated musical tale for children.[20]

In hindsight, the 1930s will be remembered as one of the most turbulent decades of the 20th century, not only as a prelude to World War II, but also as a decade in which vexing socioeconomic questions were initially posed, questions still vigorously debated by the body politic, both American and worldwide. The real message of Prokofiev's *Peter and the Wolf* was the lesson of interpersonal teamwork in the face of adversity, as opposed to mindless submission and fearfulness. In seeking to solve the ongoing civil problems of society, one is either a team player or is not. Yes, Peter is a hero, but he needs the little bird and even the cowardly hunters to successfully pull things off. As for the wolf, the composer seems to assert that, in a truly egalitarian society, everyone and everything has their designated proper place, even a wild wolf (albeit in a zoo). Otherwise, what else is one to reasonably expect from a desperate carnivorous beast except murder and mayhem?

The lesson has a certain pastoral wisdom to it. Was Prokofiev's morality tale for children inspired by the wolves of his own youth in the remote Ukraine? One would love to know. It is also worth recalling that Prokofiev himself died in comparative poverty and homeland obscurity, the latter especially outrageous given his unimpeachable stature as an international creative artist. Then again, during the 1930s, the Soviet Union, like so many other countries worldwide, struggled hard with the grinding poverty of the Great Depression, and this mentality spilled over well into the postwar era. On the other side of the world, in another hemisphere, on another continent, Latin America struggled with the exact same problem, and to canine matters of that particular time and place we now turn our attention. As for Prokofiev, let it be lastly noted that his impressive musical legacy continues to thrive among us, stronger than ever, in large part because of a canine storytelling image once so vividly conveyed and ornamented by his genius.

17

Dogs in Poverty

"A pack of dogs!" Having discovered the expression that had so stubbornly eluded him, he was elated. A pack of dogs. Obviously, backcountry people like him were no better than dogs.—Graciliano Ramos, *Barren Lives*, 20th century[1]

My late father, a man with formal training in the field of economics (possessing a greater aptitude for accurate forecasting in that science than anyone I have ever known), made it a point to travel to the former Soviet Union during the late 1970s Brezhnev era in order to see and judge the "evil empire" for himself rather than strictly rely on the reports and opinions of others.[2] That was so typically like him. He reported back to many deaf ears in our small hometown that Communism was not so much evil as it was boring, and hence destined to failure. The events of the next decade would in fact prove him correct, as he usually was about such things.

By way of favorable contrast, he selected as an example (to our astonishment), the small country of Portugal—another nation he visited during the same trip—and its larger ex-colonial satellites, particularly Brazil. Portuguese multicultural values and bold entrepreneurial spirit, my father steadfastly maintained, were a beacon for the future and should be closely studied by everyone, including Americans. It therefore seems appropriate that we should briefly focus our attention on a classic work of canine literature from the mid-20th century Brazil, in the Portuguese language by a writer with nominal Marxist sympathies. By coincidence it so happens that Graciliano Ramos de Oliveira (1892–1953) passed away only a few days after Sergei Prokofiev died in Moscow that same month (see Chapter 16).[3] Both artists, despite their considerable reputations and achievements, had suffered grievously at the hands of their own governments from time to time, although the prolonged trials and tribulations of Ramos, as a perceived Marxist living much of his life within a fascist military state, were on a far greater scale.

Latin American history is, of course, not on the radar of the average U.S. citizen or, for that matter, many non-average U.S. citizens. The long, complex history of modern Brazil—much longer than that of the United States—began in the year of 1500—less than eight years after the first voyage of Christopher Columbus—when Portuguese conquistador Pedro Álvares Cabral landed on the eastern South American coast near Porto Seguro. This was approximately midway between today's spectacular Brazilian capital of Rio de Janeiro and the remote, isolated province of Alagoas, where Graciliano Ramos was born in 1892, only a few years after the old monarchy had collapsed and slavery was abolished during the late 1880s.

The first half of 20th century Brazilian history was in turn dominated by the controversial political figure of dictator Getúlio Vargas (1882–1954), who ruled the country absolutely between 1930 and 1945, and then again (rather incredibly), by popular vote between 1951 and 1954. He committed suicide after the military—always the staunch bedrock of his support and power—finally turned irreconcilably against him. In a sense, Vargas was to Ramos what Stalin had been to Prokofiev, a lifelong nemesis and constant threat; on the other hand, Vargas was worse for Ramos because the former was fanatically anticommunist and the latter had no particular interest in cooperating with entrenched power, despite his long professional career in the Brazilian civil service. This unfortunate dynamic is underscored by comparing the many struggles of Ramos with that of his great Brazilian musical contemporary Heitor Villa-Lobos (1887–1959), who prospered under the Vargas regime, comparatively speaking, in no small part by shying away from controversy and conflict with the government. Ramos definitely lacked the doctrinal flexibility of his nemesis, Vargas, who began his long political trajectory as an enthusiastic supporter of European fascist states but backpeddled quickly after 1942 following aggressive financial outreach to Brazil by Franklin D. Roosevelt's administration, combined with the irretrievable Nazi disaster at Stalingrad on the Eastern Front during World War II.

A true son of the proletariat, Ramos was born the eldest of 16 children to lower middle class parents in remote northeastern Brazil, on the fringe of the desolate, equatorial wilderness known in Portuguese as *el sertão*. The future literary giant was destined to one day accomplish for this arid, harsh region what writer John Steinbeck (see Chapter 19) would do during the same decade for the American Dust Bowl, that is to say, immortalize it in popular fiction. Ramos appears to have held no great affection for either of his struggling parents, but the father, while consistently hapless in business matters, is credited with having the prescience to notice that his eldest son loved books and encourage this indulgence.

By the time he was school age, Graciliano had become the designated family storyteller and recalled in particular reading to his father one tale of a family lost in the woods and being stalked by wild wolves.[4] His formal education was meager and substandard, but by the time he managed somehow to complete high school he was also dabbling in journalism and writing pseudonymous poetry when not working in his father's general store. In 1914 (at age 22) he traveled to Rio de Janeiro for the first time, and in 1915 married his first wife, who died five years later in childbirth.

During the 1920s, Ramos established a foothold for himself in small-town politics while continuing to write for his own personal amusement, and in 1927 he got himself elected mayor of Palmeira dos Índios. The mayoral post, however, proved a thankless job on which he quickly soured and from which he resigned in 1930. More happily, in 1928, he married his second wife (and partner for the remainder of his life), Heloísa Leite de Medeiros. She no doubt realized that her husband's main calling in life would not be a political one. By some accident of fate or backfiring malice of his political opponents, Ramos' final written reports as ex-mayor came to the attention of the provincial governor (and noted Brazilian modernist poet), Augusto Frederico Schmidt, a learned man used to bureaucratic tedium but startled by the bracing, dry levity of Ramos' writing style, not unlike that Montaigne used when describing his forced tenure as mayor of Bordeaux during the French Wars of Religion (see Chapter 9).[5]

Thanks to the critical insight of Schmidt, electoral politics for Ramos quickly gave way to the Brazilian civil service, first with his appointment as director of the official state press, and then later as director of public education.[6] The year 1933–1934 also brought the successful publication of his first two novels. Then, in 1935, disaster struck with the Brazilian communist revolt. Although Ramos was not openly Marxist, he was perceived by the Vargas military dictatorship to be in sympathy with the rebels. Accordingly, he was arrested and, without indictment or trial, sentenced to hard labor. Fortunately, the modest literary celebrity (combined with the relative political harmlessness) Ramos enjoyed seems to have made Vargas realize that the novelist's continuing imprisonment or death would only be counterproductive to his own public relations campaign. Hence, in 1937 a 44-year-old Ramos was released from prison on unofficial probation and proceeded to try to put his life back together.

He began by writing what is now considered his masterpiece, the novel *Vidas Sêcas* (Barren Lives), which originated as a short story about the death of a dog ("Baleia") and with encouragement from his publisher grew into larger story about human relationships with the pet, as well as the animal's superior intelligence and virtue in comparison to that of its owners.[7] The positive reception of *Barren Lives* in 1938 coincided with the novelist settling permanently in Rio de Janeiro, and in 1939 he was granted a minor government post as federal inspector of secondary education. Upon the fall of the Vargas regime in 1945 following World War II, Ramos publicly declared himself an atheist and official member of the Communist Party, no doubt partly to spite those who had made his life so hard over the previous decade.[8]

Civic artistic honors accumulated even as he continued to publish works faster than ever. By the early 1950s, with Vargas coming back into temporary power and his own shaky health beginning to fail, Ramos insisted (as would my father several decades later) on taking a tour behind the Iron Curtain to see the Soviet bloc with his own eyes, even as Stalin was still alive. There he was fêted by Communist Party officials, but he seems to have reciprocated mainly with sharp criticism and skeptical wariness. Returning home, Ramos died in 1953 at age 61 from the lung cancer that resulted from the fact he was a lifelong chain smoker. His final verdict on his own substantial literary legacy was one of modest self-deprecation.[9] He firmly advocated that all writers should write exclusively from personal experience and studiously avoid everything else.[10] Towards laissez-faire capitalism Ramos remained unswervingly hostile and vocal in his implacable hatred to the very end.

At an economical 131 pages, the lean and mean text of *Barren Lives* is a literary case study in achieving the greatest emotional impact with the least amount of gesture or artifice. The story line, like poverty itself, is cyclical in structure. Fabiano, Vitória, and their two young sons are migrant ranch workers of the sertão with no property to speak of, except for an antiquated firearm and their female dog, Baleia (Whale), the latter faithfully tending to the family's needs on multiple, essential levels. As the novelist writes, "She [Baleia] was like a member of the family. There was hardly any difference to speak of between her and the boys."[11] In spite of this surprising equality between man and beast, the bond between the dog and the younger son is especially strong: "Everyone else had abandoned him; the dog was the only living being that felt any sympathy for him. He stroked her with his thin, grubby fingers and the animal curled up the better to enjoy the pleasant contact, which gave her a feeling not unlike that which she received from the warm ashes of the fire."[12]

Tragically (as in the original short story version), the aging Baleia becomes visibly ill, and the father, mistakenly fearing rabies and partly out of his own ignorance and partly from a misguided sense of duty towards family, clumsily and cruelly puts the dog down with his outmoded flintlock. Now bereft of their greatest asset, the family's already meager fortunes begin to completely disintegrate almost immediately following the dog's death. For the remainder of the tale, a dazed and confused Fabiano agonizes with recurring subconscious guilt over his premature killing of Baleia.[13] *Barren Lives* concludes with the forlorn family unit making their way to the big city in hopes of a better life, which the reader knows will in fact be even worse than the one they have been previously living. Thus Baleia's untimely death becomes symbolic and metaphorical for the family's ultimate demise, as well as for the hopeless plight of the working poor, whose typically short and hard lives are really not life at all in the civilized human sense.[14]

Fabiano's only epiphany, such as it is, comes (interestingly enough) immediately prior to his committing the great mistake of killing his family's canine pet and benefactor. As he is repeatedly abused and disrespected by wealthy ranch owners, corrupt policemen, and anyone else having slightly more material wealth than they, Fabiano stammers out the insult "pack of dogs" only to realize in the same instant this is exactly how his tormentors view him and all of the lower classes to which he belongs (see header quote). The comparison becomes all the more painful as Fabiano reflects on his family basically living in the street of a small town while he drinks cheap rum, sweats, and salivates, in appearance not unlike the rabid dogs that he so greatly fears. As for his fellow workers and victims of lower class society, he views them with nothing less than fear, loathing, and contempt—in essence, trying desperately to somehow place himself above them.

Unlike Steinbeck's Tom Joad, there is nothing noble, admirable, or particularly likable in Ramos' depiction of Fabiano. He is merely a deeply flawed human being trying to get by in a hostile environment, which in turn makes his character all the more real and visceral. His great tragic flaw, in the symbolic sense at least, is his total lack of appreciation for the family's best friend (Baleia), and, just like the greater, evil society at large, a distorted, misplaced comparison between man and dog within the natural chain of being. As a storyteller, Ramos makes almost exactly the same point modern writers from previous generations had been making for some time—from Charles Darwin to Ernest Thompson Seton to Jack London—and then places this same animal anticruelty theme within the greater context of Brazilian social justice and economic challenges faced by the people of the brutal equatorial sertão.

Half a century after *Barren Lives* first appeared in print, and following the latest demise of Brazil's military government, the world's fifth largest country enacted its new federal constitution, in 1988, which was revised in 1998. Both contained specific and express legal provisions against animal cruelty.[15] Although Ramos had dramatized the death of Baleia more as an act of deranged desperation rather than cruel abuse, he still would have surely been gladdened by the new laws. Animal anticruelty legislation had in fact been trending forward all across Western civilization since the end of World War II. Probably the most influential figure in this regard had been the renowned older contemporary of Ramos, Albert Schweitzer (1875–1965), who made direct reference to the issue in his highly publicized acceptance speech for the 1952 Nobel Peace Prize.

The Alsatian-born Schweitzer was a man of many distinguished parts, including philosopher, theologian, physician, missionary, musician, and, last but not least, strict vegetarian. Within two years of Schweitzer's recognition, and one year after the death of Ramos in 1953, the National Humane Society, which later became the Humane Society of the United States (HSUS), had been established.[16] Based in Washington, HSUS is still the largest organization of its kind and has served as an umbrella or inspiration for countless, similar-minded local groups, both in the U.S. and beyond through its growing transcontinental wing, Humane Society International (HSI), founded in 1991. Even as governments grapple worldwide with intimidating problems such as overpopulation, climate change, fair allocation of resources, and rapidly globalizing economies, the humane treatment of animals, beginning with Man's Best Friend, continues to hold a more than visible place in the pantheon of debate. This stubborn resilience, or rather, one might easily say, continually growing interest, is perhaps evidence that making a better world for mankind is impossible without making it a better place for the animal kingdom as well.

The repercussions of this emerging viewpoint can be seen everywhere across the Americas, no matter how seemingly removed from large urban areas. On April 13, 2013, this writer attended a charity fundraiser in Rothschild, Wisconsin, light-heartedly billed as "Dancing for the Paws," a valiant and successful attempt to raise money for the fiscally challenged Humane Society of Marathon County. Graciliano Ramos, had he still been alive, would have appreciated both the irreverence of style and the underlying motive behind the event. Marathon County, like thousands of other jurisdictions, is engaged in an ongoing community debate over achieving the proper balance between public financing and private charity for such endeavors during an era of shrinking revenues and resources, among many other thorny questions.[17] Similar debates are currently taking place all across the civilized world. All of this may seem a long way away from the novel *Barren Lives* and Ramos himself, a serious writer primarily concerned with human welfare, human rights, and human poverty. Yet, Ramos opted to make his greatest artistic statement on these topics through the use of a forceful and memorable canine symbol. One thing appears to be clear, however: neither public subsidy nor private charity alone seems capable of dealing with this or any other major problem. Both are obviously needed, and perhaps more than both, starting with a major shift in the cultural mindsets alluded to by Ramos in his novel.

The biggest boost to public awareness of *Vidas Sêcas* came in 1963, a full decade after the death of Ramos, when noted film director Nelson Pereira dos Santos adapted the novel into a film unusually faithful to its literary source, beginning with an on-location shoot in the sertão of Ramos' provincial Alagoas.[18] One of the founding fathers of Brazilian *Cinema Novo*, Santos had been heavily influenced by Italian neorealism of the 1940s and 1950s, and it is a safe bet that masterworks such as Vittorio De Sica's *Umberto D* (1952), showcasing a trained canine supporting star named Napoleone, had made a strong impression on him, as it had on many other viewers.[19] For the Santos film, a local stray mutt (originally named Piaba) was rescued and magnificently cast into the tragic role of Baleia.

The finished product was entered into the highly competitive 1964 Cannes Film Festival, where it won a special prize from the International Catholic Organization for Cinema and Audiovisual (the OCIC Award), and lots of publicity besides. A good part of this recognition came after the premier screening had stirred a brewing scandal with its shockingly realistic depiction of Baleia's death, causing European animal rights activists to raise an outcry of foul play. The filmmakers put a fast end to the protest, however, by bringing a more than alive and well Piaba-Baleia onto the red carpet, where the dog was treated like a human star. Thus the dog proved herself to be another notable canine actor in a very long line frustrating serious playwrights since at least the time of Johann Wolfgang von Goethe (see Chapter 11). *Barren Lives* the movie also helped to cement Ramos' reputation as one of Brazil's greatest novelists, as well as a champion of the dispossessed, both human and canine, as if the two were inseparable by any true analysis.[20]

The movie itself deserves a brief recap, given that it is a rare example of film that enhances the imagery of a novel without departing from it. The opening and closing frames show the impoverished family making its way across the sertão outback. Except at the outset they are accompanied and led by Baleia, the dog becoming a symbol of future hope, as opposed to hopelessness. Baleia's indispensable services to the family are briskly presented during the first half of the story: she hunts for and finds food (but only eats leftovers), alerts the rest of the family when anyone falters during the journey, consoles and makes the children happy when they are sad, provides bodily warmth, presides over medical attention (as a therapy dog) and leads its human pack to whatever destination is being sought out. After temporary ranch employment is found, the dog continues to earn its keep as an efficient herder of livestock and is in fact treated better by the family than the family is treated by the ranch owners.

When Fabiano briefly consorts with banditos, he is wisely herded back into the family unit by Baleia. The ill-fitting shoes and clothing of the workers is bleakly contrasted with the dog's happy freedom. In short, without the dog, the family is forlorn and lost. *Barren Lives* also contains a wealth of intimate canine cinematography. The skillfully staged (and illusory) killing of Baleia, now 60 years after the fact, still comes across as possibly the most harrowing sequence in animal cruelty ever filmed. At first she tries to run away, and then is resigned to her appalling fate, while the children grieve inconsolably and the mother makes the sign of the cross. In some ways, however, the dog's demise is far more merciful than what surely lies in store for its anchorless human family, as they trek away to the big city in their futile search for a better life. Viewers are left with the image of migratory fowl but also cannot help but ask whether the birds have more common sense than their human counterparts without any canine assistance.

The Brazilian military regime which so shaped and colored the worldview of Graciliano Ramos, after many fits and starts over the course of a full century, finally gave way in the late 1980s to a more true form of republican government. Since that time, Brazil has become a rising force on the world economic stage, similar to what my father had predicted over three decades ago. In late 2010, the country proudly elected its first female president, Dilma Vana Rouseff (b. 1947), a professed socialist and (like Ramos) former political prisoner. In 2014, Brazil will host the FIFA World Cup, and in 2016, the Summer Olympics. No doubt Brazilians will use these opportunities to showcase the many unique virtues of their society, as well as to receive criticism for its ongoing struggles against the many social ills so infuriating to Ramos during unhappier times.

The country's unique geographic location straddling both hemispheres within Pan America is symbolically appropriate, with its skies dominated by the same dog-star constellations that captured the imagination of the ancients (see Chapter 2).[21] And yet, despite its hedonistic, pagan overlay, modern Brazil in fact considers itself to be an overwhelmingly Christian, Roman Catholic nation. While one of its greatest writers insistently labeled himself a nonbeliever, a near contemporary on the other side of the Atlantic Ocean had undergone an opposite trajectory in life from atheism to faith. Both of these writers, however, despite their religious differences, shared a keen love of dogs.

18

Animal Spirituality

"And how ... but hullo! What are all these animals? A cat—two cats—dozens of cats. And all these dogs ... why I can't count them. And the birds. And the horses."
"They are her beasts."
"Did she keep a sort of zoo? I mean, this is a bit too much."
"Every beast and bird that came near her had its place in her love. In her they became themselves. And now the abundance of life she has in Christ from the Father flows over into them."—C.S. Lewis, *The Great Divorce*, 20th century[1]

If harsh, unjust political imprisonment during middle age helped to confirm an already conspicuous lack of personal religious faith for Graciliano Ramos, then it might be well said that an abundance of youthful misfortune and trauma caused a similar malaise for another great 20th century author, while nonetheless sewing the seeds for a rather unlikely conversion to religious faith at a later date. Indeed, tracing a logical trajectory for spiritual piety or lack thereof in any of these writers would appear to be a total exercise in futility. The adolescent dissipations of a Montaigne or a Saint Francis gave little hint of what would come later in terms of a completely different kind of passionate fervor. Nor would the outwardly conventional upbringings of a Goethe or a Darwin, if viewed superficially from a historical distance, suggest in any way the unconventional freethinking tendencies that assert themselves with adulthood. For purposes of this study, all that can be said with any certainty is that each of these personalities, regardless of their individual views and opinions on the afterlife, all wrote about canines with strong feelings as well. As for this commentator, I first encountered the works of Clive Staples Lewis (1898–1963) some 37 years ago as a college undergraduate and, like millions of other readers, have been drawing entertainment, enlightenment, and comfort from them ever since.[2]

Lewis was born in Belfast and baptized into the Anglo-Irish protestant church of his parents. His father was a self-made solicitor with Welsh farming roots, while his mother, a clergyman's daughter, claimed distant ancestry from the old Norman nobility. Both parents were highly educated, literate, and great lovers of books, a fortunate trait they passed on to their younger son. Famously, Lewis hated his given Christian names (Clive Staples) from infancy onwards. At age four, after beloved pet dog "Jacksie" was killed by an automobile, the child dealt with his first emotional loss by announcing to everyone that henceforth he himself would be known as "Jack."[3] This nickname or, more accurately speaking, adopted first name, stuck with him for the rest of his life, often to the confusion of those outside his immediate circle of family and friends.

Among his first great literary influences were the popular animal tales of Beatrix Potter (1866–1943), in which canines sometimes figure prominently.[4] Then, in 1908, his still relatively young mother died from cancer. Lewis was nine years old at the time. Years later he wrote that "with my mother's death, all settled happiness, all that was tranquil and reliable, disappeared from my life."[5] No sooner had this tragedy played out than the boy was shipped off by his bereaved father to public boarding school in Hertfordshire, England. Afterwards, father-son relations never seemed to fully recover (much to the later regret of Lewis) and, although going on to a brilliant academic career (winning a scholarship through competitive examination to Oxford University in 1916), by secondary school he had also became an unapologetic atheist with an expressed preference for pagan mythology and a teenage lifestyle that seems to have known few conventional inhibitions. Though counterintuitive on the surface, this intellectual rebelliousness would quickly help Lewis become an expert in languages of the past by the time his student days were over.

After turning 18, though Irish birth exempted him from conscription, Lewis left Oxford after less than a term, enlisted in the British Army, went through basic training, was commissioned an officer, and was promptly deployed to France, arriving at the Western Front on the day of his 19th birthday in late 1917. Within a matter of months, at the very height of the great German offensive in April of 1918, Lewis was wounded and narrowly escaped death from friendly artillery fire, even as his surrounding comrades were killed by the same barrage.

After a lengthy convalescence, he was demobilized and returned to Oxford, where he aggressively completed his undergraduate work plus double masters' degrees over the next five years. In 1924 he became a teaching assistant at Oxford, and then in 1925 a fellow, a post he would hold until 1954. During much of this period, Lewis cohabitated with Jane King Moore (1872–1951), an attractive Irish woman 27 years his senior and the mother of his slain war comrade Paddy Moore, with whom he had a mutual pact of family care should only one of them survive combat.⁶ It was also during this same time that Lewis began to seriously rediscover the Christian faith, particularly through the works of Scottish novelist George MacDonald (1824–1905) and British philosopher G.K. Chesterton (1874–1936).

Finally, in 1931 at age 32, Lewis recorded that he had become a believer again, unlikely enough while on a holiday trip to the zoo. He described the experience as being neither thoughtful nor emotional, but rather like awaking from a deep sleep.⁷ Also noteworthy is that, once again in his life, a close encounter with the animal kingdom seems to have triggered a permanent, inner response from him. In 1936, he published his first masterpiece, *The Allegory of Love*, still considered by many to be the finest critical study of mediaeval romantic poetry.

Initially, the Second World War had the understandable, stifling impact on Lewis of a recurring nightmare. *The Problem of Pain* (1940) was published as the Blitz and Battle of Britain were ramping up. Pulling himself together, between 1942 and 1945 Lewis delivered a series of famed radio broadcasts designed as British morale boosters from a spiritual standpoint. From the accounts of those listening in, these proved to be a resounding success and led to the immediate publication of now classic works such as *The Screwtape Letters* (1942) and *Mere Christianity* (1943–1945).

Between 1944 and 1945 the *Guardian* published installments for *The Great Divorce*, Lewis' imaginative theological novel in which the worldly allure of any and all human evil is repudiated once and for all. The story cleverly reintroduces the old, unpopular concept that, in the final analysis, all of us freely choose whether to go to Heaven or Hell, and in fact, Lewis says, many would prefer Hell but do not know it until fully understanding what both places are really like.⁸ The book, despite its revered status among true Lewisphiles, has never made it to the best-seller lists, although a motion picture is currently rumored to be in the works. This development is probably more the result of the blockbuster *Narnia* children's series, which Lewis turned to writing after the war along with additional religious works and a unique, confessional autobiography of his early life, *Surprised by Joy*, published in 1955. As things transpired, a man who married only late in life and never had children turned out to be his generation's greatest author of children's fantasy fiction, by drawing upon his own broad childhood experiences and enthusiastic love for the genre.

With the 1950s came more unexpected, dramatic changes for Lewis. In 1954 (after 30 years), he left Oxford for an academic promotion always denied him by his own alma mater and spent the remainder of his professional career at Cambridge University. Then, in 1956, defying everything that his closest friends thought they knew about him, Lewis married Joy Davidman (1915–

1960)—a Jewish American poet and divorcee with two sons, a former atheist, former member of the Communist Party, and 17 years his junior—who initiated contact with him through fan mail on behalf of her children in 1950.[9] To nearly everyone's astonishment, a warm friendship soon blossomed into the kind of romantic love that Lewis himself had written so eloquently about decades before. Happiness was fleeting, however, and Davidman soon afterwards becoming terminally ill from cancer and died in 1960.

In response to the tragedy, Lewis wrote (under a pseudonym) *A Grief Observed*, which well-meaning friends unwittingly recommended to him for reading comfort. Davidman's passing left a devastating mark on Lewis similar to the one he experienced during childhood from his mother's early death from the very same disease. Three years later, he died from heart failure on November 22, 1963, approximately one hour before President Kennedy was assassinated the same day, hence his passing was nearly unremarked by the press. In November 2013, on the 50th anniversary of his passing, a long overdue memorial to his name was placed in the Poet's Corner of Westminster Abbey. Despite his conservative orthodox reputation, Lewis' writings have exerted an enormous influence on liberal Christians and nonconformists, as well as non–Christians worldwide. The ongoing, burgeoning legacy of his children's fiction speaks for itself.

Less frequently remarked upon is that Lewis was a lifelong dog owner and enthusiast. He was also an open opponent of vivisection and animal cruelty long before either became fashionable causes. Beginning with his adopted childhood namesake Jacksie and ending with his boxer breed and late-life sidekick, Ricky, Lewis seems to have considered canine companionship a necessary and desirable part of life. All in all, there were at least eight documented dogs (and probably more) that he owned or was responsible for, not the least of which was the devilish Bruce, a creature that he expressly neither cared for (nor mourned after its death) but put up with for nearly 15 years (including the World War II years) mainly for the sake of his friend Jane King Moore and, by extension, the oath made to his fallen war comrade Paddy Moore.

Suzie, the only female dog Lewis is known to have owned, was his pet during the happy years with Joy Davidman. Papworth was another dog owned by Lewis during the crucial period of the 1920s and 1930s when he was gradually converting back to Christianity. Papworth accompanied Lewis' group on that decisive trip to the zoo in 1931. During his freewheeling school days, Lewis' intermittent companion was the independent-minded, dog-hating canine Tim, whom he later described as "the most undisciplined, unaccomplished, and dissipated-looking creature that ever went on four legs."[10] These are but a few examples. An excellent, more recent, summary of Lewis' extensive associations with domesticated canines recorded to date can be found in Bruce R. Johnson's engaging article, "All My Dogs Before Me."[11] In perusing these complex relationships, one cannot help but to notice that the many different philosophical and spiritual phases of Lewis' eventful life often corresponded chronologically to the type of dog personality he liked to simultaneously keep around his own person as a pet.

Lewis was hardly the first thinker to speculate on the nature of animal spirituality, the debate going back to ancient times. As one might expect, however, the fascination of Lewis with dogs spilled over into his serious writing, most notably in *The Great Divorce*. Here, as busloads of ghostly pilgrims to the heavenly kingdom find themselves becoming quickly disillusioned with paradise, one of them exclaims, rather ironically, "I didn't come here to be treated like a dog."[12] By contrast, the climax of the story approaches after the narrator finally realizes he is a ghost himself, being led by Lewis' literary hero George MacDonald as a kind of Beatrice-like figure out of Dante's *Commedia*. Beholding an unknown saintly resident of Heaven surrounded by dogs and other animals (see header quote), the startled narrator—at first thinking Heaven has a zoo similar to the one leading to Lewis' real-life conversion—is informed by MacDonald that divine salvation reaches these creatures through their previous earthly connections with the saint. As the great epiphany sinks in, the narrator is overwhelmed with the majestic morning sounds of paradise, which build with intensity and are similar to those often found in biblical apocalyptic literature, including the "music of hounds.[13] On the last page, the narrator awakens to find that he has dreamed the entire episode, but he also finds dark reality at that particular moment in Great Britain offers him only the blaring alarm sound of wartime air-raid sirens.

The perusal of Lewis' other major works leaves a surprisingly consistent impression of his opinions in regard to animal (including dog) spirituality, if such a phrase is appropriate. The comparatively early *Problem of Pain* includes an entire chapter on "Animal Pain" in which Lewis lays out the same idea later expressed in *The Great Divorce*, namely that "it seems to me possible that certain animals may have an immortality, not in themselves, but in the immortality of their masters.... In other words, the man will know his dog: the dog will know its master and, in knowing him, will *be* itself." Elaborating further, Lewis explains: "If a good sheepdog seems 'almost human' that is because a good shepherd has made it so."[14] Elsewhere in the same book, this mutuality of spiritual interest between superior man and inferior beast is consistently maintained: "The association of man and dog is primarily for the man's sake.... Yet at the same time, the dog's interests are not sacrificed to the man's."[15]

A few years later, in *Mere Christianity*, Lewis strikes the same note: "We treat our dogs as if they were 'almost human': that is why they really become 'almost human' in the end."[16] In conclusion, he emphasizes the same point that would be reiterated soon afterwards in *The Great Divorce*: "I think I can see how the higher animals are in a sense drawn into Man when he loves them and makes them (as he does) much more nearly human than they would otherwise be."[17] Thus the animal "theology" of Lewis maintains that the humane, compassionate treatment of any higher being—man, beast, or otherwise—has the potential to transform that creature into a more spiritual one. In essence, beast relies on man much the same way that man relies on God. The argument almost has an evolutionary ring to it, and in fact Lewis adopted the terminology of Darwin (see Chapter 11) on more than one occasion for purposes of religious discussion.

Given this steady, unchanging position of Lewis with respect to the animal kingdom, further interpretation almost becomes superfluous; and yet since he, like most great religious writers, is routinely cited by all sides in various debates, a few additional comments seem appropriate at this point. Like Saint Francis of Assisi (see Chapter 8), he views divine love as a great invisible force of natural unification. As human beings, in the worldview of C.S. Lewis, we could not separate ourselves (or our souls) from these creatures even if we wanted or tried to; or if we did, we would cease to be legitimately human as a result. Opponents of Lewis on this subject personally familiar with his rampant (and self-acknowledged) arachnophobia, were known to tease him about becoming friends with insects. To this suggestion, however, he would seriously reply that insects and other lower life forms were not part of the higher chain of being. Readers will notice that insects are not part of the vast menagerie surrounding the saintly woman in Heaven from *The Great Divorce*. An insect, say, could never bond with a human being in the same manner as a dog, cat, horse, or even a bird.[18] Thus, higher animals such as canines, according to Lewis, may well have genuine spirituality through their intimate relationships with humankind. In effect, these creatures not only have natural rights in the political sense as first asserted by Rousseau during the 18th century (see Chapter 10), they also are capable of having souls in the religious sense, via their prolonged, humane contact with mankind.[19]

Writing today about a highly speculative concept such as animal spirituality may seem extravagant until one takes any passing notice of contemporary news media. On April 15, 2013, *Time* magazine published a widely discussed feature article by Jeffrey Kluger titled "The Mystery of Animal Grief" dealing specifically with the long-debated question of whether animals emotionally mourn the deaths of other animals or humans. The article focuses in particular on the popular new book by Barbara J. King, *How Animals Grieve* (University of Chicago Press, 2013), which takes a firm positive position on the issue. These are topics which would have been near and dear to the heart of C.S. Lewis. Perhaps the thing most interesting about these current materials is the limited or zero reference to past commentators on the same subject matter, beginning with the ancient observations of writers such as Pliny and Plutarch (see Chapters 3 and 4). One wonders if old books or classic works of literature have anymore perceived relevance to modern readers in this regard. King's engaging study does cite the famous non–Western example of the Japanese Akita dog Hatchikō (1923–1935), who for an entire decade returned daily to the same Tokyo suburban train station, to wait for his dead master to return. In prewar Japan, the dog became a beloved symbol of fidelity. Another very similar example of canine loyalty in the Western world occurred very soon afterwards with the ubiquitous Italian street dog known as Fido (1941–1958), whose adoptive Tuscan owner was killed while working at a factory during a 1943 Allied air raid. For the next 15 years, Fido waited every day in vain at the same bus stop for his master's return. Like Hatchikō, upon his own death Fido was celebrated as an Italian national icon, and dogs all over the world to this day bear his honorary name.

For those readers still requiring more of the here and now for true resonance, one only need to turn on the evening news. On May 20, 2013, after a monstrous cyclone flattened the environs of Moore, Oklahoma, a small black puppy named Susie was rescued amid the wreckage, frightened but standing over the body of a dead human. Two days later, she was reunited with her owner, who had also survived the devastation and who then directed that incoming money donations be given to the Central Oklahoma Humane Society.[20] Other similar news stories of close human-canine emotional bonds in connection with the same disaster widely circulated in the aftermath of the event.

More permanent in the short-memory public consciousness than any fleeting news reports have been spectacular late 20th and early 21st century breakthroughs in motion picture special effects that allow for fantastical animal depictions to become more vividly imaginative than ever. Leaving aside the heavy-handed 1989 animated hit *All Dogs Go to Heaven* (a title Lewis would have surely objected to), the big screen adaptation of the classic *Narnia* series over the last decade has introduced a whole new generation of fans to the world of talking, human-like animals, a concept Walt Disney first took to the bank several generations ago but with far less advanced technology. It was partly for this reason that Lewis himself never wished his books to be made into movies (fearing to see his serious subject matter become cartoonish and benign). But had he lived to see what became possible after the 1960s, there is a good chance that he may have changed his mind.

First came *The Chronicles of Narnia: The Lion, the Witch, and the*

Wardrobe (2005); then, based on the resounding success of that production, followed *Prince Caspian* (2008) and *The Voyage of the Dawn Treader* (2010), all based on children's books written by Lewis between 1949 and 1954. Interestingly, the movies were made in no small part because of the huge profits grossed by J.K. Rowling's *Harry Potter* book and film franchise, which itself had been greatly inspired by Lewis' *Narnia* tales. Regarding canines (on film at least), the most prominent representatives of Lewis' Talking Animals are hostile wolves, most memorably the character of Maugrim (voiced by film star Michael Madsen), chief of the secret police for the evil White Witch (Tilda Swinton), and his presumptive second-in-command, Vardan (Jim May).[21]

Vestiges of Lewis' well-known love for domesticated dogs can be found in many of the documentaries that have been made on his life and work, as well as the biographical dramatization *Shadowlands*, made for stage (1985), television (1989), and film (1993), the last directed by Richard Attenborough and starring Anthony Hopkins and Debra Winger.[22] Lewis' canine-derived nickname, "Jack," is prominently featured in all of these works, and the final frames of *Shadowlands* feature a dog accompanying the characters as a symbol of future hope and salvation.

Arguably the most stunning (if not eccentric) film in recent years, however, involving human-like canine (or canine-like human) behavior did not derive from a C.S. Lewis book, but rather from a work almost surely influencing Lewis before he began to write *The Chronicles of Narnia*. The Miramax release of *Dean Spanley* (2008), directed by New Zealander Toa Fraser with an incredibly tongue-in-cheek screenplay by Alan Sharp and starring an all-star British cast including Sam Neill, Peter O'Toole, Jeremy Northam, Bryan Brown, and Judy Parfitt, delves into the surreal universe of dog reincarnation as a human being. The movie was based on the 1936 comic fantasy masterwork *My Talks with Dean Spanley* by Irish novelist Lord Dunsbay, aka Edward Plunkett (1878–1957), an older contemporary of Lewis, avid hunter, and World War I veteran.

At a time during the mid–1930s when Lewis was producing his great opus on mediaeval romantic poetry, the limelight-loving Plunkett was concocting a popular fictional (?) tale of a Welsh spaniel whose soul transmigrates to the body of an English village clergyman, much to the growing stunned astonishment (and spiritual enlightenment) of those around him. As readers might expect, Plunkett's dog acquires a very eloquent human voice upon its subsequent habitation of a human body. We would give a pretty penny to know exactly where and how Plunkett came up with this entertaining conceit, and so would have Lewis, we suspect. In any event, within a decade, Lewis' *The Great Divorce* had appeared in print, and soon afterwards the *Chronicles of Narnia*.

As previously noted, the final page of *The Great Divorce* reveals that the narrator has been merely dreaming but that harsh reality is far worse: the waking author falls out of his chair at the sound of air-raid sirens, and tablecloth and books from his table ("blocks of light" in the dream) fall about his disoriented person.[23] One is reminded of the wartime comment by Lewis from *Mere Christianity*—immediately following reassertion of his belief in the connection between animal and human immortality—to the effect that life itself is a nightmare from which we will all one day awaken.[24] This clearly represented Lewis' own way of coping with unpleasant reality and is not one to be lightly dismissed by any open-minded rational standard. He appears to have been consistent in this view throughout his adult life. By 1960, as Lewis was experiencing painful tragedy in the form of his wife's terminal illness, another famed but quite different kind of writer, this one on the North American continent, was trying to come to grips late in life with what he perceived as a society once more beginning to morally unhinge itself. Like C.S. Lewis, John Steinbeck was a lifelong dog-lover. But unlike Lewis, Steinbeck felt a need to take to the highway—and with canine companion in tow.

19

A Man and His Dog

> *In establishing contact with strange people, Charley is my ambassador. I release him, and he drifts toward the objective, or rather to whatever the objective may be preparing for dinner. I retrieve him so that he will not be a nuisance to my neighbors—et voila! A child can do the same thing, but a dog is better.*—John Steinbeck, *Travels with Charley*, 20th century[1]

On the surface, it might be easily asserted that C.S. Lewis and John Ernst Steinbeck, Jr. (1902–1968) had very little in common either as writers or as individuals. Closer inspection, however, reveals a number of surprising commonalities separate and apart from similar generational ties. For one, both shared a part–Irish cultural heritage and the peculiarly Irish love of storytelling with the occasional poetic lie tossed in for effect. Both were raised Episcopalian, and both fell away from the faith (Steinbeck more permanently). Both came from middle class homes with parents who instilled an early love of books and fully supported their sons' youthful talents. Both men later experienced warfare firsthand, were wounded, and had no illusions about its realities, yet neither was a pacifist in any sense of the word. Both hated fascism and feared its spread. Both writers first achieved literary renown—Lewis as a scholar and Steinbeck as a novelist—during the 1930s as the world slid into prolonged global conflict. Last but certainly not least, both men craved canine companionship. It would therefore seem appropriate at this point to address Steinbeck's underrated late masterpiece, *Travels with Charley: In Search of America* (1962), a semi-fictional travelogue that probably contains more poetic truth within its carefully crafted pages than many of the most scrupulously annotated documentaries or personal diaries.

Steinbeck was born and reared in Salinas, California, son of a German-American father and an Irish-American mother, coming of age amidst one of the world's most fertile agricultural regions, the north central coast area surrounding Monterey Bay. Barely missing World War I because of his youth,

Steinbeck entered Stanford University with great promise but left after five years without taking a degree, discovering in the process that he was incapable of studying uninteresting assigned subject matter when there was so much else of true interest around him to see, do, and, above all, write about. In 1925, like fellow-Californian Jack London before him, Steinbeck hit the road and really never stopped traveling for the remainder of his life.

Like many others of his generation, he admired the lean, visceral, and journalistic writing style of Ernest Hemingway (1899–1961); later he was inspired by the bold experimentation and oblique narratives of William Faulkner (1897–1962).[2] During the decade of 1929–1939 Steinbeck produced a string of novels that would rightfully secure his literary reputation for all time, including (but not limited to) *The Red Pony* (1933), *Tortilla Flat* (1935), and the tremendous "Dust Bowl Trilogy" of *In Dubious Battle* (1936), *Of Mice and Men* (1937), and *The Grapes of Wrath* (1939). This last work, aside from becoming a permanent symbol of depression-era economic struggle in America, was awarded a Pulitzer Prize and promptly made into a classic 1940 film starring Henry Fonda, a movie that won another bevy of awards, including an Oscar for director John Ford.

By the time World War II arrived, Steinbeck had begun a long career in Hollywood, with screen credits for his best-known titles in addition to collaboration with some of the industry's most glamorous producers, directors and actors. Soon, however, despite having achieved status as America's arguably most famous writer, restlessness got the better of Steinbeck once again, and at age 41 he went off to war in Europe, first as a news correspondent, then as a commando fighter. After getting himself wounded and shell-shocked, Steinbeck then returned home to resume doing what he had always done best: write forcefully about the exciting things that he had experienced firsthand.

Following two failed marriages caused in no small part by his incurable wanderlust, Steinbeck married a Texan divorcee Elaine Anderson, in 1950, a marriage that proved (within limits) to be the durable spousal relationship previously eluding the novelist had always sought.[3] In 1952, his acknowledged masterpiece was published, the novel *East of Eden*, which was soon thereafter turned into a 1955 screen debut vehicle for James Dean. In spite of this success, however, Steinbeck's leftist politics and cordial relations with Communist Party members made him a lightning rod for criticism during the postwar era. He was probably spared condemnation (if not more outright harassment) because of his admirable war record combined with a preeminent cultural stature.

With the coming of the late 1950s and the end of the Eisenhower era, Steinbeck began to experience the multiple health problems that would eventually kill him less than a decade later. He then decided it was time for yet another road trip. The end result was *Travels with Charley*, published in 1962 just as Steinbeck was being awarded the Nobel Prize for literature. Immediately prior to this achievement, his short novel *Winter of Our Discontent* (1961) had been mostly pilloried by critics and ignored by the reading public because it dared to cast an unfavorable light on American moral values, or lack thereof. During the early years of Camelot, now that the country supposedly had all of the answers to the problems of the postwar world, America no longer wanted to hear to kind of introspective self-criticism that Steinbeck was offering up. The public had probably been hoping more for a nostalgic redux a la *Grapes of Wrath* and *East of Eden*.[4] Steinbeck responded to this criticism by never publishing another novel, although he continued to work on a King Arthur-themed project up until his death.

Then came the Vietnam War and yet more controversy. With his younger son serving in the military, and through his friendship with war hawk Lyndon B. Johnson (from whom he had recently received the Presidential Medal of Freedom), Steinbeck was dispatched to South Vietnam in 1967 as an observer and reported back, not too surprisingly, in hearty praise of the troops and the cause for which they were fighting. War protestors were outraged. Because of close ties with family and friends, Steinbeck now found himself among the unfortunate group of old New Deal liberals caught up in defending one of the most unpopular wars in American history. A year later, in 1968, he succumbed to heart failure, having lived to see the bloody Tet Offensive forever swing the majority of public opinion against U.S. military engagement in Southeast Asia.

Published six years before Steinbeck's death, *Travels with Charley* gives an account of the author's grand, counterclockwise tour of the lower continental United States during late 1960, shortly after John F. Kennedy and Richard M. Nixon had been nominated for president by their respective political parties. This would include a rest stop in the city of Chicago that would play such a crucial role in Kennedy's November general election victory with considerable help from fellow Irish Catholic Democrat Mayor Richard J. Daley.[5] In recent years, Steinbeck's accuracy regarding places and events has been challenged by a host of critics, including some members of his own family, who all missed the point of the entire exercise, as Steinbeck no doubt knew they would at the time. As for this commentator (four years old in 1960), I can attest that, as Steinbeck and Charley passed within a few miles of my family's Michiana farm that season (near the Indiana Toll Road), the area was described by the novelist in the book with dead-on topographical accuracy and dispassionate insight.[6]

To make the long journey, Steinbeck purchased a pickup truck and specially equipped camping vehicle that he proudly dubbed *Rocinante* (after Don Quixote's broken down old horse). And of course he took his beloved French poodle, Charley (1950–1961), or, more properly, Charles le Chien (Charles the Dog), born in suburban Paris around the same time that the novelist was marrying his third wife. According to Steinbeck's detailed account, Charley was named after his own uncle, responded to commands in both English and French (the latter more quickly), was a shrewd judge of human character, a good therapy dog, a good mind reader, prone to doggie dreams, and "a born diplomat" who "prefers negotiating to fighting, and properly so, since he is very bad at fighting."[7] Throughout the trip, Steinbeck has imaginary conversations with Charley, or perhaps not so imaginary, since the dog, according to Steinbeck usually listens attentively to the writer's every utterance and responds readily with expressive looks and body language. Thus equipped, a quixotic Steinbeck set out with *Rocinante* and Charley (as a kind of Sancho Panza sidekick) to explore a postwar America that he felt a deep personal need to reconnect with.

Despite continuing perceptions that by then his powers as a writer had diminished, never was the great novelist's acerbic wit and eye for detail any sharper. At this point in history, he was probably America's most famous and celebrated man of letters, one soon to win the Nobel Prize. But he noted that throughout his journeys, absolutely no one recognized him or made any comment or even showed the slightest curiosity regarding the name *Rocinante* inscribed on his camper.[8] To repeat, this was in 1960. He complains about the media and "all the polls and opinion posts, with newspapers more opinion than news so that we no longer know one from the other."[9] Steinbeck saves his sharpest barbs, however (and surprisingly enough), for recreational hunters, prefacing his comments with acknowledgment of political incorrectness, despite the fact that he was a hunter in his youth and was packing several firearms for the trip, including a scoped rifle.

Tearing into the incompetent sportsmen of Maine for several pages, he protests that "I have nothing against the killing of animals. Something has to kill them, I suppose." The novelist, former hunter, and wounded war veteran then qualifies his criticism: "I know there are any number of good and efficient hunters who know what they are doing; but many more are overweight gentlemen, primed with whiskey and armed with high-powered rifles." He might as well have been writing about today. Steinbeck concludes: "Somehow the hunting process has to do with masculinity, but I don't know quite how."[10]

He softens his stance somewhat in the state of Wisconsin when he encounters a mass of wild turkeys ("a reservoir for Thanksgiving") while admiring the vast natural beauty and agricultural bounty of the region.[11]

When confronted with two curious but nonthreatening coyotes along Route 66 in the Mojave Desert that do not seem to upset Charley from inside the camper, he cannot bring himself to shoot them. Instead he leaves dog food behind.[12] By this time during his trek across the United States, Steinbeck had developed more respect for canines than for many of his fellow countrymen, not unlike Ibn al-Marzubān from 10 centuries earlier (see Chapter 6). He recalls the recent complaints of a highly respected journalist friend who had made similar exploratory rounds: "I haven't seen anything but cowardice and expediency. This used to be a nation of giants. Where have they gone?"[13] Steinbeck had set out in search of the real America, but in the end he became disillusioned with what he found.

The most painful moments come during the second half of the trip after reaching the Pacific coast. Charley's health begins to suffer and competent veterinarians are hard to find. Upon reaching the Golden State, Steinbeck laments, "I find it difficult to write about my native place, northern California."[14] A Monterey County homecoming to his mostly Republican family was marked by bitter, knock-down, drag-out political arguments with his sisters.[15] Then came Texas, a state where John F. Kennedy would be assassinated three years later. Again there were unpleasant family obligations: "Even if I wanted to avoid Texas I could not, for I am wived in Texas and mother-in-lawed and uncled and aunted and cousined within an inch of my life."[16] Texas turned out to be not so bad, however, with a compassionate veterinarian in Amarillo able to help to ease Charley's escalating health problems.[17] The remainder of the journey below the Mason-Dixon line was not so pleasant, and Steinbeck admitted, "I faced the South with dread."[18] His worst fears were confirmed in New Orleans, a city he loved, which in late 1960 had become a center of activity for the infamous "Cheerleaders"—a highly organized group of middle-aged white women gathering daily to shout vile, unprintable obscenities at black (and some white) children as they bravely attended recently integrated public schools.[19] A demoralized Steinbeck described the event as "a kind of frightening witches' Sabbath" leaving him shaken to the very core of his being.[20] After that, he rushed back home to the friendly confines of the Northeast. Upon finally returning to New York City, he admittedly sobbed in relief, begging amused or pitying traffic cops to allow him more hurried passage through detoured streets.

In the final analysis, Steinbeck had little uplifting or encouraging to report as a result of his cross-country U.S. travels. All of the best anecdotes, and everything most positive, seems to flow from his routine encounters with the animal kingdom and his dog, Charley, in particular. In short, Charley comes across as much smarter and much more compassionate than most of Steinbeck's fellow Americans. Early in the book, with respect to Charley, the novelist exclaims, "What strength of character, what a friend!"[21] Towards the final pages, he pays further tribute to his canine companion as a creature not burdened by irrelevant or irrational concerns. Steinbeck reflects that "he [Charley] doesn't even know about race, nor is he concerned with his sisters' marriage." As for any other comparison to the intelligence of mankind, the verdict of the author is loud and clear: "I've seen a look in dogs' eyes, a quickly vanishing look of amazed contempt, and I am convinced that basically dogs think humans are nuts."[22]

Sprinkled among these random musings are a continuing series of canine adventures and interludes. Alluding to the Roman legend of Romulus, Remus, and the she-wolf that nursed them (see Chapter 4), Steinbeck reflects on how humans raised by wolves are reportedly more animal-like, while dogs raised by humans (such as Charley) almost become human, echoing the animal theology of C.S. Lewis (see Chapter 18).[23] At one point (in the Dakotas) the novelist crosses paths with a traveling actor accompanied by a performing dog described as a "partner" who "[s]teals the show when he feels like it."[24] One is reminded of the great theater acting dogs of the past, from ancient times to those more recent, in particular another poodle which so greatly aggravated the delicate stage sensibilities of Johann Wolfgang von Goethe (see Chapter 11).

In Montana, Steinbeck cannot help but to repeat that one of his older writing acquaintances had been a cavalry officer in the brutal military campaign against Chief Joseph during the 19th century, noting that the dogs belonging to the Native Americans opted to stand by them loyally to the end as they were being wiped out.[25] Against this backdrop of inspirational canine virtues, some to be readily found in wolves and coyotes of the wild, Steinbeck draws a mostly dark portrait of American citizenry at the conclusion of the Eisenhower presidency, one that was spiritually void, rife with bigotry, pettiness, shrill opinions, and willful ignorance.

Although its primary focal point with respect to the animal kingdom is horses rather than dogs, it would be remiss not to mention, at least in passing, Steinbeck's classic early novella from the 1930s, *The Red Pony*.[26] This surely semi-autobiographical work tells the coming of age story of its young California-born-and-raised boy hero Jody and delves into the timeless mysteries of life, death, and rebirth—lessons learned through the boy's relationships with farm animals. As in *Travels with Charley*, mortality and tragedy loom everywhere in *The Red Pony*, but somehow the cycle of existence continues forward and even occasionally thrives beyond all expectations.

Of secondary but noteworthy interest in Steinbeck's unflinching tale of rural childhood awareness is Jody's insensitive interactions with Doubletree Mutt and Smasher, two working ranch dogs whom he treats badly and whose solid, faithful virtues he completely underappreciates. This human ingratitude towards useful farm animals becomes symbolic of Jody's immature state of mind at the beginning of the story—a mindset that will change quite profoundly by the end. It may well have been that Steinbeck's fawning indulgences towards Charley many decades later was a kind a compensation for the somewhat less fortunate dogs he probably knew as a child.

Fittingly, *The Red Pony* was made into a worthy 1949 feature film by director Lewis Milestone, the movie boasted a dynamic soundtrack written by Aaron Copland, and starred a distinguished cast led by Robert Mitchum and Myrna Loy. In 1973, a television remake starred an aging Henry Fonda and Maureen O'Hara and won a Peabody Award; composer Jerry Goldsmith won an Emmy for his soundtrack. According to a recent note in Wikipedia, President Barack Obama in 2010 raised some eyebrows by purchasing a copy of *The Red Pony* for his daughters while in St. Petersburg, Florida.[27] Steinbeck would have been proud.

Unmentioned thus far in this study is the immeasurably vast quantity of canine photographic art produced over the last two centuries, a popular genre from almost the moment photography was invented. No attempt here will be made to categorize or classify this boundless body of material, although as good a place as any to begin (regarding domesticated dogs, at least) is the 160-page 2007 coffee table book *These Were Our Dogs*, by Libby Hall, or perhaps the 128-page *The Best Dog in the World* (2007) by Donna Long. Both survey vintage photographic images from many different periods and places around the globe. With respect to 20th century American writers, any naysayer or skeptic doubting whether Steinbeck actually owned a dog named Charley or whether reciprocal affection between dog and master was real need only glance at the cover photo for the 1980 Penguin Modern classics edition, clearly depicting both in a pose of mutual admiration. Today, Charley's grave may be found on the grounds of Steinbeck's Pacific Grove cottage in Monterey County.

Steinbeck's American contemporary writing colleagues also enjoyed being photographed with dogs. Ernest Hemingway's staged and unstaged poses with dogs are collector's items. Perhaps the most famous is with Negrita, one his four Cuban-born canine associates. Meanwhile, in 1947, Steinbeck's favorite American contemporary, William Faulkner, pulled off what is arguably the best-known human-canine photo op in literary history when he posed at his backwater Mississippi home for Henri Cartier-Bresson with two pet terriers. One dog stretches his hind legs on cue in the opposite direction that Faulkner stretches his right arm that same instant and the other dog stands attentively on guard between them.[28] This list, of course, could go on forever merely with respect to modern writers of domestic fiction. Suffice it here to say that Steinbeck belonged to a milieu in which relationships between humans and dogs seemed to be growing closer and more intimate than ever before in history.

As many a perceptive critic from the past has noted, some of the most profound moments in *Travels with Charley* occur when Steinbeck records "conversations" with his dog. Anyone who has ever been a dog owner will immediately recognize what is going on in these passages. At first, Charley simply "listens" to Steinbeck's comments, rants, and complaints. Then, somehow, Charley transforms into an active participant, communicating with Steinbeck through his eyes and body language, though not actually speaking in the manner of, say, Toto in the later *Oz* books by L. Frank Baum (see Chapter 13). *Travels* is, after all, supposed to be nonfiction. Instead the novelist transcribes his own interpretation of Charley's doggie language, based on the not-too-unreasonable assumption that Charley understands what he is talking about, or at least thinking and feeling in general terms. In a sense, Charley was the ultimate sounding board, one helping a great novelist to answer his own pressing philosophical questions about modern life. We suspect that this is a very old conversation between humans and canines, ongoing since mankind first domesticated wild wolves possibly as long as 100,000 years ago. Nor is it likely to end any time soon. People may cease to speak to one another, but people and dogs, never. Curiously enough, around the same time Steinbeck's "imaginary" and soon-to-be best-selling conversations with a dog were being recorded, an unhappy autistic teenage girl, one destined to later change the way in which most of us think about communication between humans and animals, was entering a New Hampshire private school for gifted special needs children. Like many of the great scientific minds preceding her in this field, Temple Grandin was, among other things, an animal enthusiast, dogs included.

20
Last Word in Social Beings

Through all the years dogs have been living with humans they've developed a lot of ability to read people, to know what people are thinking and what they're likely to do.—Temple Grandin, *Animals in Translation*, 21st century[1]

You have to know your dog, and you have to know your dog as an individual, not just as a member of a particular breed.—Temple Grandin, *Animals Make Us Human*, 21st century[2]

During the final chapter of John Steinbeck's *Travels with Charley*, after the novelist is traumatized by several close encounters with hardcore racism in the South, he decides that his long road trip is over and begins to make a beeline for home and New York City. As he races northward, Steinbeck ponders "how can you explain that Charley knew it was over too?"[3] Apparently his beloved pooch was somehow suddenly aware that his master had been deeply troubled by recent events and was now in the home stretch of what had been, up until that point, a leisurely journey. Charley fully cooperates in facilitating a fast and seamless return leg in any manner that it was in his power as a dog to do. Somehow, he had picked up on Steinbeck's urgency and changed his own behavior accordingly.

Experienced dog handlers know perfectly well that phenomena like these occur all of the time, but those less fond of canines might attribute them to the overly vivid imaginations of the owners. During the late 20th century, after Steinbeck's death in 1968, the scientific community would begin to study such things in earnest, and the results consistently proved in favor of domesticated dogs being capable of fantastically quick studies of human behavior, moods, and language. This situation belied the skepticism that denied animals possess such talents. It is to the extraordinary life and work of one of these pioneering figures in the study of animal behavior that we now turn our full attention.

It must be viewed as somewhat of a paradox that the most influential architectural designer of modern slaughterhouse facilities is also one of the leading activists against animal cruelty, as well as a prominent spokesperson in bettering public understanding of human autism. Then again, like Albert Schweitzer before her (see Chapter 17), Temple Grandin (b. 1947) is no ordinary individual; she is a person of many accomplished parts. A Bostonian by birth, Grandin was diagnosed with autism—at least to the extent that the condition was then understood—before the age of three.[4] She did not speak until the age of four.

Fortunately for her (and for us), her mother, Eustacia, refused to accept flawed conventional medical opinions of the time and worked tirelessly to give her handicapped daughter the semblance of a normal life. She also had a supportive maternal aunt, Ann Brecheen, living on an Arizona cattle ranch, who later proved pivotal in her development. Nonetheless, by the time Grandin reached regular school age, she had been labeled "retarded"—to use the politically and factually incorrect term common to that era—by most of her uncomprehending teachers and classmates. As time would prove, however, she was not retarded—quite the contrary, in fact. Even at this early, unhappy stage, there were signs of future greatness. Arts, crafts, and draftsmanship came effortlessly to her, a seeming disconnect that would continue to startle dismissive critics right up through the beginning of her professional career.

After being thrown out of high school for retaliating against bullies, Grandin was enrolled by her mother as a freshman boarding student in the famed Hampshire Country School, then known as the Mountain Country School of Rindge, New Hampshire. It was here that she encountered her first, and surely most important, academic mentor, William Carlock, a nonaccredited science teacher with a NASA background who, for whatever reason, took a keen interest in the young Grandin and her unusual intellectual abilities, helped her turn her grades around, and acted as her trusted guidance counselor for the remainder of his life. She graduated from high school in 1966 (giving a commencement speech), then earned a psychology degree from nearby Franklin Pierce College in 1970. Twenty years prior to this, hardly anyone would have imagined, let alone predicted, such achievements, and yet this was only a prelude of things yet to come.

During the summer of 1965, before her senior year in high school, Grandin stayed on her aunt's Arizona cattle ranch and unknowingly first came into prolonged contact with her future livelihood.[5] The first thing there that engaged her attention was an improvised squeeze chute, a primitive but humane device used to calm down nervous livestock by applying gentle pressure to their restrained bodies. Grandin then insisted that her hesitant aunt allow the machine to be used on herself and was more than pleased with the result. Upon returning to New Hampshire for her senior year, she constructed a similar device for personal use, much to the consternation of other students and school administrators, the latter condemning the practice as perverse.

Undeterred, and once again with Carlock's help, she turned the human squeeze machine into a legitimized college science project. After undergraduate studies, she moved back to Arizona to work on her master's degree, switching from psychology to animal science after more exposure to her aunt's cattle ranch and the bustling meatpacking industry where she felt most at home.[6] She got a job manning nearby feedlot chutes in 1971, and in 1972 her first livestock article was published. Grandin had simply walked up to the managing editor during a rodeo and asked if she could submit a piece. Thus began a long and prolific writing career. That same year Grandin designed her first cattle chute, and in 1973 she was admitted access to the local Swift processing plant, where she was immediately invited by the manager to stun (i.e., kill) some cattle, possibly as a test of nerve. Not only did she pass with flying colors, Grandin later described the event in quasi-religious terms, comparing the slaughtering act to animal sacrifices practiced by ancient cultures.

In 1974, Grandin designed her famous "Stairway to Heaven" cattle chute for Swift, innovative in its overarching concern for the humane treatment of livestock right up to and through the point of death.[7] Crucially, the new approach proved profitable for investors, as calm animals directly translated into more efficiency and less waste. In 1975, Grandin received her master's degree from Arizona State University, by which time her career as a facility designer was off and running with hardly a pause ever since. Later she declared that "animals saved me."[8]

The 1980s and 1990s also proved to be fruitful for Grandin. While earning her doctoral degree at the University of Illinois at Urbana-Champaign, she designed her first fully integrated masterpiece in 1983, the John Wayne Red River Feedlot near Phoenix. It is now estimated that at least one-third of existing cattle processing facilities worldwide have been influenced by her work. Soon afterwards, in 1986, her memoir, *Emergence: Labeled Autistic*, was well-received, followed by *Thinking in Pictures: My Life with Autism* in 1995. That same year, the Oliver Sacks collection, *An Anthropologist on Mars*, featured Grandin as the last of its seven case studies, taking its title from one of her own quotations. In 1990, she was awarded a professorship at Colorado State University. She has since become a regular speaker for the Autism Society of America, as well as a leading advocate against all forms of animal cruelty.

Grandin is not a vegetarian and is particularly critical of vegan lifestyles as being unhealthy.[9] Instead, Grandin is a proponent of symbiosis, or "a mutually beneficial relationship," between living things.[10] Like Darwin before her (see Chapter 11), she controversially believes in the reality of animal emotions, and like C.S. Lewis (see Chapter 18), even more controversially, in animal spirituality.[11] A lover of dogs since early childhood, her frequently unusual observations and often unorthodox advice are constantly being sought out, despite her official reputation as an industry livestock expert. Fully cognizant of evolutionary law, she is opposed to the outlawing of vicious breeds such as pit bulls on the novel grounds that unethical breeders would then simply develop new varieties of "criminal dogs."[12]

More recently, in 2010, the stunning HBO biopic *Temple Grandin* brought her inspirational life story to an even wider, international, audience. Directed by Mick Jackson and featuring a stellar cast led by Claire Danes, David Straitharn, Julie Ormond, and Catherine O'Hara, the film won a bevy of highly deserved awards, including an Emmy for its striking minimalist soundtrack composed by Alex Wurman. In anticipation of and in tandem with this public awareness breakthrough appeared two terrific treatises by Grandin (both cowritten with Catherine Johnson), *Animals in Translation* (2005), and its sequel, *Animals Make Us Human* (2009). Today, at age 67, there are few if any individuals more respected than Grandin in multiple fields, crossing the fluid boundaries of scientific inquiry and cultural awareness.

In the opening pages of *Animals in Translation*, Grandin lays out what could well be described as the great thesis of her life. With the authority of personal experience she asserts that "autistic people can think the way animals think."[13] Then, for the sake of those who might believe she had misspoken, Grandin repeats herself: "Animals are like autistic savants. In fact, I'd go so far as to say that animals might actually *be* autistic savants."[14] For her, human autism—a handicap in the conventional sense—thus becomes an advantage with respect to the understanding of animal behavior. By being autistic, Grandin and others like her are able to empathize better with nonhuman sentient life forms. This basic premise is at once both surprising and yet (upon reflection) common-sensical.

Like human autistics, higher animals, including canines, are typically dismissed as inferior beings despite obviously possessing many sensory, mental, and physical capacities beyond those of their "normal" human counterparts. Grandin's revolutionary ideas about autism were well-timed to find a growing acceptance, not only among the scientific and business communities, but among the general, nonscientific public as well. This is evidenced (on an over-simplified and somewhat misleading level) by cultural touchstones such as the 1988 Oscar Award-winning film *Rain Man*, directed by Barry Levinson and starring Dustin Hoffman and Tom Cruise. Grandin's view of autism as a kind of mental bridge between man and beast, however, had much broader implications. When combined with intelligence, knowledge, and experience, autistic qualities—that is, thinking visually with acute sensory perception—could literally become a type of communications translator between humans and animals. This is to imply that the ultimate dog "whisperer" (or any animal "whisperer" for that matter) could, under the right circumstances, probably be a human autistic savant.

As a trained scientist, Grandin accepts without any hesitation the recently established direct genetic link between domesticated dogs and wild wolves (see introduction). Citing the 1990s research at UCLA led by Robert K. Wayne, she emphasizes the stark revelation that "genetically dogs are juvenile wolves" with a less-than-significant 0.2 percent variation in DNA between the species.[15] More specifically, she states, "Dogs are genetic wolves that evolved to live and communicate with humans."[16] As she explains it, "during evolution dogs went through a process called pedomorphosis, which means that dog puppies stop developing earlier than wolf cubs do. It's a kind of arrested development."[17] The theory was in fact nothing new, but it had been finding a more receptive audience over the last decade.

Old preconceptions and prejudices against wolves had been challenged ever since 1944 when pioneering conservationist Adolph Murie (1899–1974) published his seminal study, *The Wolves of Mount McKinley*, as expressly noted by Grandin.[18] She then goes one better, joining a growing chorus of breeders and owners by asserting that more "wolfish" traits in dogs are probably desirable and preferable, in that these breeds tend to get along better with other canines (as do wolves with each other) through instinctive submissive behaviors. In short, "wolfishness" is now seen as a good thing in dogs; moreover, mutts or mixed breeds tend to have more of these traits and are therefore calmer, shyer, and more emotionally stable than purebreds (i.e., less likely to attack humans or other dogs).[19] Grandin even goes so far as to note that wolves tend to be more monogamous than dogs because they are more "mature" animals, though not necessarily more social or trainable.[20]

Exactly how and when domestication occurred is still a mystery, although she cites modern research begun in Russia during the late 1950s with the domestication of foxes that has begun to shed some light on the process.[21] Above all, she reminds us, "that dogs have the ability to anticipate human actions through close observation of human behavior." For example, dogs, unlike wolves and other pets, always look at their master's faces for cues and direction.[22] One is reminded once again of John Steinbeck's imagined (?) "conversations" with his dog, Charley, while maintaining physical closeness and eye-to-eye contact (see Chapter 19).

Grandin's general observations on domesticated dogs are too numerous and varied to be adequately presented within this limited space, but a few selected examples will give a flavor for her consistent lack of conventionality.

Describing dogs as "hyper-social predators" and "smell geniuses" who "need people" and "social companionship," she repeatedly emphasizes that dogs (unlike, say, cats) cannot be trained without "social approval" and are "hyper-sensitive to everything we do."[23] In short, "a dog is happy when you're happy."[24] Like humans, dogs seem to have a conscience, even a religious sense at times ("I don't think that anyone can rule it out"), and sometimes suffer psychological diseases normally associated with humans such as Post Traumatic Stress Disorder (PTSD).[25]

Unlike "normal" humans, however (and like autistic humans and other animals), dogs appear to lack Freudian illusions such as denial or repression. To a canine, something simply is or is not (see Chapter 2).[26] Grandin, like many great canine observers of the past such as Montaigne (see Chapter 9), is particularly impressed with the abilities of working guide dogs, and (more recently), the experimental training of seizure-predicting dogs.[27] Rather brilliantly, she hypothesizes that modern-day leash laws, while absolutely necessary, are also probably having an effect on the continually ongoing evolution of dogs by inhibiting their socialization skills with other dogs, as well as possibly being the underlying cause of a statistical uptick in biting incidents over the last few decades.[28] If her theory on leash laws is correct, the implication is clear: not only are dogs changing with respect to their ingrained social tendencies but probably their human owners are changing as well with respect to the same behaviors.[29]

As one may well surmise from these valuable insights, Grandin has become a much sought after source of advice by owners for doggy training and discipline. In *Animals Make Us Human*, the first animal-specific chapter in the book (titled "A Dog's Life") contains over 35 pages of sound rules, tips and suggestions (some quite humorous), supplementing those from *Animals in Translation*. Going against the conventional wisdom of using forced submission in training, she notes this method can backfire because "someday, when your back is turned, he [your dog] will bite you in the butt."[30]

Invisible shock fences, so popular nowadays, are considered far from foolproof since dogs, as rational beings, are quite capable of weighing the risks and rewards of taking a temporary hit in order to achieve a concrete, desired objective. Some will even run a gauntlet simply to make their escape. Grandin refers to this canine behavior (quite accurately) as "doing their own doggie version of reality testing"—unlike many humans who prefer not to do this, it is tacitly implied.[31]

Many of her suggestions are unorthodox. Because she believes too much restraint is a bad thing, typical taboo behavior such as dogs getting on furniture or playing tug of war is for her okay.[32] Since canines have hyper-socialized tendencies, use of doggie role models—using a well-behaved dog to help calm down an untrained one—is encouraged.[33] As a firm believer in animal emotions, Grandin advocates that, in general, any good dog training must be tied to reinforcing those emotions. While rejecting the traditional argument that canines naturally gravitate towards pack behavior, she acknowledges that pack situations can and often do happen under forced or unnatural circumstances, and that these pack mentalities "can be incredibly dangerous to humans."[34] Likewise (it is rather strongly inferred), a human pack mentality can be an incredibly dangerous, albeit unnatural, thing for other humans as well. In effect, for Grandin, domesticated dogs become the last and final word in social beings, even more so than human beings themselves.

Some of Grandin's most nuanced, and hence most underappreciated, thinking comes on the topic of government regulation. In a stance applying not only to canines, but to all domesticated animals, she is, on one hand, a firm believer in government regulation and a leading activist voice for stronger controls against all forms of animal cruelty, abuse, and misuse. On the other hand, she feels that government itself has lost its way in this regard. As an example, she writes at length about the United States Department of Agriculture (USDA), harking back to the 1950s, 1960s, and 1970s, as a "golden age" in which anonymous, underpaid USDA field staff were viewed by many (herself included) as heroes and innovators.[35]

Today, however, she notes that much of the regulatory progress made in those previous times could never now be achieved for at least two good reasons. The first, and perhaps most damning, is that a majority and ever increasing number of government employees are desk jockeys with little or no field experience, hence capable only of what Grandin terms "abstractification"—attempted theorizing with no basis in hard reality—which in turn accelerates political polarization and gridlock.[36] Many are career bureaucrats who came up through the ranks of the Civil Service, as opposed to the ranks of the real world, as Grandin did. The second problem she cites is that special interests on all sides of the political spectrum have gained far too much influence over the regulatory process. In the old days, Grandin recalls, when a problem needed quick solving by government, "they just did it; they didn't get everyone's permission."[37] All of these sage observations would seem to have important implications for the ongoing development of effective regulatory law in relation to all canines, both domesticated and wild (see Chapter 1).

In terms of pure ground level, "just do it" type of hands-on experience, perhaps Grandin's biggest influence of late on the world of dog training is represented by the growing, widespread use of the "Thundershirt" and similar products. The Thundershirt is a body-wrap device used to calm nervous animals during turbulent weather or other stressful events that cause canine anxiety. While some dog-owners and non-owners have questioned its value for all pets in all situations, I can personally attest to its effectiveness in many cases, a highly welcomed antidote by both dog and owner. Grandin credits the invention of the dog-specific device (or "Anxiety Wrap") to professional trainer Susan Sharpe, while also noting that Sharpe admittedly got the original idea by reading Grandin's earlier, fascinating articles about the squeeze chutes she developed to calm down livestock, as well as herself during stressful school days.[38]

The development of the doggie Thundershirt is thus a perfect example of a humane, progressive advancement in technology rooted in longstanding personal experience—beginning with Grandin's Arizona ranch days—that became popular and successful before government regulators or big business concerns realized it even existed. No one sought permission, no one was consulted in an ivory tower, no one concocted any elaborate for-profit scheme; instead, an emergency situation was simply addressed in hands-on fashion, the solution worked, and that was that.

Many of the ideas championed by Grandin with respect to canines were well summarized in the recent PBS *Nova* installment "Dogs Decoded," which first aired on November 9, 2010. Beginning with the irrefutable direct genetic link between dogs and wolves, the program proceeds to highlight the even more remarkable and uniquely close link between dogs and humans, suggesting once again that ongoing human and canine evolutions are inseparably tied together. In terms of contemporary pop culture, however, perhaps the best place to look for these new trends is in the visual arts, especially since Grandin maintains that animals, like human autistics, are visual thinkers. One such example consists of two recent outstanding children's books illustrated by superstar animator Carter Goodrich, *Say Hello to Zorro!* (2011) and *Zorro Gets an Outfit* (2012), both named after the ubiquitous pug Zorro, who moves so contentiously through the ongoing story line. All of Grandin's favorite themes, from the virtues of doggie socialization to the dangers of pack mentality, can be found in Goodrich's hilarious renderings as we follow the canine misadventures of Zorro, Mister Bud, Dart, Eddie (and the boys), as well as their kitty-cat nemesis, Slim. The highly strung Dart even wears a Thundershirt-like body wrap. As for Zorro, he may well be a distant artistic descendant of English painter William Hogarth's beloved pug Trump (see Chapter 10).[39]

As of this writing, Temple Grandin's incredible life story is of course still unfolding. Who knows what new breakthroughs and insights she has yet to offer, although what she has already provided could easily fill and satisfy several lifetimes. In hindsight, one of the bigger lessons of her improbable career seems to be that none of us, no matter how talented or special, are able to accomplish much left merely to our own individual devices. Grandin's mother and aunt were clearly indispensable figures of support and encouragement during her youth. Then in 1960, when the late William Carlock decided to take a professional teaching interest in the troubled teenaged misfit recently expelled from high school for fighting, he did a great service not only to the teenager in question, but to the rest of humanity as well, not to mention a good portion of the animal kingdom. Grandin then went on to have many other important mentors in both the academic world and the cattle industry who helped to shape her into the international figure she has become—mentors, alas, too numerous to list here.

In reviewing the first seven decades of her life, it might well be said that, in the end, we as individuals all become the sum of those people and other living beings who influenced and encouraged us throughout life. Taking this thought further, perhaps the "individual" parts of us might be overrated and ultimately ineffective in terms of achieving meaningful accomplishments for society. Since it now appears that dogs are indisputably the most social living creatures under God's dominion, could it possibly be that these same animals exert heavy sway over our human personalities and thoughts as well? The correct answer, it would seem, is suggested by the rhetorical nature of the question itself.

21

Summary

> *Many people today find it hard to believe and some would really rather not know, even when confronted with overwhelming scientific evidence, that the gentle dog which follows them about with such unquestioning devotion is a comparatively recent descendant of the wolf, a creature whose very name is associated with savagery and cunning from our earliest childhood memories of Little Red Riding Hood.—*
> Terence Clark[1]

In a modern American nation made up of tremendous contradictions and polar opposites, the great state of Wisconsin is, in many respects, a place most dramatically representative of these conflicts, and nowhere are they better illustrated than in local attitudes towards canines. Dogs are both loved and scorned, but mostly loved; wolves are admired and reviled, but mostly reviled. These differences of opinion are often expressed and debated with a vehemence typically reserved for politics and religion. "Love me, love my dog" goes the oft-quoted, ancient adage.[2] Likewise, the 1984 hit song "Will the Wolf Survive?" by Los Lobos (translated literally, "The Wolves") has recently found resonance in the Badger State, even though, strictly speaking, the song itself is not about wolf preservation but rather an allegory for struggling multicultural bands within the popular music industry. Nevertheless, the comparison is apt.

The American gray wolf, after being pushed to the brink of extinction—an end result which an alarming number of thoughtless voters would in fact favor—has made an impressive comeback over the last quarter century, only now to be threatened once again with more liberalized hunting laws all across the upper Midwest and beyond. As any experienced hunter knows, for every wolf legally "harvested" there will be scores of others illegally and wantonly slaughtered by emboldened gun enthusiasts as proponents of the new legislation either applaud or look the other way in full tacit approval.[3]

As for Man's Best Friend, challenges of a different nature have arisen.

With the recent rise of widespread economic hardship in this country (and state) over the last decade, particularly in rural areas, news reports of animal cruelty, frequently aimed at dogs as the intended or unintended victims, have also risen at an alarming rate. Most of us can see these revolting stories on a daily basis simply by turning on our television sets or computers. Community indignation will sometimes follow, other times, not so much. In Wisconsin, many citizens have voiced objection to the use of dogs as trackers for the newly legalized wolf hunts, but to date, official efforts to eliminate the practice (one that is unique to this state) have fallen short.[4]

Leaving aside this single contentious issue, other news reports of abandoned and abused dogs, not to mention those oftentimes beheld with our own eyes during the course of everyday affairs, must rank as among the more disturbing sights offered by contemporary life. Such acts against a domesticated animal, particularly a dog, which has been bred over thousands of years for the sole purpose of seeking human companionship and approval, should be viewed as heinous in the extreme. If we assume the offender is otherwise mentally competent, then one can only attribute this level of human cruelty to cowardice, as did Montaigne long ago during the European Wars of Religion (see Chapter 9). In any event, these are the types of vexing disunities routinely being presented to any thoughtful observer of modern American culture.

More uplifting are regularly appearing news reports of ongoing canine fidelity, loyalty, and courage in the face of tremendous adversity. In addition to recent accounts of doggie heroism and survival in the wake of the Oklahoma tornado disasters (see Chapter 18), relatively newfangled social media such as Facebook and YouTube continue to accumulate emotional, moving testimonials to the seemingly closer-than-ever bonds between humans and their canine pet associates. Many of these postings, a number of which feature such items on personal blogs and Web sites, can be unbearably maudlin in sentiment, while others are difficult to believe even for those of us possessing a very high opinion of animal intelligence and capabilities. "Nature-Faker" hawks of the past such as Theodore Roosevelt and John Burroughs (see Chapter 15) no doubt are still turning in their graves over some of the unrealistic claims made by these reports.

On the other hand, many other accounts are quite real and no less poignant for their stark realism. To give just one isolated example, former Arkansas governor and presidential candidate Mike Huckabee recently posted a heartfelt obituary for Jet, his beloved hunting Labrador retriever of some 15 years. Governor Huckabee and this writer may disagree on many religious, political and social issues, but one thing that we do agree upon was his profound closing comment: "Some people doubt that dogs go to heaven, but I don't have any doubts. If heaven is a place for the best, then Jet will be there."[5] Thus not all of contemporary Internet and media traffic in this regard is negative, sordid, or depressing; on the contrary, much of it displays positive reassurance, frequently offering exceptional role models (both human and canine) which we find admirable and noble.

Getting back to Wisconsin and, for that matter, much of the upper Midwest, it appears that the ongoing efforts of humankind to reach consensus over the legal status and rights of canines over the last 4,000 years (see Chapter 1) have of late shifted focus in response to modestly expanding wild wolf populations. Having nearly been completely wiped out of the lower 48 states by the mid-20th century, the gray wolf in 1973 received official protected federal status as an endangered species. It has since been making a steady comeback, with now an estimated 6,000 wolves existing mostly in the Rocky Mountain and Great Lakes regions.[6] This in turn has prompted, only 40 years later, a recent, likely-to-pass congressional proposal to the U.S. Fish and Wildlife Service for removing wolves from their current protected status. Protections from targeted geographic areas containing the largest populations were in fact removed in 2011–2012, thus prompting many states, including Wisconsin, to offer a limited wolf hunting season. In a state with a longstanding reputation for natural conservation, as well as one with a substantial and active Native American presence, the new and pending legislation has created public controversy unlikely to be quelled any time soon regardless of how temporary or intended final political decisions are made.

Recall that, historically, Wisconsin has been a place attracting the residency of many famous conservationists, the distinguished ranks of whom have included Increase Lapham (1811–1875), Carl Schurz (1829–1906) and John Muir (1838–1914).[7] With respect to wild wolves, however, surely the most famous Wisconsinite was Aldo Leopold (1887–1948), in his younger days a professional wolf bounty hunter who, like Ernest Thompson Seton a generation before him (see Chapter 14), came around to strongly believe that the indigenous American gray wolf needed active preservation rather than aggressive eradication.[8] Leopold was particularly scornful of the commonly held and oft-quoted view that wolves represent a major threat to local deer populations, themselves the primary targets of most hunting sportsmen. He not only found it absurd that any wild species should be hunted or wiped out simply so that another more plentiful species could continue to be more easily hunted by sportsmen, but also rightfully questioned the shaky and spotty statistical data on which these dubious arguments are oftentimes based.[9]

Let us not be misunderstood. Farmers defending their livestock have every right to kill a predatory wolf or any other natural threat to their livelihood. Current and traditional laws already make allowances for this. Simple arithmetic, however, deflates the extent of the alleged, exaggerated, threat. In Wisconsin, for example, a state consisting of over 65,000 square miles—much of it rugged, wild terrain—most everyone agrees that there are currently about 800 wolves roaming around unrestrained. As one gun-owning farmer in the north woods recently remarked to me, exactly how much damage can 800 small animals do to a territory this size? Enough to declare open season? This overreaction to a highly localized problem calls to mind Saint Francis' famous rebuke to the Italian town of Gubbio during the 13th century (see Chapter 8).

As for self-defense, any big or small animal (or animal pack) is certainly capable of attacking a human, although instances of wolf-on-human assaults in the lower 48 states are virtually unknown within modern memory. Regarding safety concerns over domesticated dogs, that is what leash laws are for— to protect people and animals, including the dog on the leash, even if such a precaution may not be foolproof.[10] The same Wisconsin hunters using dogs in the pursuit of wolves would seem to have little cause to complain about dogs being threatened. For smaller pets, an eagle is just as much of a risk in this regard, but we do not shoot eagles, at least last time that I checked. Finally, the allure of killing such creatures for mere recreational sport (or out of pure superstition) totally escapes me. Many gun owners feel the same, as it is hoped these pages have demonstrated.[11]

Long ago, highly accomplished hunters such as Ernest Thompson Seton concluded that wolf hunting lacked any true legitimacy as a sport, and nowadays far too many self-professed hunting sportsmen do not measure up to Seton's admirable standards of outdoorsmen. John Steinbeck once quipped that any criticism of hunters whatsoever was an open invitation for trouble (see Chapter 19); yet Wisconsin public opinion is far from being monolithic in this regard. Even as we proceed to deplete the wolf population, one can behold the artistic image of a wolf on state auto license plates proudly labeled "Endangered Resources." More locally, as these words are being written, a dramatic new wolf sculpture is being installed in the popular outdoor garden of the Woodson Art Museum in Wausau, Wisconsin.[12] Perhaps powerful artwork like this might one day accomplish what legislators, voters, and activists have failed to accomplish thus far (see Chapter 16).

Canine legislation and regulation has come a long way since the Laws of Eshnunna (see Chapter 1), and its growing international reach is far too broad in scope to summarize herein. However, a few selected examples are in order simply to demonstrate the diversity and complexity of these issues. A fairly progressive neighboring state such as Illinois goes so far as to make specific legislative provision for the creation of doggie trusts in personal wills and estate planning. A more regressive state such as South Dakota (recently ranked last in this regard by HSUS), does not even make animal cruelty a felony criminal act. Whereas Wisconsin has since 2012 allowed dogs to be used for purposes of wolf hunting, California expressly disallows the use of hunting dogs for the tracking of certain animals (bears and bobcats), while its single known surviving wild wolf not only continues to enjoy federal protection, but has become somewhat of a media celebrity in its own right.[13]

More recently, Michigan joined Wisconsin, Minnesota, Montana, Idaho, and Wyoming in legalizing wolf hunts, undercutting ongoing efforts to bring the issue to a voter referendum. Interestingly, the Michigan spokesperson favoring the new legislation belongs to a group called the Upper Peninsula Bear Houndsmen Association, named after a concept that is now an illegal activity in California.[14] The point to underscore here is that canine legislation for both dogs and wolves has lately become so divisive and complicated that, like many other similar issues in the public arena, legislation and enforcement appear to be rapidly devolving to local authorities. Nor is anything resembling political consensus on any of these issues anywhere currently in sight, although some very broad and long-term trends seem to be emerging. One is that people (and voters) in general seem much more aware of these conflicts and often appear genuinely surprised to learn that many other citizens (both on the same and opposite sides of the political aisle) do not share identical opinions on these same issues. Accordingly, the opinion gaps remain wide, but at least these gaps now are obvious to anyone not living in self-imposed isolation.

Nor can anyone escape these debates by seeking refuge in a local bookstore. Recent releases of canine literature are more visible than ever, presumably because someone is voraciously buying these books and hence making it profitable for publishers. A comparatively serious American writer such as Jon Katz has made a career of sorts by specializing in doggie nonfiction, sharing with readers his personal interactions with intelligent animals typically far too interesting to have been simply made up from the human imagination. On a more dramatic, visceral level, the Emmy Award–winning film and photographic work of Jim and Jamie Dutcher on the wild wolves of the Idaho Sawtooth Mountains, among whom the couple lived for six years, between 1990 and 1996, continues to provide the reading public with a wealth of tangible factual information on subject matter usually dominated by misinformation and false preconceptions. Their latest picture book, *The Hidden Life of Wolves* (2013), published by National Geographic with a foreword by Robert Redford, in many ways represents a ringing confirmation of the new and controversial ideas on wild canines being embraced within the scientific community by prominent figures such as Temple Grandin (see Chapter 20).

Of particular note are benign interactions between wolves and humans as if the beasts were family dogs, calling to mind similar socializations witnessed in earlier times by writers such as Ernest Thompson Seton and Jack London (see Chapter 15).[15] The visual legacy created by the Dutchers is in fact so stunning—humans and wolves living improbably and in harmony at close quarters together—that it would seem to throw some insight on how humans were able to first transform wild wolves into domesticated dogs. During the distant past, this generational process was of course surely accomplished at gradual stages which were prolonged and incremental.

Hopefully, the tone of this book, despite its obvious pro-canine bias, has avoided equating dogs with wolves or, for that matter, humans with canines. Charles Darwin, Jack London, C.S. Lewis, and other famous writers throughout history sometimes opted to view their human characters through the eyes of canines with similar reverence, as if their mortal masters were deities of sorts. In point of fact, however, it is London's canine hero, Buck, from *The Call of the Wild* who, in the end, becomes an adopted Native American deity, and whose spirit lives on indefinitely among the wild wolves of the great continental northland, not to mention among the reading public. As for our own speculation on the matter, it most likely short-changes canine intelligence and instinct to presume they view us with too much awe. In all likelihood, canines see us for what we humans really are—superior beings in terms of intellectual sophistication and mechanical technology, but otherwise quite mortal and fallible. Steinbeck probably had it right when he wrote that dogs think we are crazy but still love us in spite of it all. That is why they feel a need to protect us, experience anxiety on behalf of our welfare, and even sometimes mourn us when we pass. This is also why writers and poets throughout the ages have been inspired by them.

We sense how these creatures really know our true selves, and yes, even feel animal emotions towards us. Perhaps C.S. Lewis (see Chapter 18) hypothesized correctly, or at least closest to the truth, when he suggested that dogs and other higher animals have a share in the Great Spirit (to borrow a Native American phrase) through their close relationships and interactions with the good people caring for them. The alarming corollary to this same theory is that they are quite capable of sharing in our damnation as well, as brilliant writers the caliber of Johann Wolfgang von Goethe were quick to seize upon (see Chapter 11). In either event, these domesticated canines often appear to be an integral, inseparable part of our very being, even when we tragically attempt to reject or scorn them.

Lovers of other intelligent, domesticated or semi-domesticated pets—cats, horses, lower primates, seafaring mammals (such as dolphins), even birds—may well make similar and quite legitimate arguments. Wild and domesticated canines, however, remain uniquely apart in their intimate or hostile relationships with humans and, one might add, with each other as well. For one, our human relationship with canines is much older (older by far, in fact) than with any other nonhuman living being, extending well beyond the memory of Western civilization and recorded history. One might easily characterize the partnership (for that is what it truly has been) as biblical in breadth and scope. If one chooses to read the Bible literally, then chapter one of Genesis has man and "all the wild creatures" being created by God on the sixth day, which means that humankind's direct interaction with canines began immediately, for all practical purposes.[16] Even if one is not a biblical literalist, there can be no denying that domesticated dogs represent the apotheosis of human collaboration with the animal kingdom.

And yet wild wolves were also there from the beginning, or, to be more accurate, they were there first, ahead of the dogs, according to today's scientists. Mankind somehow took what he first despised (the wolf) and slowly molded it into what he later cherished (the dog), thereby transforming himself in the process. Today, thousands of years later, perhaps tens of thousand of years after the fact, seemingly little has changed. We tend to love dogs and hate wolves. Many, if not most, people would say that the latter should be significantly downsized or completely eliminated. Such an attitude, we submit to the patient reader, is short-sighted and (to borrow a neat descriptor from Jack London) dangerously homocentric. You cannot separate the wolf from the dog any more than you can the dog from the human, or, dare we say, the human from the canine.

Chapter Notes

Introduction

1. Grandin and Johnson, *Make Us Human*, 26.
2. Douglas Brewer, among many others who agree, has written that "the overwhelming evidence to date, however, points to the wolf (*Canis lupus*) as the sole ancestor of the domestic dog (*Canis familiaris*)" (2).
3. Pythagorean philosophers among the ancient Greeks held similar views (see Chapter 5).
4. We are particularly interested in frequent contemporary claims for new ideas that in fact often have written precedent going back thousands of years.
5. My goal is to maintain primary attention on the historical writer in question, rather than promote my own ideas on any particular topic.
6. Johns, 10.
7. Cats may sometimes rule the roost but must be considered usurpers in this regard.
8. Brewer, 1.
9. Johns, 16.
10. If domesticated dogs predate the agricultural revolution, it may well be asserted that they were also essential to its later development.
11. Brewer, 2.
12. Ibid., 23.
13. Ibid., 25.
14. Ibid., 28, 50.
15. Ibid. (comment by Adrian Phillips), 95.
16. If a dog represents all that is best in man, as a wise person once remarked (a comment widely attributed to Étienne Charlet), then it might also be said that a wolf represents all that is worst in man; nevertheless, a more nuanced view seems to be emerging of late. Wolfish traits in both dogs and humans are now frequently seen as potentially good things (see Chapter 20).
17. See, for example, those offered by Webster's or the OED.

Chapter 1

1. Wasik and Murphy, 19, 241*n*, citing the more recent (2001) English translation by Wu Yuhong.
2. Genesis 11:31, 15:7. "Ur" is a Sumerian word for dog (among other meanings). See comment by Terence Clark in Brewer, 71.
3. Albrecht Goetze, the first English translator of these fragments, deduced that the Laws of Eshnunna probably predated the reign of Dadusha, but he remained uncertain as to their true author or exact date of composition (15).
4. The surviving Eshnunna tablets are generally considered by archeologists to be private copies rather than official ones. That fact may have ensured their preservation in that they were under the proverbial radar of subsequent invaders.
5. Goetze, 1.
6. This kingdom became the Republic of Iraq in 1958.
7. Goetze, 133.
8. Wasik and Murphy, 19–20, 241–242*n*, citing Yuhong.
9. To be more precise, the joke is less about the long distance traveled by the convalescent (the malady was taken very seriously) and more about culture clash between various Mesopotamian city-states. See Wasik and Murphy, 17–18, 241*n*, citing Andrew R. George.
10. Black and Green, 70.
11. This symbolic use dates back at least to

the Old Babylonian Period, roughly contemporary with the Eshnunna tablets. See Black and Green, 40, 60, 70, 101.

12. Black and Green, 70, 101.
13. Johns, 26.
14. Ibid., 34–35.
15. See Shakespeare's *Julius Caesar*, III.i.273.
16. Black and Green, 70.
17. Johns, 17, 34–35, 50, 118–119.
18. Ibid., 26, 48, 56–57. An extraordinary group of five molded, painted, and inscribed terra cotta figurines used for talismanic purposes and recovered from the site of Nineveh (48) are also illustrated in Black and Green, 70.
19. Hammurabi is sometimes equated with the biblical king Amraphel of "Shinar" (Genesis 14:1). This historical association, however, is tenuous at best.
20. Near exact reproductions of Hammurabi's Code can also be viewed in a number of museums, including the Oriental Institute at the University of Chicago.
21. *The Code of Hammurabi, King of Babylon*, trans. Robert Francis Harper (University Press of the Pacific, 2002), xii. Harper, along with C.H.W. Johns (see note 22 below), completed the earliest English translations of the code shortly after its discovery in 1901. The original subtitle of this volume dates the code to 2250 BCE but that has since been revised to a more recent date by a majority of scholars, reflecting an ongoing debate regarding the general uncertainty of any Mesopotamian dating more remote than the first millennium BCE.
22. The Harper translation (see note 21 above) uses "mighty bull" (5); Johns prefers "charging bull" but acknowledges in his commentary that "rabid buffalo" was a legitimate reading and would have even been considered a compliment by Hammurabi, though some modern readers might be offended by the word choice. See *Babylonian and Assyrian Laws, Contracts, and Letters*, by Claude Hermann Walter Johns (Charles Scribner's Sons, 1904), 389, 391.
23. Wasik and Murphy, 16–17.
24. Salukis are mentioned in some of the earliest Sumerian writings, circa 3500 BCE See Wasik and Murphy, 25, 242*n*, citing Katharine Rogers.
25. In particular, the works of Veronese are noteworthy in this regard.
26. The saluki is the mascot of Southern Illinois University. The dominant confluence of the Mississippi and Ohio River valleys in this region has always been known in the Midwest by the slightly derogatory nickname of "Egypt." Some maintain that the saluki's name is derived from the Arabic pronunciation of Seleucus, general of Alexander the Great and founder of the Seleucid Empire in the Middle East after the latter's death at Babylon in 323 BCE Another theory is that the Arab word "al-Salūqī" had simply become synonymous with hunting hounds by the modern era. See comments by Terence Clark in Brewer (73) and Abdel Haleem in the introduction to al-Marzubān (xxvii–xxviii).
27. Speculation has been that the MWD was probably a German or Belgian Shepherd breed. See "Who's the Dog Hero of the Raid on Bin Laden?," *New York Times*, May 4, 2011, and "Belgian Malinois: The Dog that Took Down Osama Bin Laden?," *Huffington Post*, May 5, 2011. A German Shepherd MWD was portrayed as part of the task force in the 2012 award-winning film by Kathryn Bigelow, *Zero Dark Thirty*.

Chapter 2

1. *Egyptian Book of the Dead*, chapter 30B, plate 3 (caption).
2. William J. Dobson, "Tunisia's Lessons for Repressive Regimes," *U.S. News and World Report*, January 20, 2011.
3. The "Arab Spring"—a phrase coined by American journalists—was first sparked on December 18, 2010, when Tunisian street vendor Mohamed Bouazizi of Sidi Bouzid self-immolated in protest of being denied a permit and thus permission to continue his livelihood. Within a year of this event, the governments of Tunisia, Libya, and Egypt were all overthrown by popular uprisings. Algeria and Morocco also experienced disturbances. For more on the long and sometimes overlapping history of suicide or martyrdom protests in Tunisia, see my earlier study *Perpetua of Carthage: Portrait of a Third Century Martyr* (McFarland, 2007).
4. Probably the best-known Hollywood portrayal of Pharaoh Rameses II was by Yul Brynner in Cecil B. DeMille's *The Ten Commandments* (1956).
5. *The Papyrus of Ani* draws upon a number of much older sources, including the "Pyramid" and "Coffin" texts, elements of which date back to the earliest known periods of Egyptian civilization.
6. Johns, 83.

7. Ibid., 88.
8. *Egyptian Book of the Dead*, 147 (comment by Ogden Goelet).
9. Of these three, only the golden jackal is still found in northern Africa, while the black-backed and side-striped varieties are sub-Saharan in habitat.
10. See, for example, *Egyptian Book of the Dead*, with extended commentary on this topic by Ogden Goelet, 144–145.
11. Grandin and Johnson, *Translation*, 91.
12. Ibid., 92–93.
13. Egyptian artwork typically emphasizes these heightened canine senses by slightly exaggerating the sizes of ears, noses, eyes, etc.
14. *Egyptian Book of the Dead*, 155 (comment by Ogden Goelet).
15. Another function of *The Papyrus of Ani* (if not its primary function), was to improve the chances of the deceased for achieving eternal bliss by offering spells (or cheats, if you will) to get past the merciless test scales of Anubis.
16. Johns, 82–88.
17. Ibid., 196–197.
18. Dan Vergano, "Museum Returns King Tut Artifacts," *USA Today*, November 11, 2010.
19. Brewer, 94.
20. On a lighter note, the saluki is today the college mascot of Southern Illinois University (see Chapter 1), whose most famous representative, fittingly named King Tut, is buried beneath a miniature pyramid near the university stadium.
21. Sopdet was the Egyptian name given to the star (known as Sothis or Sirius in Greek), gradually becoming deified in its own right, and viewed as a manifestation of Isis, supreme goddess of the Egyptians.
22. Johns, 26, 58–59.
23. The location of this town has never been established, and its very historical existence is questioned.
24. During the Roman civil wars, as well as long afterwards, the Nile River Valley's status as breadbasket to the Mediterranean world first became a decisive factor in almost all large-scale political and military decision-making.
25. Contrast, for example, Greek provocation of the Maccabean Revolt in the Holy Land around the same time period, sparked by unsuccessful Hellenist attempts to supplant local religious customs.
26. Good artistic representations of Hermanubis can been found in Johns, 91.

27. Sopdet could be viewed as the sibling or cousin of Anubis, depending upon which ancient Egyptian text one is reading.
28. As of this writing (early 2013), Egypt is in the vacillating throes of violent civil disturbances following its Arab Spring revolution, with a new Islamist constitution being drafted. Whatever the outcome of these turbulent events, we are confident that the traditional Egyptian love affair with the saluki breed will remain constant.
29. The Rosetta Stone was misnamed after the Nile Delta town of Rashid in which it was discovered by a French soldier circa 1799.

Chapter 3

1. Pliny the Elder (translation by Harris Rackham), 101.
2. Pliny the Younger later gave an impressive bibliography of his uncle's literary output and writing habits in a letter to Baebius Macer. See Pliny the Younger, 87–90.
3. Pliny the Younger, 166–168, 170–173.
4. Ibid., 167.
5. Ibid., 168.
6. Grant, 10.
7. Pliny the Elder, Book VIII, pp. 60–61.
8. Werewolf stories had become popular in the Roman world long before this as well, making appearances in works by writers such as Ovid and Virgil.
9. Pliny the Elder, Book VIII, p. 61.
10. Brewer, 85 (Adrian Phillips quoting S.J. Crockford).
11. Pliny the Elder, Book VIII, pp. 101–102. Not all Roman commentary on dogs was positive. Julius Caesar once criticized the overindulgence of Roman matrons towards their lap dogs as undermining civic resolve for purposes of national defense (or, more accurately, international conquest).
12. Pliny the Elder, Book VIII, p. 102.
13. Pliny the Younger, 171.
14. Pliny the Elder, Book VII, pp. 103–104.
15. Ibid., Book VII, p. 103. The assertion is debatable, but (on the other hand) yet to be disproved.
16. Ibid., Book VII, pp. 103–104.
17. Ibid., Book VII, pp. 59, 105.
18. Ibid., Book VII, pp. 105–107.
19. Ibid., Book VII, p. 105.
20. Ibid., Book VII, p. 106.
21. A good illustration and commentary by Adrian Phillips can be found in Brewer 87, 90.

22. Burglary was a common problem for affluent Romans, as Pliny himself noted. See Grant, 82.
23. The House of Menander, named after the ancient poet portrayed in one of its interior frescoes, was in fact owned by the maternal family of the notorious Poppea, wife of the emperor Nero. See Grant, 38, 101–102.
24. Grant, 18.
25. Ibid., 20.
26. Immediately coming to mind are reports that dogs and other animals fled from an approaching tsunami which struck Sri Lanka in 2010, while many soon-to-be human victims stayed near the waterfront.
27. See "Love Among Pompeii's Ruins Extends to Dogs" by Elisabetta Povoledo in the *New York Times*, July 15, 2010.
28. Also in typically southern Italian manner, the wordplay of the program's name is the result of director Giacomo Bottinelli, formerly a student of philology, objecting somewhat to the popular English translation of the phrase.
29. Since the destruction of Pompeii, Vesuvius has erupted 70 times, the last eruption occurring in 1944. See Grant, 23–24.
30. The five emperors in question for the year 68 CE were Nero, Galba, Otho, Vitellius, and Vespasian, the latter Pliny's being friend who emerged victorious from the conflict, 11 years before the eruption of Mount Vesuvius.

Chapter 4

1. Plutarch (translation by Dryden/Clough), Vol. I, p. 28. English translator John Dryden uses the unsual word "dug" for a female animal's nipple.
2. Plutarch "Pythia" translation by A.O. Prickard.
3. Plutarch, "Why the Pythia Does Not Now Give Oracles in Verse," Chapter IX. Plutarch does not use the names of Vesuvius or Pompeii, but rather summarizes the recent destruction caused by volcanic activity at "Cumae and Dicæarchia [Puteoli]," located in the same vicinity.
4. Plutarch, Vol. I, p. xi.
5. Ibid., Vol. I, p. xii.
6. Ibid., Vol. I, p. xi.
7. Ibid., Vol. I, p. xxiii.
8. As a parallel Greek biography to that of Romulus, Plutarch appropriately chooses Theseus, legendary founder of Athens.
9. Plutarch, Vol. I, pp. 25–27.
10. Ibid., Vol. I, pp. 28–32. The rape of the Sabine women has been a popular subject in the arts ever since. On a contemporary, more polite, level, the 1954 film *Seven Brides for Seven Brothers*, with words and music by Mercer and DePaul ("Sobbin' Women"), is one such lighter example.
11. Ibid., Vol. I, pp. 33–47.
12. Ibid., Vol. I, pp. 50–51.
13. The abandoned twins were also nourished with morsels from a woodpecker, another creature (besides the wolf) deemed holy to the war god Mars. See Plutarch, Vol. I, p. 27.
14. Plutarch (translation by Harold Cherniss), "On the Intelligence of Animals," chapter 8 (*Moralia*, Volume XII).
15. Ibid., chapter 1. See also note 18 below.
16. Ibid., chapter 5.
17. Johns, 104–109.
18. For further discussion, see my own study on this subject matter in *DeVere as Shakespeare: An Oxfordian Reading of the Canon* (2006), chapter 24.
19. Polybius (translation by W.R. Paton), *The Histories*, Volume III, Book 6, Section 22.
20. Many of Connolly's fascinating essays and artistic exercises can be found in numerous volumes under his name published by Greenhill Books of London.
21. For example, many of these reenactors likely have little appreciation for the sacred associations of the wolf to the Latin war god Mars.

Chapter 5

1. Diogenes Laërtius (trans. R.H. Hicks), *Lives of Eminent Philosophers*, Vol. II, p. 63.
2. Plutarch writes as follows: "The Athenians were, from the beginning, great enemies to wolves...." He adds that the lawgiver Solon set prices for captured wolves to bought and sold, perhaps implying practical uses for these animals. See Plutarch, Vol. I, p. 121.
3. Roman emperor Alexander Severus (208–235 CE) was born in modern-day Lebanon and given an honorary first name after the Macedonian conqueror, Alexander the Great. Representing the last descendant of emperor Septimius Severus, Alexander Severus is generally regarded by historians as a good ruler who, among other virtues, tolerated Christians (and was possibly sympathetic towards them

as well), but eventually fell afoul of the military, leading to his ultimate demise.

4. Paul the Hermit, generally regarded as the first Christian recluse, according to tradition fled from the Decian persecution to the deserts of Egypt circa 250 CE.

5. Derived from "cynos" (dog). See Brewer (Adrian Phillips), 101.

6. Diogenes Laërtius, Vol. II, p. 27.

7. Asked by the auctioneer what his skill was, Diogenes replied, "In ruling men." Then pointing to Xeniades of Corinth, he said, "Sell me to this man; he needs a master." Xeniades, for his part, later admitted that "a good genius entered my house." See Diogenes Laërtius, Vol. II, p. 77.

8. Diogenes Laërtius, Vol. II, pp. 79-81.

9. Ibid., 29-31, 55.

10. Ibid., 49.

11. Ibid., 27-29.

12. Ibid., 41.

13. Ibid., 59-61.

14. Plutarch, *Life of Timoleon*, Vol. II, pp. 337.

15. Diogenes Laërtius, Vol. II, p. 45.

16. Ibid., 69.

17. Ibid., 63.

18. Ibid., 35, 41. Plutarch retells the same famous story in his *Life of Alexander*, Vol. I, p. 149.

19. Diogenes Laërtius, Vol. II, p. 35.

20. Ibid., 47.

21. Ibid., 65, 79. According to a disputed tradition related by Plutarch in his treatise "Thrice-Greatest Hermes," Alexander's general Ptolemy, after inheriting his Egyptian kingdom upon Alexander's death, had imported a statue of the god Pluto from Sinope, hometown of Diogenes. In Egypt, this image then became amalgamated with those of the longstanding Egyptian supreme god Osiris. As Greek god of the underworld, Pluto (and later Serapis as well) was often depicted with Cerebus, the multiple dog or wolf-headed guardian of Pluto's domain.

22. Ibid., 79.

23. Ibid., 81.

24. Suetonius (Robert Graves translation), 286-287.

25. Excellent artistic representations for most of these figures can be viewed in Johns, 27-29, 61.

26. Alexander's "Companions" were his designated, elite bodyguards and cavalry.

27. Sinop has a number of tourist attractions named after Diogenes ("Diyojen" in Turkish), including a hotel and disco bar.

Chapter 6

1. From the opening of the book's second section, appropriately subtitled "Man's Best Friend." See Ibn al-Marzuban, 8. Fidelity of domesticated dogs had also been praised much earlier in history by Pliny the Elder (see Chapter 3).

2. Stager writes that "in the cosmology of the Persian Zoroastrians, dogs rank next to humans in both this world and the next." See "Why Were Hundreds of Dogs Buried at Ashkelon?" by Lawrence Stager, *Biblical Archaeology Review* (July, 2010).

3. Another one of his monikers from a surviving text indicates that al-Marzubān was active in and around the outskirts of Baghdad. See Ibn al-Marzubān, ix, xii.

4. Ibn al-Marzubān, ix. The name of al-Marzubān also bears some similarity to the foremost Persian-born Arabic scholar of that same epoch, Abū Bakr Muhammad ibn Zakariya al-Razi (841-926).

5. Ibid., xii-xiii, xvii, 26, 37 (note 53).

6. Ibid., xxvi.

7. Ibid., xv.

8. Interestingly, the opening of the text is dated to the year 991 CE some 70 years after the author's death, perhaps representing a deliberate attempt by al-Marzubān or his editor to appeal to future reading generations, an effort which has indeed succeeded way beyond that limited time span. See Ibn al-Marzubān, 1, 35 (note 1).

9. Ibn al-Marzubān, 3.

10. Ibid., 28.

11. Ibid., xxxii-xxxiii.

12. Origins of the English phrase "Man's Best Friend" in reference to dogs are usually dated to early 19th century England, although Professor Haleem's use of the same label within this organizational context seems quite appropriate.

13. Ibn al-Marzubān, 10, 22. Pliny gives several examples. Plutarch, of course, wrote of the legendary founding of Rome by Romulus and Remus.

14. Ibid., xvii, 19-20.

15. Ibid., 33-34, 38 (note 62). Later still, the French legend of the dog-saint Guinefort would seemingly spring from the same tradition (see Chapter 8).

16. Ibid., xxix.

17. See English translation by M.A.S. Abdel Haleem (Oxford University Press, 2004), 67. See also discussion by Brewer (Terence Clark),

77. The Qur'an mentions dogs (possibly) in two others contexts. Sura XVIII (verse 9) names one "al-Raquim," often interpreted as a faithful dog belonging to the Companions of the Cave (Haleem, 183, note b). Sura VII (verse 176) unfavorably compares an unrepentant sinner to an insensible dog (Haleem, 107), alluding, interestingly enough, to the same unchangeable canine qualities considered a virtue by al-Marzubān in the header quote for this chapter. See also discussion by Haleem in introduction to Ibn al-Marzubān xxviii–xxix.

18. The author attempts to bolster his thesis on the authority of the Prophet Muhammad and his family, but these are not derived from supportable traditions, as underscored by translator Haleem. See Ibn al-Marzubān, xvi.

19. See the New Jerusalem Bible English translation and notes. Remnants of this cultural attitude carry over to the New Testament, for example, in Luke 16:22, where dogs lick the sores of Lazarus as a healing gesture.

20. Rashi was mostly active in Troyes, the Champagne region of France, a geographic area no doubt more favorably inclined towards domesticated dogs than the Middle East of the crusading era. He is still viewed by many Hebrew scholars as the definitive commentator on the Torah and Talmud. Rashi wrote in a French environment that was (comparatively speaking) more intellectually friendly and open, not unlike that of early 10th century Baghdad during the time of al-Marzubān. This same intellectual climate in France would soon encourage the activity of early Arthurian poets, including the great Chrétien de Troyes.

21. Canaan dogs currently serve as MWDs (Military Working Dogs) for the Unit Oketz of the Israel Defense Forces.

22. See "In Israel, a Battle to Save the Ancient Canaan Dog" by Nicholas Brulliard, *Washington Post*, March 27, 2012.

23. Stager rules out the possibility of Egyptian practice on the sensible grounds that the dog skeletons were not mummified.

Chapter 7

1. Marie de France, trans. Eugene Mason, 12.

2. "Lycanthropy" is defined by *Webster's* as "a mental disorder in which one imagines oneself to be a wolf" or "the magical power to transform oneself or another into a wolf." Factual cases of the former have been documented but not the latter.

3. Several of the animal fables from Marie's *Ysopet* involve canines.

4. The dedication is simply addressed to a "most noble and courteous King."

5. See my earlier study on this subject matter, *Chrétien de Troyes and the Dawn of Arthurian Romance* (McFarland, 2010).

6. Marie underscores this source by taking the trouble early in the tale to distinguish the Breton word for "werewolf" ("Bisclavret") and the Norman word for the same ("Garwal"). Brittany and Normandy, one should recall, were adjacent regions in northwestern France.

7. Latin authors also frequently touched upon themes of lycanthropy, including Ovid (*Metamorphoses*), Virgil (*Eclogues*), and Petronius (*Satyricon*).

8. Similar poetic tales of noblemen werewolves possessing a good side, coming soon after Marie's *Bisclavret* at the turn of the 13th century, included the anonymous *Guillaume de Palerne*, *Melion*, and *Biclarel*, the latter two having an Arthurian setting. These works probably either imitated Marie, drew upon a common source, or both. Sometimes the human-to-wolf transformation is attributed to magic rather than lycanthropy. Thomas Malory also included a similar story in his *Le Morte d'Arthur*, first published in 1485.

9. For example, it was the same violent and unpredictable barons of King Henry II who murdered Saint Thomas à Becket in 1170.

10. Translator Eugene Mason uses the variant spelling "Bisclaravet."

11. Marie credits Breton minstrels as the sources for her *lais*.

12. Marie also writes (in reference to her own efforts) that "he who would keep himself unspotted from the world should search for knowledge, that he might understand." This has been understandably interpreted to imply that she herself was a monastic.

13. His *Were-Wolves* book was subtitled *Being an Account of a Terrible Superstition*.

14. The 2007 BBC adaptation of the same story, *Jekyll*, was more explicit in this regard. Besides Stevenson, Alexandre Dumas and G.W.M. Reynolds, among several other noted writers, previously dabbled in the genre of werewolf fiction.

15. Immediately prior to Housman's achievement, prominent English writers such as Arthur Conan Doyle ("A Pastoral Horror," 1890) and Rudyard Kipling ("The Mark of the Beast,"

1891) had experimented with short stories delving into werewolf legends.

16. A 1961 film, *The Curse of the Werewolf*, was loosely based on this novel.

17. The film was directed by Stuart Walker, with stunning makeup effects by Jack Pierce. Warner Oland, despite his purely Swedish ancestry, eventually became best known for his portrayal of detective Charlie Chan, although he had also appeared in Josef von Sternberg's 1932 classic *Shanghai Express* with Marlene Dietrich. In 1978, the late Warren Zevon's well-known song *Werewolves of London* was inspired by the 1935 film. The previous year (1977), Ray Davies and the Kinks had also written and recorded a song about lycanthropy, "Full Moon."

18. Lugosi earlier achieved stardom with his vampire portrayal in *Dracula* (1931).

19. An identically titled TV series, *She-Wolf of London*, aired in 1990–1991, starring Kate Hodges.

20. One is also reminded of Walt Whitman's oft-quoted observation on Shakespeare's history plays as being dominated by "wolfish earls," one of whom (in his opinion) may have been the true author, lending additional fodder to the authorship debate. See my previous study, *DeVere as Shakespeare* (McFarland, 2006).

21. *Prince Caspian* was the second installment of Lewis' acclaimed *The Chronicles of Narnia* series (1950–1956), eventually made into a successful feature film (2005) with financial backing from Disney.

22. Also, who can forget the campy and comedic werewolf-like makeup of Eddie Munster from *The Munsters* TV series of the mid–1960s?

23. The late 1970s produced a bumper crop of distinguished werewolf fiction. In addition to Brandner's *The Howling*, novelist Whitney Strieber wrote *The Wolfen* (1978), which was later made into a 1981 film feature. Angela Carter produced a number of short stories including "The Company of Wolves" (1979), also later made into a movie (1984). The two latter works both portray werewolves in a semi-sympathetic light.

24. Lupin's first and last names are suggestive. "Remus" and the same character's pseudonym "Romulus" both hark back to the twin brother founders of Rome, who were saved as abandoned infants by the milk of a she-wolf (see Chapter 4). "Lupin" recalls *lupus*, the Latin word for wolf.

25. Lupin had been infected as a child by a bite from his evil werewolf counterpart, Fenrir Greyback.

26. Meyer's four novels in the series have been *Twilight* (2005), *New Moon* (2006), *Eclipse* (2007), and *Breaking Dawn* (2008). These in turn became five feature films between 2008 and 2012.

27. These sequels included *Full Moon* (2009), *Dark of the Moon* (2009), and *Shadow of the Moon* (2010).

28. Over the last decade, distinguished fiction writers such as James Patterson (*Maximum Ride*, 2006) and Anne Rice (*The Wolf Gift*, 2012) have adopted werewolf themes for their novels.

Chapter 8

1. *Little Flowers* (translation by Dom Roger Hudleston), 57–58. A similar sentiment by Saint Francis is preserved in his "Blessing of Brother Leo," where death from wild beasts is considered to be a potential price paid in obedience to God's will. See *S. Francis*, 166.

2. Raphael Brown has also produced an excellent updated translation of *The Little Flowers of Saint Francis*. See his introduction, 13. The American city of San Francisco is of course named after the saint as well.

3. So wrote English philosopher Thomas Hobbes (1588–1679), with respect to society without the government of kings.

4. One of the earliest short biographies of Francis, *The Mirror of Perfection*, sometimes ascribed to his close companion Brother Leo, quotes the saint as comparing Franciscans to "Knights of the Roundtable." See *S. Francis*, Section 72.

5. Things came to a head when Francis had a vision while praying at the chapel of San Damiano outside of Assisi, where a voice directed him to repair God's ruined house. Francis took this to literally mean the run-down chapel itself, and he promptly sold some of his father's expensive fabrics to raise money for the purpose. In retrospect, the vision clearly referred to the Roman Catholic Church as a whole.

6. Wolf symbolism and iconography associated with Gubbio first appeared in the late 13th and early 14th century. See *Little Flowers* (Brown), 322.

7. Pope John Paul II declared Francis the patron saint of ecology in 1979.

8. "Lady Poverty" was the phrase coined by Francis in reference to the Franciscan vow of poverty, a good example of the strong influence that troubadour poetry had upon the saint's frequent mode of expression.

9. One believable anecdote is that Francis offered to endure a trial by fire to prove the truth of the Christian faith against any Islamic opponent, to which the sultan sensibly replied that he did not know of any Muslims who were willing to undergo such a test.

10. Franciscan Brother Elias had in fact preceded Francis to the Holy Land by two years in 1217, arriving at the coastal city of Acre in Galilee.

11. This controversial event has since become an iconic benchmark of the Christian faith, inspiring countless artists and writers who contemplate it.

12. Francis reportedly requested that he be buried among criminals. The request was not honored. Instead his body was enshrined below his namesake basilica in Assisi.

13. The oldest surviving manuscript of *The Little Flowers* dates from 1390 and is found today in Berlin. As a qualifier, the French poet Henri d'Avranches alluded to the legend as early as 1290. See *Little Flowers* (Brown), 321–322.

14. Nonetheless, if Brother Leo was in fact the author of *The Mirror of Perfection*, he does not mention the Wolf of Gubbio. Raphael Brown (*Little Flowers*, 27) remarks, accurately enough, that it would not have been considered politically correct to depict a recently canonized saint shaking hands with a wolf, as Francis does in *The Little Flowers*, possibly explaining the disfavor of the story in the official view of the institutional church.

15. There are genuine and believable anecdotes about Francis being dismissive towards the fear of wolves. There is another story of him converting to the Franciscan order a criminal in the vicinity of Gubbio whose nickname was "Wolf" among local residents. This same friar subsequently became known as "Frate Lupo" ("Brother Wolf"), accompanying Francis to Spain, Lupo died in 1291. See Brown, 320–322.

16. On this point, see the discussion by Arthur Livingston in his introduction to the *Little Flowers*, xiii–xv.

17. On a more sophisticated level, the Wolf of Gubbio might be read as a parable of evolutionary domestication from wolf to dog.

18. As a side note, there is no indication that Saint Francis, despite his aestheticism, was a vegetarian. On the contrary, according to *The Mirror of Perfection*, he had a weakness for good fish and "sweetmeat" mostaccioli. See *S. Francis*, Sections 111–112.

19. See *Little Flowers*, Chapter XVI. *The Mirror of Perfection (S. Francis*, Section 140) recounts the preference of Francis for hooded larks, whose behavior reminded him of the monks themselves.

20. See, for example, *Mirror of Perfection (S. Francis*, Sections 119–120).

21. See *Mirror of Perfection (S. Francis*, Section 114).

22. This author attended the 2011 annual Blessing of the Animals service at the Episcopalian Church of the Ascension located in remote Hayward, Wisconsin, and can attest to the warm and enthusiastic vibe of the congregation on that day. My previous attendances on the same feast day at different churches in different cities have been no different.

23. The Welsh village of Beddgelert features a mound, the alleged grave of Gelert, which appeared during the 18th century to promote tourism. The name of the village is thought to be in fact derived from that of an early religious figure, which if true would offer an example of a human saint being replaced in the popular imagination by a canine.

24. It is now generally agreed that Saint Roch is an amalgamation of several historical figures.

25. For an artistic depiction of the legendary Saint Roch and his dog-savior companion, see Johns, 27.

26. Merson had obviously taken the trouble to read *The Little Flowers*, since the final sentences of Chapter XXI (59) meditate on this aftermath, noting that "all the people received him [the wolf] courteously, feeding him with great pleasure, and no dog barked at him as he went about."

27. See www.sacredartpilgrim.com.

Chapter 9

1. Montaigne, trans. M.A. Screech, 516.

2. Montaigne was born during the long reign of French king Francis I, who was succeeded in 1547 by his son Henry II.

3. Henry II was succeeded in 1559 by the adolescent King Francis II, who died a year later in 1560 and was succeeded by Charles IX.

4. Upon the death of Charles IX in 1574,

he was succeeded as king by Henry III. After the assassination of Henry III in 1589, Henry IV became the rightful heir to throne but was not crowned until 1594, following his mastery of Paris and defeat of the Catholic League, which continually opposed him.

5. In a bitterly ironic coda, King Henry IV (1553–1610) of France was later assassinated by a fanatical French monk who doubted the monarch's true inner commitment to Roman Catholicism.

6. Montaigne's famous circular library-study, which contained thousands of volumes, still stands today.

7. Montaigne's mother, who long outlived her husband (but is rarely mentioned by her son), was descended from a Jewish Marano (i.e., Christian convert) family of the Iberian Peninsula. In her defense, she would have understood a thing or two about the need for religious tolerance.

8. Henry IV reportedly intended to make Montaigne one of his royal counselors before learning of his death in 1592.

9. Montaigne, xxi, 628.

10. Only a small portion of Montaigne's essay in fact touches upon Sebond directly; mostly it consists of original commentary.

11. Montaigne, 517.
12. Ibid., 520.
13. Ibid., 536–537.
14. Ibid., 525, 531.
15. Ibid., 524.
16. Ibid., 518.
17. Ibid., 521.
18. Ibid., 518.
19. Ibid., xxxii.
20. Ibid., xxxi.

21. Montaigne wrote a separate essay, *On Presumption*, a vice which he viewed as a major contributing factor to the Wars of Religion. The inscribed motto in his own château library read, "Que sçay-je?" (What do I know?).

22. Montaigne, 787.

23. Montaigne makes a direct comparison to human cruelty towards both animals and fellow humans during the ancient Roman games in the arena. See Montaigne, 481–482, 484–485.

24. Montaigne, 488.

25. Ibid., 481, 488.

26. It is now generally agreed, though disputed as to the exact degree, that Catherine helped to instigate the massacre through undue influence over her son, King Charles IX.

27. Griffith's *Intolerance* presents the Saint Bartholomew's Day Massacre as one piece of a larger cinematic tableau that includes the fall of Babylon, the crucifixion of Christ, and (rather surprisingly) the tragedy of some misguided 20th century social workers.

28. There are several known artistic depictions of Diane de Poitiers as the goddess Diana accompanied by dogs, another famous one being the 1549 statue *Diana with a Stag* by Jean Goujon, also today at the Louvre.

Chapter 10

1. Locke, Section 116, p. 180.

2. Thus the English, railing so fanatically a century later against the execution of King Louis XVI during the French Revolution, had committed the same act themselves in 1648 under the cloak of legality and legitimacy. This time frame does not include the period of 1648–1651 in which parliamentarian forces consolidated their victory with successful, albeit brutal, campaigns in Ireland and Scotland.

3. Strictly speaking, the English Civil War involved a religious aspect, i.e., temporary overthrow of the Episcopalian Church of England by Presbyterians. Parliamentarians, however, objected less to Episcopalians than to the alleged unrestricted rights of their monarch and his abusive use of that power.

4. The modern variations of the breed, including the Cavalier King Charles spaniel, so named after Royalist noblemen of the English Civil Wars, are in fact distant, partial descendants of similar dogs from the 17th century and were also popular among Tudor monarchs of the previous dynasty. For striking artwork dating from the 18th and 19th centuries, see Johns, 134–135.

5. The military career of Locke's father was brief and unsuccessful. He appears to have been deactivated after the early Royalist victory at Bristol in 1642, leading eventually to reform of the Parliamentarian armed forces into the highly successful "New Model Army."

6. As a sign of the favor in which he was now held, Locke was among Queen Mary's retinue upon her triumphant entry to England in 1688.

7. No doubt Locke had also personally witnessed throughout his life the unfortunate consequences of political power held by those lacking in good education, no matter how otherwise well-intentioned they may or may not have been.

8. Locke, Section 116, pp. 180–181.
9. Ibid., 1.
10. Ibid., 9.
11. Ibid., 12–13. At one point, Locke quotes Montaigne directly (Section 91, p. 149).
12. Ibid., Sections 167, 177, 189, pp. 219–220, 234, 242.
13. Ibid., 65.
14. Jean-Jacques Rousseau, *A Discourse on the Origin and Basis of Inequality Among Men*, preface (translated by G.D.H. Cole).
15. Rousseau quotes Plutarch's well-known essay on the same subject in reference to the vegetarian followers of Pythagoras.
16. The exact extent of Rousseau's influence on the Founding Fathers of the United States has been recently disputed due to his undeniable, posthumous sway over the architects of the somewhat more violent French Revolution. There can be no denying the American connection, however, particularly in reference to American Francophiles such as Thomas Jefferson.
17. Voltaire, *The Philosophical Dictionary*, trans. H.I. Woolf (New York: A.A. Knopf, 1924).
18. American victory at Saratoga in 1777 in fact directly led to French alliance with the U.S., a crucial and indispensable factor later leading to British defeat.
19. Thomas Jefferson's complex relationship with dogs is detailed on Monticello's website, www.monticello.org.
20. Jefferson famously wrote near the end of his life that the problem of slavery in America was like holding a wolf by the ears—not a fun thing to do, but letting go could be worse.
21. This letter was written to Peter Minor of Albemarle County, Virginia, after word of similar disturbances in Pennsylvania had come to Minor's attention. See www.monticello.org.
22. Jefferson wrote in reference to Lafayette's appetite for power, for which his "canine" adjective would still be quite appropriate.
23. See Johns, 140–141.
24. European continental art would begin to exhibit the same tendencies, although these would be carried to their apotheosis by English portrait painters of the 18th century.
25. Hogarth may have been influenced by Dutch masters of the 17th century who experimented with similar devices, such as Gerard ter Borch (1617–1681), based for a time in London, and who enjoyed including dogs in his works, such as the masterful *A Boy Cleaning His Dog's Coat*. See Johns, 184–185.
26. Gainsborough and Reynolds, as direct professional rivals, rather expectedly seem to have rarely tackled identical subject matter in their work.
27. By "American colonists" I am of course referring to the 13 original colonies and not those parts of the Americas settled by the Spanish or French.
28. It was natural that Jefferson, as a lifelong Francophile, would, with one mark of his quill, both assist Napoleon in his war against Great Britain and achieve the largest territorial expansion of the United States in history, not including the Declaration of Independence (also mostly authored by Jefferson).

Chapter 11

1. Goethe (trans. Walter Kaufmann), 401. The somewhat unusual word "caitiff" refers to a mean or cowardly person.
2. Goethe was educated in the arts and sciences, especially languages. He does not appear to have been an enthusiastic outdoorsman before traveling to Italy in 1786.
3. "Wolfgang" in the archaic German approximately means canine-like pathfinder, in the complimentary sense. The meaning of the name is reminiscent of the Egyptian wolf-headed deity Wepwawet, viewed by the ancients as a god who opened all roads (see Chapter 2). Whether Goethe was sensitive about his middle name is unknown.
4. Goethe also achieved a reputation as a published scientist and naturalist, although his preference was for botany and, unlike Darwin after him (see Chapter 12), he did not seem especially interested in the animal kingdom.
5. *Sturm und Drang* took its name from a 1776 German play of the same title by Friedrich Maximilian Klinger that dealt with the then-ongoing American Revolution.
6. The most tragic of Goethe's German contemporaries in this regard was surely Wolfgang Amadeus Mozart (1756–1791).
7. The historical Doctor Faust was also said to have owned a shaggy black dog. See Woods, 229.
8. Woods, 229.
9. Goethe's early biographer, Henrich Düntzer, draws upon Goethe's own memoir. *Tag- und Jahres-Hefte*, for an account of this incident. See Heinrich Düntzer, *Life of Goethe*, trans. Thomas W. Lyster, vol. 2 (Macmillan, 1883), 194.
10. Düntzer, vol. 2, p. 352–353.

11. Operatic and extended musical treatments of the Faust legend since Goethe's stage version have been composed by Berlioz, Schumann, Liszt, Gounod, Boito, and Busoni, among others.
12. Woods, 229–230.
13. Ibid., 230–232.
14. Goethe's personal attitude towards Bonaparte seems to have been at best ambivalent. Politically conservative, Goethe supported German independence and its traditional monarchy. In 1808 at Erfurt, a 60-year-old Goethe was summoned by Bonaparte for a discussion of literature over breakfast.
15. Woods, 230–234. Perhaps the best-known literary example of this genre is the 1901–1902 novel *Hound of the Baskervilles* by Arthur Conan Doyle (1859–1930), in which the alleged satanic Hellhound is eventually revealed to be a rather ordinary country guard dog.
16. Lord Byron's dog Boatswain died at five years of age and was buried on his estate, the grave marked by a large monument inscribed with Byron's lengthy poem in praise of the animal's virtues.
17. The Brothers Grimm included in this same collection the tale of "The Wolf and the Seven Young Kids," in which the Big Bad Wolf is ultimately destroyed as well.
18. Perrault's older, more sinister version of "Little Red Riding Hood" is part of his collection popularly known in English as *Mother Goose Tales*.
19. In spite of Aesop's frequent use of the Big Bad Wolf motif, these fables also exhibit an extraordinary sympathy for and sensitivity towards the animal kingdom, including dogs, one reason why John Locke so endorsed them for children (see Chapter 10).
20. Johns, 136–137.
21. As any experienced dog owner knows, these animals can instantly detect human fear of them and will often focus on that individual as a consequence, either to harass that person or attempt to win them over.

Chapter 12

1. Darwin, 23.
2. Ibid., 157–158.
3. Josiah Wedgwood was namesake of his father, who founded the pottery manufactory. The Wedgwood family fortune would prove indispensable to Darwin's future professional advancement and achievement.
4. The beagle dog breed is of course famous for its hunting prowess.
5. Dickens, a close contemporary of Darwin, died in 1870. He was known to have supported Darwin's theory of evolution. Dickens was also a well-known dog-lover who often incorporated sympathetic dog characters into his fiction.
6. Based on the 2001 book by Canadian novelist Yann Martel.
7. In the popular parlance, "Darwin Award" winners refer to those who about bring their own demise, through stupidity or ignorance.
8. Regarding human evolution and survival, Darwin tended to believe (somewhat quietly) that education or the lack thereof would be the deciding factor in determining prosperity, if not survival from extinction.
9. Darwin describes in wonderment how male hummingbirds routinely fight each other to the death (698). This author has personally witnessed hummingbird pugnacity, when my shepherd mix was once fearlessly "buzzed" by a hummingbird for intruding on its feeding ground. The poor dog retreated in fear back into the house.
10. Darwin, 452.
11. Ibid., 188.
12. See *The Voyage of the "Beagle,"* by Charles Darwin (Modern Library, 2003), 162–163. In contrast to the natural, instinctive viciousness of birds, Darwin observed certain dog breeds as being specially bred and trained for killing, such as the diminutive Argentine "Leoneros" terriers capable of baiting pumas (282).
13. The Falkland Islands wolf is the only canine breed known to have become extinct in modern times.
14. Darwin, 307. Darwin predicted their extinction in his journal (Seen 7 above, pp. 205–206). He also noted the presence of wild dogs in Argentina, as well as the unusual respect shown towards him by locals viewing his credentials as "El Naturalista Don Carlos" (134).
15. Darwin, 398–399.
16. Ibid., 452.
17. Ibid., 453.
18. Ibid., 455–456.
19. Ibid., 451–452. Again, this author has personally witnessed the same phenomenon: in his case, a German Shepherd-Collie mix learning while young how to bath and groom itself like a cat.
20. Ibid., 461.
21. Ibid., 473, 476.
22. Ibid., 470. Who among dog owners has

not witnessed an intelligent animal pause and deliberate between two potential courses of action to decide if a potential reward sufficiently justifies the risk of punishment for disobedience?

23. Ibid., 838.

Chapter 13

1. Baum, vol. 4, p. 315.
2. See commentary from "The Oz Books" by Gore Vidal, *New York Review of Books*, December 3, 1964.
3. Tragic events associated with this same time and place included the murder of Chief Sitting Bull in 1890 and a general massacre at Wounded Knee in 1891.
4. By some estimates, Chicago (in the wake of the Great Fire of 1871) was then the fastest growing city in the world.
5. According to a well-known anectdote, Baum instantly manufactured the name "Oz" after his audience of children demanded a name and he noticed the letters "O–Z" labeling the second half of his filing cabinet.
6. This author was fortunate to have grown up with a first edition of the book owned by my parents which, many years later, mysteriously vanished.
7. In 1976, Chicago honored its Baum heritage by naming a North Side playground Oz Park.
8. Baum's books written under the feminine pseudonym of Edith Van Dyne were particularly successful.
9. Baum, vol. 1, p 5.
10. In the film, Toto causes Dorothy to be caught in the cyclone after biting (with some justification) Miss Gulch, who later in Oz transforms into the Wicked Witch of the West (both played brilliantly by Margaret Hamilton).
11. The grisly aftermath of this scene is illustrated by Denslow in the book with an unsuccessful attempt at humor. Baum also portrayed a wolf unfavorably in his final posthumous work, *Glinda of Oz* (1920).
12. Baum (*Little Wizard Stories of Oz*), 27–28. Billina is another one of Baum's inspired animal creations, harking back to his younger days as a self-made authority on chicken breeding.
13. Baum has never been lionized in Kansas. Apart from having never lived there (and in fact having abandoned the plains states in favor of Chicago and Hollywood), moving Dorothy's family to Oz in his sixth book of the series represented a betrayal of sorts, if you happen to live in Kansas. Also Baum's attempt to attribute Toto's temporary muteness to his Kansas origins may have struck the wrong note with some readers. Baum's own relocation to Hollywood that same year (1910) possibly reflected his own view that Hollywood now represented (to him, at least) a new land of dreams and unfulfilled ambitions.
14. Baum, Volume 3, p. 489.
15. Ibid., 489–490.
16. Ibid., 490.
17. Ibid., 701.
18. Baum, vol. 4, pp. 268–271.
19. Ibid., 271.
20. Ibid., 311.
21. Ibid., 312.
22. Ibid., 315.
23. Ibid., 388.
24. Ibid., 423.
25. See "Following the Yellow Brick Road Back to the Origins of 'Oz'" by NPR staff, April 15, 2013.
26. Dorothy, the Scarecrow, the Tin Woodman, and the Cowardly Lion have in more recent times often been held up as symbols of gay pride. Baum would likely have approved. Except for the Tin Woodman, who is given an often-suppressed backstory of a heterosexual relationship, romance has no place in the Land of Oz. Baum rightfully considered it boring to pre-teenage children. The attractive corollary to this storytelling principle is that gender bias and sexual preference become irrelevant, thus in the final analysis, we are all equal as human beings; moreover, ones not much superior to the animal kingdom surrounding us.
27. *Wicked* was subsequently turned into a 2003 mega-hit musical by composer Stephen Schwartz, rivaling the 1939 MGM production in popularity and box office, although time will tell as to whether it has similar staying power.

Chapter 14

1. Seton, 13.
2. Although Seton's 1898 publication of *Wild Animals I Have Known* predated Baum's *The Wonderful Wizard of Oz* by two years, Baum had moved to Chicago by 1891 and likely began concocting the Oz fantasies as bedtime material for his children soon afterwards. The basis for Seton's account of Lobo and Blanca

dates from factual events of 1893–1894. In addition, Seton's view represents a much more modern outlook of wolf behavior. Hence, in this collection of essays, Baum is given precedence in terms of chronology.

3. Thompson's parents, like many others in the Durham-Northumberland region of England, were of Scottish ancestry.

4. Family tradition held that the Thompsons came to England after the failed Scottish rebellions of the 18th century.

5. Courtaud ("Bobtail") was the leader of a man-eating wolf pack that terrorized the outskirts of Paris during the 15th century. The Beast of Gevaudan was the leader of a man-eating pack of wolves or wolf hybrids killed in 1765 or 1767 (two large wolves were shot) in rural south central France. Seton relates both traditions in his wonderfully titled *Mostly About Wolves* (1937).

6. Witt, 15–17.

7. Disney had previously given treatment to the same subject matter in *The Legend of Lobo* (1962), and more recently, in 2007, the BBC had produced its own documentary.

8. "Lobo" in Spanish literally means "wolf"; "Blanca" is the feminine form of "white."

9. Seton, 45.

10. Ibid., 53.

11. Seton's first priority was always the Woodcraft Indians, later breaking with the BSA because of what Seton felt were militaristic tendencies. What he would have thought of today's ongoing controversy over homosexuality in the BSA is impossible to say.

12. The pelt of Lobo is still preserved today at the Philmont Museum.

13. Seton also devoted time to proving and defending factual claims of writers he felt had been unjustly treated during the controversy, such as Charles "Buffalo" Jones.

14. Seton, 9, 11.

15. It was Roosevelt who coined the term "Nature Fakers."

16. Seton, 12.

17. In this sense, both Seton's books and his extensive activities as a youth organizer were closely connected.

18. Seton, 11.

19. Today, this author (through the efforts and encouragement of his wife) is an enthusiastic, backyard bird watcher.

20. Darwin, 741.

21. It should be added that Seton's casual sidebar illustrations are no less engaging.

22. As this is being written, the largest assemblage of Gromme's work is on full glorious display at the Woodson Art Museum in Wausau, Wisconsin.

Chapter 15

1. London, 92–93.

2. Ibid., 251.

3. London's personal nickname eventually became "Wolf."

4. Specifically, many elements from London's *The Call of the Wild* were taken from *My Dogs of the Northland* (1902) by Egerton R. Young, a charming book, though not written with a fraction of London's poetic skill or dramatic tension.

5. For a humorous, alternative view of Teddy Roosevelt's presidency, see Gore Vidal's essay "Theodore Roosevelt: An American Sissy" from the *New York Review of Books*, August 13, 1981. London's acerbic article appeared in *Collier's Weekly*, September 5, 1908. In regard to Roosevelt, London used the highly insulting descriptor of "amateur."

6. London presents Buck as a kind of Nietzschean super dog. Like almost every artist of his generation, London had been influenced by the German philosopher Friedrich Nietzsche (1844–1900), who died just three years before the novel was published.

7. London, 93.

8. The final paragraph of the novel is satisfyingly poetic, comparing Buck's wild howls as he leads the wolf pack to the "song of a younger world." See London, 101.

9. London, 257.

10. Ibid., 292.

11. For example, White Fang's gradual domestication and mating with a collie, despite his three-quarters wolf lineage, is a demonstration of Darwin's evolutionary theories.

12. London, 9.

13. Above all, London's canine characters and their journeys represent symbols and allegories for human beings.

14. This was over two years between the first successful transatlantic flight by Charles Lindbergh.

15. Balto went on to become a film star and media darling. After his death in 1933, his body was preserved by the Cleveland Museum of Natural History.

16. Seppala's survival of the notorious Norton Sound "ice machine" was due to more than mere luck; as noted by Charles Darwin during

the previous century (see Chapter 11), sled dogs are celebrated for their extrasensory abilities to detect and avoid thin ice, as well as to consciously economize and minimize their weight when forced to travel across it.

17. Togo, because of his advanced age, lived less than five years after the serum run. After humane euthanization in 1929, his body was first displayed in the Peabody Museum (where his skeleton is still housed) and today may be viewed at the Iditarod Museum in Wassila, Alaska.

18. The Iditarod was named (somewhat appropriately) after an obscure and isolated ghost town along the traditional route.

19. See "Iditarod Dog Found 7 Days After Disappearing from Team" by Katie Kindelan, http://abcnews.go.com, March 15, 2013. The flip side to this happy ending, however, is that PETA routinely monitors and criticizes Iditarod mushers for alleged (and sometimes very real) cases of animal cruelty. For instance, one sled dog died in a snowstorm during the 2013 race after it had been dropped off at a checkpoint to recover from a minor injury.

20. Lassie had actually been the name of another fictional collie from a British short story by Elizabeth Gaskell, published in 1859, the same year as Charles Darwin's *On the Origin of Species* (see Chapter 12).

21. Strongheart was the doggy stage name for the German shepherd's true and rather elaborate moniker from the old country, Etzel von Oeringen.

22. It's a well-known—and humorous—fact that Lassie from the 1943 film and subsequent 1954 television series was portrayed by a male collie (and later, his descendents); hence the Lassie of Hollywood was, in actuality, a laddie.

Chapter 16

1. Prokofiev (22).

2. The old joke goes that the United States has more in common with Russia than any European country: large geographic expanse, vast agricultural resources, a highly religious populace, emphasis on military prowess, deemphasis on education in favor of superstition, and a considerable appetite for lording it over other cultures and countries.

3. This is based on the total number of recordings made, comfortably outpacing all other competition.

4. Ukraine has always had its own separate national identity, as more recently demonstrated by its becoming an independent state after the fall of the Soviet Union in 1991. This factor alone probably always caused Prokofiev to be somewhat of an outsider in Moscow.

5. Lina Llubera Prokofiev (1897–1989), born Carolina Codina in Madrid, was imprisoned by the Stalinist government in 1948, approximately seven years after she and Prokofiev were separated. She permanently left the Soviet Union in 1974. Upon her death in London she was survived by their two sons and eight grandsons.

6. In 1935, Prokofiev had published his Music for Children, Op. 65, and Children's Songs, Op. 68. In 1933, he had written the successful soundtrack (Op. 60) for the satirical anti-czarist film *Lieutenant Kijé* (1934).

7. This victim was none other than Marshall Mikhail Tukhachevsky (1893–1937).

8. The most spectacular of these propaganda musical works was *Cantata for the 20th Anniversary of the October Revolution*, Opus 74, a composition dominating most of the composer's time in late 1936 and early 1937. Prokofiev ended up shelving the work for unspecified reasons, probably due to justified anxiety over whether it would be favorably received.

9. Koussevitzky had known Prokofiev since his student days at the Saint Petersburg Conservatory.

10. Mendelson, who died in 1968, married Prokofiev in 1948. The legitimacy of this second marriage has always been contested by Lina Prokofiev and her family, although Mendelson and Prokofiev were a couple until his death in 1953.

11. Shostakovich, unlike Prokofiev, long outlived Stalin and during the subsequent two decades was able to somewhat enjoy his international celebrity.

12. Peter's use of a rope to capture a wild wolf recalls similar real-life feats by Ernest Thompson Seton (see Chapter 15).

13. Prokofiev, 49.

14. Ibid., 54.

15. Ibid., 56.

16. Program titled *Legends, Tales and Myths* performed February 24, 2013, at the Sentry Insurance Theater venue in Stevens Point, Wisconsin, including works by Prokofiev, Mussorgsky, Stravinsky, and Debussy. The town is also home to the environmental specialization University of Wisconsin at Stevens Point (UWSP) and Wisconsin Conservation Hall of Fame.

17. Wisconsin is the only state to allow the use of dogs for this purpose. This clause of the legislation is currently being appealed in a legal action. An estimated 815 to 880 wolves and 213 packs currently live in Wisconsin. See "Plaintiffs File Appeal in Wolf Hunting with Dogs Lawsuit" by Paul A. Smith, *Milwaukee Journal Sentinel*, April 12, 2013.

18. Act 169 was passed and signed into law in 2012 after legitimate concerns from farmers over defense of their livestock escalated into a politicized sporting issue.

19. For Disney's version, the narrator was well-known American actor and voice-over artist Sterling Holloway.

20. Other prominent past artists affected by the decision included Pablo Picasso, Alfred Hitchcock, Virginia Wolf, Igor Stravinsky, and C.S. Lewis (see Chapter 18). Justice Ginsberg wrote the majority opinion for the court. See "Public Domain Works Can Be Copyrighted Anew, Supreme Court Rules" by Adam Liptak, *New York Times*, January 18, 2012.

Chapter 17

1. Ramos (Dimmick translation), 80.
2. As a descriptor for the Soviet Union, the bombastic phrase "evil empire" was popularized by President Ronald Reagan.
3. Prokofiev died on March 5, 1953, and Ramos on March 20, 1953.
4. Ramos, x.
5. Augusto Frederico Schmidt (1906–1965) was Ramos' first major patron, publisher, and distinguished poet in his own right. After the fall of Vargas, Schmidt also came back into political prominence as a United Nations ambassador for Brazil.
6. In 1930, Ramos and family relocated to the provincial capital of Maceió.
7. Ramos, xxiv. "Baleia" was later republished in 1946 with a new title ("The Dog") as part of the Ramos collection "Incomplete Stories."
8. Though professedly unreligious, Ramos reportedly enjoyed reading biblical scripture during his leisure time more than any other material.
9. The personal eccentricities of Ramos were the stuff of legend: antisocial but generally well disposed towards children; indifferent to food, music and clothing; grumpy and contrarian as a conversationalist; physically lazy but writing everything by hand rather than typewriter; a lover of off-color language. See www.vidaslusofonas.pt/graciliano_ramos2.htm.

10. Ramos, xv–xvi.
11. Ibid., 87.
12. Ibid., 57
13. Ibid., 111, 117.
14. The title of Ramos' novel (*Vidas Sêcas*) is actually a pun, translating literally as "Dry Lives"—a reference both to the parched climate of the *sertão* and to the empty barrenness of the human characters' fates.
15. Although Brazilian law treats animals as personal property, it aggressively punishes abuse and misuse of animals as a waste of natural resources.
16. Shortly after the formation of HSUS, *101 Dalmations*, the 1956 anti-cruelty novel by Dodie Smith, became a best-seller and basis for the Disney film franchise.
17. Other similar questions remain vexing. For example, to what extent should these shrinking resources be devoted to different dog breeds (i.e., pit bulls), or dogs versus cats and other pets, since rescued dogs are, statistically speaking, much easier to give away for adoption than other pets.
18. The Santos film version of *Barren Lives*, though highly visible at the 1964 Cannes Film Festival, was not released in the United States until 1969.
19. For De Sica's *Umberto D*, the dog character of Flike (played by Napoleone), loyal canine companion to the main human character of Umberto, had set a new standard for canine sentimentality and pathos in postwar film.
20. Santos later went on to make a fine film version of Ramos' *Memórias do Cárcere* (1983), about the time spent by the novelist as a political prisoner.
21. Brazil's distinctive, brightly colored flag of green, gold, and blue primarily features star emblems representing the Canis Major and Canis Minoris constellations.

Chapter 18

1. Lewis, 119–120.
2. Not to be confused with his older, more socially conscious contemporary, American novelist Sinclair Lewis (1885–1951).
3. Lewis later described the unhappy event as "my first religious experience." See Lewis' autobiographical *Surprised by Joy: The Shape of My Early Life* (Harcourt Brace, 1955), chapter 1 ("My First Years"). This title was taken from a line by poet William Wordsworth.

4. Potter's popular animal fables in turn led Lewis and his older brother Warren to compose their own "Boxon" tales, a youthful precursor to the famous *Narnia* series.

5. Movingly, Lewis later recalled how as a child he prayed for his mother's recovery, but his prayers were not answered, contributing to his temporary loss of religious faith. See *Surprised by Joy: The Shape of My Early Life* (Harcourt Brace, 1955), chapter 1 ("My First Years").

6. Lewis' relationship with Moore continues to be a topic of controversy and speculation. Was a she a friend, substitute mother figure, lover, or all of these things? One thing is for certain, he remained loyal through her illness and death during the late 1940s and early 1950s.

7. See *Surprised by Joy: The Shape of My Early Life* (Harcourt Brace, 1955), chapter 15 ("The Beginning"). Lewis officially joined the Anglican Church of his parents and baptismal infancy to the disappointment of his Roman Catholic friend and Oxford colleague J.R.R. Tolkien (1892–1973), author of *The Lord of the Rings* and other notable fantasy works.

8. The same unorthodox concept has been used by a number of writers in the English language, from John Milton (1608–1674) to George Bernard Shaw (1856–1950).

9. Lewis and Davidman were married in a civil ceremony that year and then in 1957 again with an Anglican religious ceremony, somewhat controversially at the time since Davidman was a recent (1954) divorcee. Besides his World War I experience in France, the only other time Lewis left England was to go on a Greek holiday with Davidman in 1960.

10. See *Surprised by Joy: The Shape of My Early Life* (Harcourt Brace, 1955), chapter 10 ("Fortune's Smile").

11. Pastor Johnson's delightful article, dated January 27, 2011, can be found at the website for the Humane Society of the United States, www.humanesociety.org.

12. Lewis, 31.

13. Ibid., 145.

14. See *The Problem of Pain* (HarperCollins, 1940/2001), chapter 9 ("Animal Pain"), 143–144. The same "civilizing" idea recalls Jack London's novel *White Fang* (see Chapter 16).

15. See *The Problem of Pain*, (HarperCollins, 1940/2001), chapter 3 ("Divine Goodness"), 35–36.

16. See *Mere Christianity*, (Simon and Schuster, 1943-1945/1996), Book 4, chapter 7 ("Let's Pretend"), 167.

17. Ibid., chapter 8 ("Is Christianity Hard or Easy?"), 171.

18. Here Lewis parts with some philosophers who have observed that even lowly insects are capable of displaying human-like behavior in isolated instances. Instead, Lewis focuses on human behavior towards the creature itself ("He [man] does not house-train the earwig or give baths to centipedes"). See *The Problem of Pain* (HarperCollins, 1940/2001), chapter 3 ("Divine Goodness"), 36. Nevertheless, he admits not knowing where exactly to draw the line in this regard: "How far up the scale such unconscious sentience may extend, I will not even guess" (136). A few years later, in *Mere Christianity*, Lewis even suggests that the same idea may be extended further beyond sentient beings: "I can even see a sense in which the dead things and plants are drawn into Man as he studies them and uses and appreciates them" (171–172).

19. This topic was debated by the Inklings, an informal group of Oxford intelligentsia of which Lewis was a longstanding member. See note 21 from "All My Dogs Before Me" by Bruce R. Johnson, January 27, 2011, posted at the website for the Humane Society of the United States, www.humanesociety.org. For a more in-depth discussion of this topic, see "Some Dogs Go to Heaven: Lewis on Animal Salvation" by Gregory Bassham from *The Chronicles of Narnia and Philosophy: The Lion, the Witch, and the Worldview* (Carus, 2005).

20. See "Dog Guards Dead Owner's Body after Oklahoma Tornado Disaster" by Cavan Sieczkowski, *Huffington Post*, May 22, 2013.

21. Though not portrayed in film, the final book of Lewis' *Narnia* series, *The Last Battle* (1956), has the Talking Dogs joining the forces of good.

22. Debra Winger received an Oscar nomination for her performance as Joy Davidman. The film was also nominated for best screenplay.

23. Lewis, 145–146.

24. See *Mere Christianity* (Simon and Schuster, 1943–1945/1996), Book 4, Chapter 8 ("Is Christianity Hard or Easy?"), 171–172.

Chapter 19

1. Steinbeck, 65.

2. Both Hemingway and Faulkner were dog owners who occasionally wrote about dogs

as well, though not as famously as did Steinbeck in his 1960 travelogue.

3. Steinbeck's first wife was Carol Henning, whom he married in 1930 and divorced in 1941. His second wife was Gwyndolyn Conger, whom he married in 1942, fathered two sons with, and divorced in 1948.

4. This trend began to gradually reverse almost immediately after 1962. By 1963, literary works critical of American culture such as Eliot Asinof's *Eight Men Out* were finding favorable reception among critics and audiences. See my own study in this area, *Eliot Asinof and the Truth of the Game* (McFarland, 2012).

5. Steinbeck treated himself to the plush Ambassador East hotel while having a resentful Charley boarded and groomed (115, 123–124). In Chicago, Steinbeck rendezvoused with his wife, who, according to later third-party accounts, actually spent a good deal of time with her husband during the road trip.

6. Steinbeck, 114.

7. Ibid., 9, 112–113, 128, 165, 179, 207, 259. At one memorable point in the story, Steinbeck has a deep philosophical conversation with Charley on the overrated value of having personal roots in a particular geographic place. He concludes: "Perhaps we have overrated roots as a psychic need" (see pp. 103–114). Quite appropriate considering the source!

8. Ibid., 7.

9. Ibid., 273.

10. Ibid., 56–57.

11. Ibid., 126–128. This was long before the Wisconsin Dells had been unpleasantly transformed into the "Water Park Capital of the World."

12. Ibid., 212–213.

13. Ibid., 168.

14. Ibid., 194.

15. The novelist admitted that his own liberal political views had been formed mostly in response to the inept Republican presidential administrations of the 1920s. See Steinbeck, 198–199.

16. Steinbeck, 227.

17. Ibid., 234–235.

18. Ibid., 244.

19. Ibid., 252–259.

20. Ibid., 258.

21. Ibid., 47.

22. Ibid., 269.

23. Ibid., 128.

24. Ibid., 148.

25. Ibid., 160.

26. The first periodical installment of *The Red Pony* first appeared in 1933, very early during Steinbeck's writing career, as *The Gift*.

27. Wikipedia references "President's Pick of Franzen's 'Freedom' Stirs Ruckus" by Colette Bancroft, *St. Petersburg Times*, August 29, 2010.

28. The original print reportedly sold in 2005 for $4,000.

Chapter 20

1. Grandin and Johnson, *Translation*, 177.

2. Grandin and Johnson, *Make Us Human*, 61.

3. Steinbeck, 275.

4. Leo Kanner was the first scientist to define autism in 1943, only seven years before Grandin was diagnosed.

5. At Mountain Country School, one of the main attractions for Grandin was student horseback riding privileges, the love of which first taught her anger management. Hands-on experience with cattle at her aunt's Arizona ranch followed in quick succession. According to her memoirs, all personal conflicts before this time had been resolved with fisticuffs.

6. Grandin gradually became less interested in psychology as a specialized field, especially after an anticlimactic meeting with B.F. Skinner during her collegiate years, as well a growing abhorrence and distrust of experimental animal behaviorism (see Grandin and Johnson, *Translation*, 10, 16).

7. "Stairway to Heaven" was taken from the title of a popular Led Zeppelin song that same year.

8. Grandin and Johnson, *Translation*, 4.

9. Grandin and Johnson, *Make Us Human*, 297.

10. Ibid., 297.

11. Ibid., 301.

12. Ibid., 61.

13. Grandin and Johnson, *Translation*, 6.

14. Ibid., 8.

15. Ibid., 86.

16. Grandin and Johnson, *Make Us Human*, 2. The human-canine evolutionary relationship goes back at least 14,000 years, well before the development of agriculture (see Chapter 1), and possibly as long as 100,000 years ago (see *Translation*, 176, and *Make Us Human*, 32.

17. Grandin and Johnson, *Make Us Human*, 34.

18. For example, it is becoming more accepted now that wild wolves do not naturally live in packs with alpha males leading them.

Grandin traces the scientific establishment of a direct genetic link between dogs and wolves to the end of the 20th century, via the previously cited UCLA study. See Grandin and Johnson, *Make Us Human*, 26, 28.

19. Grandin and Johnson, *Make Us Human*, 38–39, and *Translation*, 83. She even postulates, based on observation, that darker fur is preferable in this regard (see *Make Us Human*, 59–60). The most "wolfish" breed is currently considered to be the Siberian huskie, often the working sled dog of choice in arctic regions (see Chapter 16), while the gentle King Charles spaniel (see Chapter 10) is considered the least "wolfish" (see *Make Us Human*, 34–36).

20. Grandin and Johnson, *Translation*, 108.
21. Ibid., 237–238.
22. Nor will a wolf's gaze, like that of a dog, follow the pointed finger of a human (Grandin and Johnson, *Translation*, 177).
23. Grandin and Johnson, *Translation*, 169–170, 287, and *Make Us Human*, 25, 64, 66–67. She notes that "dogs can train themselves" through reinforcement of "our social reactions" to them (*Make Us Human*, 25).
24. Grandin and Johnson, *Make Us Human*, 2.
25. Grandin and Johnson, *Translation*, 195, 258–260.
26. Ibid., 91–92. To clarify, if a dog "pretends" not to be afraid of a dangerous situation, it is attempting to diffuse a conflict, as opposed to denying the existence of the situation as a human might do. Also dogs usually hate any disguises that attempt to distort reality (Halloween costumes, for example). See also 47, 93.
27. Grandin and Johnson, *Translation*, 246, 288.
28. Grandin and Johnson, *Translation*, 159–161, and *Make Us Human*, 41–42.
29. Grandin remarks, "I think humans have probably evolved some innate ability to read dog language, or at least to learn to read it quickly" (Grandin and Johnson, *Translation*, 177).
30. Grandin and Johnson, *Translation*, 166.
31. Ibid., 226–228.
32. Grandin and Johnson, *Make Us Human*, p 56.
33. Grandin and Johnson, *Translation*, 234.
34. Ibid., 168–169.
35. Ibid., 29.
36. Ibid., 27–29.
37. Ibid., 28.
38. Grandin and Johnson, *Make Us Human*, 54.
39. Amazingly, Goodrich is not a dog owner; however, he credits quality time spent with a dog-loving brother for providing his dead-on accurate story material (see www.readeo.com/readeos-jenny-brown-talks-with-carter-goodrich).

Summary

1. Brewer (comment by Terence Clark), 49.
2. Also the title of a forgettable 1975 hit song by British-Canadian pop music artist Peter Shelly.
3. This writer once saw a wolf running full tilt in the wild at a pace of approximately 30 mph. Admittedly, it would take a superb marksman to hit such a moving target; but then again, why would anyone want to kill this magnificent creature merely for recreational sport?
4. See "Plaintiffs File Appeal in Wolf Hunting with Dogs Lawsuit" by Paul A. Smith, *Journal Sentinel*, April 12, 2013.
5. "Mike Huckabee Shares Touching Story of Former First Dog's Passing" by KARK 4 news, posting from *Arkansas Matters*, updated January 17, 2013.
6. See "Gray Wolf to Lose Endangered Species Protection as Numbers Rise" by Lenny Bernstein, *Washington Post*, June 7, 2013.
7. Scientist and naturalist Increase Lapham, born in upstate New York, is usually credited with being the founder of the Wisconsin conservation movement. Carl Schurz was a German immigrant-refugee who went on to become an American Civil War general, U.S. senator, foreign ambassador, and secretary of the interior; he was also known as the "Father of the Forest Preserve." John Muir, a Scottish-born immigrant to Wisconsin, later became the most famous naturalist and author-advocate of his generation in favor of natural conservation.
8. Aldo Leopold first came to Madison, Wisconsin, in 1924 as a federal employee and later assumed his very influential professorship there at the University of Wisconsin.
9. Leopold's classic work *A Sand County Almanac* (1949) carries the similar profound impact of personal experience combined with common sense also found in Ernest Thompson Seton's earlier *Wild Animals I Have Known* (see Chapter 14).
10. A dog on a leash can of course still be attacked, especially by coyotes or other dogs; nonetheless, a dog off a leash is even more

likely to be attacked in a similar situation. In the event of such attacks, one is inclined to ask if the human leash holder was at fault.

11. The recent wolf-phobic, mediocre and arguably allegorical film *The Grey* (2011) features a professional wolf hunter (played by Liam Neeson) feeling deep empathy for his quarry, even as he and his human companions become the hunted.

12. Featured exhibits in this regard include several canine-related works by American born artists Chapel (b. 1948) and Gwynn Murrill (b. 1942). The Leigh Yawkey Woodsen Art Museum in Wausau has long been known for its dedication to naturalist themes. Other works with similar images by Owen Gromme (1896–1991) and Charley Harper (1922–2007) have also recently been displayed there.

13. The lone wolf, popularly known as OR-7, wandered into northern California from Oregon looking for a mate, it is believed. See "California's Lone Gray Wolf Gets Protections from the State" by Carly Schwartz (AP), *Huffington Post*, updated October 4, 2012.

14. See "Michigan Wolf Hunting Law Signed by Gov. Rick Snyder Clears Way for Season to Be Created" by John Flesher (AP), *Huffington Post*, May 8, 2013.

15. See "Wolves Have Strong Family Values" by Juliet Eilperin, *Washington Post*, February 20, 2013.

16. The phrase "all the wild creatures" is drawn from the New Jerusalem Bible, English translation.

Selected Bibliography

Baum, L. Frank. *The Little Wizard Stories of Oz.* Wizard of Baum, 2013.
_____. *Oz, the Complete Collection.* Vols. 1–5. Aladdin, 2013.
Black, Jeremy, and Anthony Green. *Gods, Demons, and Symbols of Ancient Mesopotamia: An Illustrated Dictionary.* Illustrated by Tessa Rickards. University of Texas Press, 1992.
Brewer, Douglas. *Dogs in Antiquity.* With Terence Clark and Adrian Phillips. Aris & Phillips, 2001.
Darwin, Charles. *The Descent of Man.* Modern Library, 1977.
_____. *The Origin of Species.* Modern Library, 1977.
Diogenes Laërtius. *Lives of Eminent Philosophers.* Translated by R.H. Hicks. Vols. 1–4. Loeb Classical Library, 1925.
The Egyptian Book of the Dead: The Book of Going Forth by Day, Being the Papyrus of Ani, Royal Scribe of the Divine Offerings. Translated by Dr. Raymond D. Faulkner. Additional translations by Dr. Ogden Goelet, Jr. Introduction by Carol A.R. Andrews. Chronicle, 1994.
Goethe, Johann Wolfgang von. *Faust.* Original German and new translation and introduction by Walter Kaufmann. Doubleday, 1961.
Goetze, Albrecht. *The Laws of Eshnunna.* Vol. 31. Annual of the American Schools of Oriental Research, 1951–1952.
Grandin, Temple, and Catherine Johnson. *Animals in Translation: Using the Mysteries of Autism to Decode Animal Behavior.* Harvest, 2005/2006.
_____. *Animals Make Us Human: Creating the Best Life for Animals.* Mariner, 2009/2010.
Grant, Michael. *Cities of Vesuvius: Pompeii and Herculaneum.* Phoenix, 1971/2001.
Ibn al-Marzubān. *The Book of the Superiority of Dogs Over Many of Those Who Wear Clothes.* Translated and edited by G.R. Smith and M.A.S. Abdel Haleem. Aris & Phillips, 1978.
Johns, Catherine. *Dogs: History, Myth, Art.* Harvard University Press, 2008.
Lewis, C.S. *The Great Divorce.* HarperCollins, 1946/2000.
The Little Flowers of Saint Francis of Assisi. Translated and with an introduction by Raphael Brown. Doubleday, 1958.
The Little Flowers of Saint Francis of Assisi. Translated by Dom Roger Hudleston and with an introduction by Arthur Livingston. Heritage Press, 1930/1965.
Locke, John. *Some Thoughts Concerning Education.* Edited and with an introduction, notes, and critical apparatus by John W. and Jean S. Yolton. Clarendon Press, 1989.
London, Jack. *The Call of the Wild.* Bantam, 1981.
_____. *White Fang.* Bantam, 1981.
Marie de France. *French Mediaeval Romances: From the Lays of Marie de France.* Translated by Eugene Mason. Aegypan, 1911/2007.
Montaigne, Michel Eyquem de. *The Complete Essays.* Translated by M.A. Screech. Penguin, 1987.

Pliny the Elder. *Natural History.* Translated by Harris Rackham. Harvard University Press, 1940.
Pliny the Younger. *The Letters of Pliny the Younger.* Translated and with an introduction by Betty Radice. Penguin, 1963.
Plutarch. *The Lives of the Noble Grecians and Romans.* Dryden translation edited and revised by Arthur Hugh Clough. Vols. 1, 2. Modern Library, 1992.
Prokofiev, Sergei. *Peter and the Wolf: A Musical Tale for Children.* Opus 67. Libretto as reprinted in Chandos recording number 8511, 1987.
Ramos, Graciliano. *Barren Lives [Vidas Sêcas].* Translated and with an introduction by Ralph Edward Dimmick. University of Texas Press, 1965.
S. Francis of Assisi: His Life and Writings as Recorded by His Contemporaries. Translated by Leo Sherley-Price. A.R. Mowbray, 1959.
Salisbury, Gay, and Laney Salisbury. *The Cruelest Miles: The Heroic Story of Dogs and Men in a Race Against an Epidemic.* W.W. Norton, 2003.
Seton, Ernest Thompson. *Wild Animals I Have Known.* Charles Scribner's Sons, 1913.
Steinbeck, John. *Travels with Charley: In Search of America.* Penguin, 1962/1986.
Suetonius. *Twelve Caesars.* Translated by Robert Graves. Revised and with an introduction by Michael Grant. Penguin, 1957/1979/1989.
Thiel, Richard P. *Keepers of the Wolves: The Early Years of Wolf Recovery in Wisconsin.* University of Wisconsin Press, 2001.
_____. *The Timber Wolf of Wisconsin: The Death and Life of a Majestic Predator.* University of Wisconsin Press, 1993.
Wasik, Bill, and Monica Murphy. *Rabid: A Cultural History of the World's Most Diabolical Virus.* Viking, 2012.
Witt, David. *Ernest Thompson Seton: The Life and Legacy of an Artist and Conservationist.* Gibbs Smith, 2010.
Woods, Barbara Allen. "The Devil in Dog Form." *Western Folklore* 13, no. 4 (October 1954). Western Folklore Society.

Index

Abraham 12
Aesculapis 50
Aesop 4, 62, 89, 143, 197
Akhenaten, Pharaoh 24
Alexander Nevsky 141
Alexander the Great 25, 31, 37, 43, 44–52, 58–59, 188, 191
Alexander III, Czar 138
Al-Jāhiz 55
All Dogs Go to Heaven 160
Al-Malik al Kamil, Sultan 71
Al-Raquim 192
An American Werewolf in London 66
An American Werewolf in Paris 66
Ammit 23
Amraphel, King 188
Andersen, Hans Christian 109–110
Anderson, Elaine 164
Antisthenes 47
Antonius (Pius) 37
Antony, Mark 25
Anubis 20–21, 23, 25–26
Arabian Nights 55–56
Argos 50, 107
Aristotle 47, 49
Asinof, Eliot 203
Aubrey, Saint 62
August, Duke Karl 96, 98–99, 101–103
Aurelius, Marcus 37
Autobulus 40–41

Baquir, Sayid Taha 12
Baring-Gould, Sabine 64
Barren Lives (film) 151–152, 201
Baum, L. Frank 4–5, 112–121, 170, 198

Beagle, HMS 103, 105–106
Becket, Saint Thomas à 192
Bin Laden, Osama 18, 188
Black, Jeremy 13
Blok, Vladimir 142
Boétie, Étienne de la 79
Bonaventure, Saint 72
Borch, Gerard ter 196
Bottinelli, Giacomo 35, 190
Bouazizi, Mohamed 188
Brecheen, Ann 172, 179, 203
Brewer, Douglas 6, 187, 191
Brown, Raphael 69, 73, 193–194
Buffy the Vampire Slayer 67
Burroughs, John 125–126, 181
Buttree, Julia 125
Byron, Lord 101, 197

Cabral, Pedro Alvares 147
Caesar, Augustus (Octavian) 25
Caesar, Julius 25, 41, 189
Caligula 35
The Call of the Wild (film) 136–137
Carlock, William 172–173, 179
Carter, Angela 193
Cartier-Bresson, Henri 169
Catherine d'Medici 183–184
Cave Canem 32, 34
Cerebus 22, 50, 191
Charles I 86
Charles II 86
Charles IX 78, 194–195
Charlet, Étienne 187
Charybdis 50
Chesterton, G.K. 156
Chrétien de Troyes 62, 192

Cicero 48
Clark, Terence 180, 187–188
Clarke, Mr. and Mrs. Edward 88
Cleopatra VII 25
Columbus, Christopher 144
Conan Doyle, Arthur 192, 197
Conger, Gwydolyn 203
Connolly, Peter 43, 190
Constantine 46
Coolbirth, Ina 131
Crockford, S.J. 189
Curse of the Werewolf 193

Dadusha 15, 187
Daley, Richard J. 165
Dante 158
Darius III 51
Darwin, Charles 2, 4–5, 51, 82, 103–113, 128–129, 134, 150, 154, 158, 173, 185, 199–200
Darwin, Emma Wedgwood 107
Darwin, Robert 105–106
Darwin, Susannah Wedgwood 105
Davidman, Joy 156–157, 202
Dean Spanley 161
Denslow, W.W. 115–116, 198
Diaghilev, Sergei 139
Diana (Artemis) 33–34, 50, 84, 195
Diane de Poitiers 84, 195
Dickens, Charles 197
Diocles of Peparthus 38
Diocletian 46
Diogenes Laërtius 45–52
Diogenes of Sinope 4, 9, 45–52, 76, 81, 191
Dionysius the Younger 48

Disney, Walt 50, 141, 144, 160, 193, 199, 201
Dobson, William J. 19
Dogs Decoded 178
Dracula (film) 193
Dryden, John 190
Duamutef 21
Dubois, François 83
Dumas, Alexandre 192
Dunsbay, Lord 161
Düntzer, Heinrich 196
Dutcher, Jamie 184–185
Dutcher, Jim 184–185

Eddy, Sherwood 106
The Egyptian Book of the Dead (The Papyrus of Ani) 19–27
Eisenhower, Dwight D. 164
Eleanor of Aquitaine 62
Elias, Brother 194
Elizabeth I 84
Endore, Guy 65
E.T., the Extra-Terrestrial 66
Eusebius 37

Faulkner, William 164, 169, 202
Faust, Doctor (historical) 196
Fiorelli, Giuseppe 33
Fitz Randolph, Lewis V. 124
FitzRoy, Robert 105
Fleming, Jim 143
Florus, Lucius Mestrius 37
Francis I 78, 194
Francis II 194
Francis of Assisi, Saint 2, 9, 68–78, 102, 108, 142, 158, 183, 193–194
Frankenstein Meets the Wolfman 165
Freud, Sigmund 22, 176

Gage, Matilda Joslyn 114–115
Gage, Maud 114–115
Gainsborough, Thomas 93–94, 196
Galba 190
Gallatin, Grace 125
Gaskell, Elizabeth 200
Gelert 56, 74, 194
George, Andrew R. 187
Gérôme, Jean-Léon 50
Gibbon, Edward 37
Glazunov, Alexander 139
Goelet, Ogden 23, 189
Goethe, Johann Wolfgang

von 5, 94–103, 152, 154, 168, 185, 196–197
Goetze, Albrecht 13
Golan v. Holder 144
Goodrich, Carter 178, 204
Goujon, Jean 195
Grandin, Eustacia 172, 179
Grandin, Temple 2, 4, 22, 170–179, 184, 203–204
Grant, Ulysses S. 114, 117
The Grapes of Wrath (film) 164
Green, Anthony 13
The Grey 205
Grimm Brothers 101–102, 197
Gromme, Owen J. 129, 199, 205
Guinefort, "Saint" 74, 191
Gula 13–14, 17, 50, 59

Hades (Pluto) 50, 191
Hadrian 37
Haleem, Abdel 55–56, 188, 191–192
Hall, Libby 169
Hammurabi 15–17, 188
Harper, Charley 205
Harper, Robert Francis 16, 188
Hawthorne, Rachel 68
Hearn, Michael Patrick 118
Hecate 50
Hemingway, Ernest 164, 169, 202
Henning, Carol 203
Henri d'Avranches 194
Henry, O. 5, 119
Henry II (English King) 62, 169, 192
Henry II (French King) 78, 194
Henry III 80, 195
Henry IV 78–80, 195
Henslow, John Stevens 105
Hermanubis 26
Hermes 26
Hobbes, Thomas 193
Hogarth, William 92–93, 178, 196
Homer 50
Horus 21
Housman, Clemence 65
The Howling 66, 193
Huckabee, Mike 181
Humane Society of the United States (HSUS) 151, 184, 202
Hussein, Saddam 11

I Was a Teenage Werewolf 66
Ibn al-Marzubān 53–61, 167, 191–192
Ibn Zakariya al-Razi 191
Intolerance 83
Isis 24–26

James II 87
Jefferson, Thomas 90–92, 94, 196
Jekyll (film) 192
Jesus 2, 7, 29, 57–58, 69, 195
John Paul II, Pope 193
Johns, Catherine 6–7, 14, 23, 42, 102
Johns, C.H.W. 16, 188
Johnson, Bruce R. 156, 202
Johnson, Catherine 174
Johnson, Jack 132
Johnson, Lyndon B. 165
Jones, Charles "Buffalo" 199
Jonson, Raymond 125
Joseph, Chief 168
Justinian I 53

Kaasen, Gunnar 135
Kanner, Leo 203
Katz, Jon 184
Kennedy, John F. 157, 165, 167
King, Barbara 159
Kipling, Rudyard 4, 126–127, 134, 192
Kittredge, Charmian 131–132
Klein, Johann Adam 102
Klinger, Friedrich Maximilian 196
Kluger, Jeffrey 159
Koussevitzsky, Serge 141, 200

Lady and the Tramp 50
Laelaps 50
Lafayette, Marquis de 92, 196
Landseer, Edwin 50–51, 110, 112
Lapham, Increase 182, 204
Laws of Eshnunna 2, 11–18, 183
The Legend of Lobo 199
Leite de Medeiros, Heloísa 148
Lenin, Vladimir 139
Leo, Brother 72, 194
Leopold, Aldo 182, 204

Index

Lewis, C.S. 2, 66, 153–163, 168, 174, 185, 193, 201–202
Lewis, Sinclair 201
Lewis, Warren 202
Life of Pi 106
Lindbergh, Charles 199
Livingston, Arthur 194
Llubera (Prokofiev), Lina 139, 144, 200
Locke, John 2, 83, 86–95, 195, 197
London, Jack 2, 126, 129–138, 150, 164, 185, 199, 202
Long, Donna 169
Louis XVI 195
Lucretius 81
Luther, Martin 78

Ma'at 23
MacDonald, George 156, 158
Macer, Baebius 189
Maddern, Elizabeth 131
Malory, Thomas 192
Malthus, Thomas 106
Margaret of Valois 78, 80
Marie d'Anjou 62
Marie de France 60–70, 76, 78, 192
Marlowe, Christopher 98
Mars 38–39
Marshall, Newton 135
Martel, Charles 53
Martel, Yann 197
Mary (Bloody), Queen 84
Mary II 87, 195
Mason, Eugene 192
McGuire, Gregory 119
Memórias do Cárcere 201
Mendelson, Mira 141, 200
Menzel, Rudolphina 58
Merson, Luc-Oliva 75, 194
Meyer, Stephenie 67, 193
Milton, John 202
Minor, Peter 196
Montaigne 6, 31, 35, 46, 76–86, 88, 92, 98, 109, 148, 176, 181, 194–195
Moore, Jane King 155, 157, 202
Moore, Paddy 155, 157
Moses 20
Muhammad 52–53, 192
Muir, John 175, 182, 204
Mulla Dust 59
The Munsters 193
Murie, Adolph 175
Murphy, Monica 13, 16
Murrill, Gwynn 205
Mussorgsky, Modest 200

Napoleon Bonaparte 20, 111, 196, 197
Nebuchadnezar II 14
Neill, John R. 116
Nero 29, 35, 37, 190
Nerva 37
Newton, Isaac 87, 107
Nicholas II, Czar 139
Nietzsche, Friedrich 199
Nixon, Richard M. 165
Nowlan, Gwendolyn 5
Nowlan, Robert 5

Obama, Barack Hussein 169
O'Keefe, Georgia 125
Orthos 50
Osiris 21–23, 25, 191
Otho 190, 192
Ovid 183, 189

Page, Dorothy G. 135
Patrick, Saint 62
Patterson, James 193
Paul, Saint 29, 37
Peacham, Henry 88
Peritas 25, 51, 52
Perrault, Charles 102, 197
Peter, Saint 29, 37
Peter I, Czar 142
Petronius 192
Philip II of Macedon 37, 47–49
Phillips, Adrian 189
Picasso, Pablo 201
Pictor, Quintus Fabius 38, 40
Plato 45, 47–49
Pliny the Elder 2, 4, 6, 9, 28–35, 37, 40, 43, 50, 56, 61–62, 76, 133, 160, 191
Pliny the Younger 28–29, 31, 37, 189–190
Plotinus 46
Plutarch 4, 25, 35–45, 47, 50, 56, 62, 76, 81–82, 98, 160, 190–191, 196
Polybius 43
Poppea 190
Potter, Beatrix 155, 202
Poveledo, Elisabetta 34
The Princess of Montpensier 83
Prokofiev, Gabriel 144, 200
Prokofiev, Oleg 144, 200
Prokofiev, Sergei 5, 9, 137–145, 147, 200–201
Ptolemy Soter 25, 191
Puget, Pierre Paul 51

Queen Margot 83

Rachmaninoff, Sergei 139
Rain Man 174
Rameses II, Pharaoh 20, 24, 188
Ramos, Graciliano 146–154, 201
Rashi 58, 192
Reagan, Ronald 201
The Red Pony (film) 169
Redington, Joe, Sr. 135
Remus 37, 39, 41–42, 63, 133, 168, 191, 193
Reuven, Yaron 13
Reynolds, G.W.M. 192
Reynolds, Joshua 93–94, 196
Rice, Anne 193
Rivière, Briton 111
Roch, Saint 174, 194
Rogers, Katherine 188
Romulus 37, 39, 41–43, 45, 63, 133, 168, 190–191, 193
Roosevelt, Franklin Delano 147
Roosevelt, Theodore 5, 122, 126, 132, 181, 199
Rosetta Stone 189
Rothberg, Abraham 134
Rouseff, Dilma Vana 153
Rousseau, Jean Jacques 89–91, 159, 196
Rowling, J.K. 67–68, 161

Sacks, Oliver 173
Saladin 71
Salisbury, Gay 135
Salisbury, Laney 135
Sats, Natalya 140
Sayles, John 66
Schiller, Friedrich 99
Schmidt, Augusto Federico 148, 201
Schubert, Otto 76
Schurz, Carl 182, 204
Schweitzer, Albert 150–151, 172
Screech, M.A. 80, 82
Scylla 50
Seavey, Martin 135
Sebond, Raymond 80–82, 195
Seneca 83
Senecio, Quintus Sosius 37
Seppala, Leonard 135–136, 199
Serapis 49
Seton, Anya 125

Index

Seton, Ernest Thompson 2, 4–5, 121–130, 134, 137, 150, 182–183, 185, 198–200, 204
Seven Brides for Seven Brothers 35, 190
Severus, Alexander 46, 190
Severus, Septimius 190
Shadowlands 161
Shaftesbury, Earl of 87–88
Shakespeare, William 14, 35, 42, 65, 98–99, 193
Shanghai Express 193
Sharpe, Susan 178
Shaw, George Bernard 202
She-Wolf of London (film) 65
She-Wolf of London (TV series) 193
Shostakovich, Dimitri 138, 140
Sitting Bull, Chief 198
Soclarus 41
Socrates 47–48
Solon 45
Sopdet (Sothius-Sirius) 24–26, 32, 189
Stager, Lawrence 59, 191–192
Stalin, Joseph 139–141, 143, 147, 149
Steinbeck, John 147, 150, 162–171, 203
Stevenson, Robert Louis 64, 110, 192
Stoker, Bram 65
Stravinsky, Igor 138–139, 201

Strieber, Whitney 193
Suetonius 50

Tacitus, Cornelius 29
Temple Grandin (film) 174
The Ten Commandments 188
Theseus 190
Thiel, Richard P. 143
Thomas of Celano 72
Tiberius 29
Titus 29–30, 35
Tolkien, J.R.R. 202
Trajan 37, 43
Tukhachevsky, Mikhail 200
Tutankhamun, Pharaoh (King Tut) 23–24, 189
Twain, Mark 5, 119, 127

Uglolino of Montegiorgio 72
Umberto D 201

Vargas, Getúlio 147, 149, 201
Vereticus, King 62
Vespasian 30, 35, 50, 81, 190
Vidal, Gore 78, 199
Vignoli, Farpi 75
Villa-Lobos, Heitor 147
Virgil 189, 192
Vitellius 190
Voltaire 90–91, 99

Wallace, Alfred Russel 106
Wasik, Bill 13, 16
Wayne, Robert K. 175

Wedgwood, Josiah 105, 197
Wedgwood, Josiah, II 105, 107, 197
Wepwawet 21, 39, 196
The Werewolf (1913 film) 65
The Werewolf (1956 film) 66
Werewolf of London 65, 193
The Werewolf of Paris 65
White Fang (film) 136
Whitman, Walt 193
William III (of Orange) 87
Witt, David 123
The Wizard of Oz (film) 115, 120
Wolf 66
Wolf, Virginia 201
The Wolf That Changed America 124
The Wolfen 193
The Wolfman (1941 film) 65
The Wolfman (2010 film) 66
Woods, Barbara Allen 101, 197
Woodson Art Museum, Leigh Yawkey 183, 205
Wordsworth, William 201

Xeniades 191

Young, Egerton R. 199
Yuhong, Wu 13, 187

Zero Dark Thirty 188

www.ingramcontent.com/pod-product-compliance
Ingram Content Group UK Ltd.
Pitfield, Milton Keynes, MK11 3LW, UK
UKHW041957140426
5217IPUK00015B/837